The Historical Monuments of Nakhichevan

Special acknowledgement is made to the A.G.B.U. Alex Manoogian Cultural Fund for financial assistance in the publication of this volume.

The Historical Monuments of Nakhichevan

Argam Ayvazian

Translated by Krikor H. Maksoudian

Wayne State University Press   Detroit   1990

94 93 92 91 90   5 4 3 2 1

Library of Congress Cataloging-in-Publication Data
Aĭvazîan, Argam.
   [Nakhijevani patmachartarapetakan hushardzannerĕ.
English]
   The historical monuments of Nakhichevan / Argam
Ayvazian; translated by Krikor H. Maksoudian.
       p.   cm.
   Translation of the rev. text of: Nakhijevani
patmachartarapetakan hushardzannerĕ.
   Includes bibliographical references and index.
   ISBN 0-8143-1896-7 (alk. paper)
   1. Architecture, Armenian—Azerbaijan S.S.R.—
Nakhichevanskaîa A.S.S.R. 2. Nakhichevanskaîa A.S.S.R.
(Azerbaijan S.S.R.)—Antiquities.   I. Title.
NA1492.7.A3513 1990
720'.947'91—dc19   88-38939
                                                   CIP

Invaluable assistance was provided by Edmond Azadian,
chairman, A.G.B.U. Alex Manoogian Cultural Fund, who acted
as publishing consultant.

Argam Ararati Ayvazian, a historian, bibliographer,
and journalist, was born in the village of Arinj,
Nakhichevan Autonomous Soviet Socialist Republic, in
1947. After receiving his elementary education in his
native village, he went to Yerevan where he attended the
state university. His field of specialization is the study of
the cultural history and historical monuments of
Nakhichevan ASSR. At present he pursues his studies
and research in Yerevan with the Commission of Preservation of Ancient Monuments of Armenia. He is the author of the following books: *The Historico-Architectural
Monuments of Nakhichevan* (1978), *Agulis* (1984), *Jugha*
(1984), *The Armenian Monuments of Nakhichevan ASSR: A
Comprehensive List* (1986), and *The Memorial Monuments
and Sculpture of Nakhichevan* (1987).

The translator, Krikor H. Maksoudian, received his
A.B. from Harvard College, his M.A. from Boston College, and his Ph.D. from Columbia University. He has
published a translation of Hovhannēs Draskhanaker-
tets'i's *History of Armenia* and numerous journal articles.

The manuscript was edited by Lois Krieger. The book
was designed by Joanne Elkin Kinney. The typeface for
the text and the display face is Meridien 54.

Manufactured in the United States of America.

Contents

Illustrations

Translator's Note

The Historical Monuments of Nakhichevan is a semi-popular work of great importance about a region of historic Armenia which is now an autonomous republic within the borders of Azerbaijan SSR. Until 1918, Nakhichevan, and especially the district of Goght'n in the south, had a large Armenian population. According to statistics, in 1903 there were within the jurisdiction of the prelacy of the Armenian Church of Nakhichevan ninety-four functioning churches and twelve major monasteries, in addition to several other abandoned and dilapidated religious and strategic sites.

Many of the Armenian inhabitants of Nakhichevan moved out of their ancestral villages and towns in 1918 to escape the invading Ottoman armies. During the encounters in the summer of 1919 between the Armenians and the Muslim insurgents, forty-five Armenian villages were destroyed and ten thousand Armenians massacred. Nakhichevan was finally annexed to Azerbaijan in 1924. During the ensuing decades, the Armenians who had survived the massacres and remained in Nakhichevan gradually moved to Soviet Armenia, abandoning their native soil and their ancient and medieval sanctuaries. Argam Ayvazian has rendered a great service to scholarship by visiting the Armenian towns and villages in this region and providing us with a physical description of the topography and the historical sites.

The history of the region has been sufficiently covered by earlier historians; there are also monographs on some of the districts and monastic institutions. Ayvazian, however, has produced a comprehensive study on the region and presents new information, otherwise impossible to obtain, about the historical background of the districts, towns, and villages, their geographical position and topography, the interconnecting highways and byways, the scriptoria, and the present state of preservation of the monuments. He also provides photographs and better and more precise measurements and descriptions of the architectural features of each monument than earlier studies. The physical evidence is always supplemented with inscriptions, colophons, archival material, and citations from original sources.

Ayvazian's work will be useful not only to students of Armenian architecture and antiquities, but also to those in the fields of European and Middle Eastern art and architecture, Middle East studies, church history, and so on. This work was translated from the Armenian manuscript of the author. It contains more factual material than what is presented in the Armenian edition published in Erevan in 1978 and seems to be a revision of the Russian edition published in Erevan in 1981.

Armenian place names and words have been transliterated according to the Library of Congress system.

Krikor H. Maksoudian

There is evidence that humans have lived in Nakhichevan since the earliest stages of civilization. Stone Age tools, especially those of the Neolithic and Chalcolithic periods, that were discovered in a prehistoric salt mine[1] in the middle of the nineteenth and early part of the twentieth century and the remains of richly pigmented earthenware and other items (found in Kiul-T'ap'a,[2] Karmir Vank',[3] Shaht'akht, and other ancient sites) reveal that Nakhichevan even in prehistoric times was one of the important agricultural and cultural centers of Transcaucasia.

During the summer of 1976,[4] on one of the levels of the Nakhichevan salt mine, a hall was discovered that was part of the ancient mine and is similar in shape to a contemporary football field. At present this site is considered the oldest known mine in the USSR. There archaeologists have discovered remains of ovens, wooden couches, earthenware, basalt axes, tools made out of horn, and other items. Primitive miners' carvings on the walls of the hall are also significant—according to scholars, they represent calculations.

The artifacts found in this mine, which dates from the end of the third millennium B.C. to the beginning of the second, reveal beyond any doubt that solid salt was mined both by the open-pit and underground methods. It has been shown that more than twelve thousand tons of salt had been mined from the recently discovered hall. Such quantities would have allowed the early inhabitants of Nakhichevan not only to secure the amounts needed for their own consumption, but also for other lands.

A number of historical facts and the building techniques used in the construction of fortresses (Arba, Chahuk, Ernjak, Giran) and aqueducts of the prefeudal period give us reason to conclude that the area of historic Nakhichevan in the eighth century B.C. fell within the boundaries of the state of Urartu.[5] During the formative period of the Armenian people, from the seventh to the second centuries B.C., Nakhichevan emerged as an Armenian political entity and was within the limits of the Orontid Kingdom, which had taken control of the state of Urartu. Subsequently, until the end of the ninth century, Nakhichevan was, according to the historical sources, a district of the province of Vaspurakan (in historic Armenia). At the beginning of the tenth century, the Bagratid King Smbat I liberated Nakhichevan from the Arab [Sadjid] emirs and handed it over to the princes of Siwnik'.[6] Beginning with the eleventh century, Nakhichevan was constantly harassed and raided by the Seljuk Turks and then by the Mongols, the Ottomans, and the Safavids of Iran, who established their rule there at different times.

At the beginning of the nineteenth century Nakhichevan was ruled by a Persian khan. In 1828, through the provision of the Russo-Persian Treaty of Turkmanchay, the Khanate of Nakhichevan, together with its historic districts and eastern Armenia, was annexed to Russia. Thereafter, the administration of Nakhichevan and its districts was integrated into that of the Armenian District, also formed by the Russians in 1828, and then in 1849 into that of the territory of the Khanate of Erevan, which was preserved until the middle of 1918.[7] On February 9, 1924, Nakhichevan was organized as an autonomous republic within the structure of the Azerbaijan SSR and occupies a territory of 5,363 square kilometers.[8]

Since Nakhichevan was for centuries located on one of the crossroads of ancient trade routes, it was frequently raided and burned by foreign invaders. Nevertheless, her geographical position contributed to the quick recovery and development of her towns and villages. In the past, the major commercial routes from Ecbatan to Artashat, Siwnik' to Nakhichevan, and Nakhichevan to Archēsh had a major significance for this region. The early fortresses, fortified towns, cities, villages, and religious and cultural centers of Nakhichevan were built along the main roads of the Bagratid period that ran from Maragheh to Dvin and Dvin to Partaw[9] and across the nearby plains.

Nakhichevan contained the Goght'n, Ernjak, Nakhichevan (Nakhchawan), Chahuk-Shahapunik', and Sharur districts, which occupied the area extending over the plains and hilly regions on the left bank of the Arax River and were surrounded by the Zangezur and Vayk' mountains. On the towering peaks and flanks and in the valleys of these districts and along the sides of rarely frequented roads and paths there are many medieval architectural monuments and landmarks that are still standing.

The architectural monuments in the districts of Nakhichevan present a great deal of variety. Among them there are primitive dwelling sites, Bronze Age strongholds, ancient fortified towns, fortresses, medieval monasteries, churches, *khach'k'ars* [crosses carved on slabs], and graves that have been obscured throughout the centuries or destroyed by frequent foreign attackers. Nonetheless, these buildings and monuments have survived through restoration. Our catalog of Armenian historical architectural monuments and of archaeological sites in Nakhichevan contains more than 4,500 individual structures. This estimate is not final, and it does not take into account all of the Armenian monuments built before the nineteenth century. During the period of the Ildegizid rule (1136–1225), about ten renowned Seljuk and Azerbaijani monuments were built in the cities of Nakhichevan, Ordubad, and Karabaghlar. In the pre-Soviet period and during the last few decades, these have been thoroughly studied and abundant literature exists on them. Recently another concise study has been published[10] that covers all of the Azerbaijani architectural monuments in Nakhichevan.

We must note with sadness, however, that to this day Nakhichevan, so rich in antiquities and monuments, has not yet been the topic of a specialized study. It would be sufficient to state that during the past sixty or seventy years no study has been published about the Armenian monuments of Nakhichevan. We come across specific descriptions and notes about these monuments only in general works of a topographical, geographical, ethnographical, demographical, or religious nature from the end of the nineteenth and early twentieth centuries (A. Sedrakian, Ghewond Alishan, M. Smbatian, Eruand Lalayian, Garegin Hovsēp'ian). In these works one will find information on only the most outstanding monuments. Despite this, the pages dedicated to the renowned monuments of Nakhichevan in the works of the meritorious Alishan, Lalayian, Sedrakian, Smbatian, and Hovsēp'ian have exceptional value, since today they take the place of unavailable or destroyed original sources.

Research on the historical and architectural monuments of Nakhichevan reveals that the major dwelling places were surrounded by comprehensive systems of defensive structures. Especially important examples of these systems are at Arba, Chahuk, Ernjak, Giran, and Shahaponk'. The numerous medieval monastic complexes, churches, and *khach'k'ars*, dating from the twelfth to the seventeenth century, were constructed with original architectural technique. The most common types of religious structures built were domed churches with four pillars and basilican churches with a nave and two aisles. The architectural solutions that were employed in these buildings are similar to those used in the same types of structures found in Siwnik' and the districts of Vaspurakan.

As a result of centuries of devastation and destruction, the majority of the architectural monuments in the districts of Sharur, Nakhichevan (Nakhchawan), and Chahuk, which are close to the Arax River, have been in ruins for a long time. A greater number of monuments have been preserved in the districts of Goght'n, Ernjak, and Shahapunik', parts of which are located in mountainous areas far away from the well-traveled main roads. A significant number of monuments were destroyed in the fifteenth and sixteenth centuries during the battles between the Ottomans and the Safavids that were fought on Armenian soil. The Turkish historian Pechevi-Ibrahim, describing the brutality of the Ottoman army marching from the plain of Ararat to Nakhichevan and Siwnik', states:

> On the twenty-seventh day they reached the plain of Nakhichevan. Out of fear of the victorious army, the people deserted the cities, villages, houses, and places of dwelling, which were so desolate that they were occupied by owls and crows and struck the onlooker with terror. Moreover, they [the Ottomans] ruined and laid waste all of the villages, towns, fields, and buildings along the road over a distance of four or five days' march so that there was no sign of any buildings or life.[11]

In addition to such atrocities, natural disasters and earthquakes measuring up to eight points on the Richter scale occurred at different times and wrought great destruction.[12]

The purpose of this study is to present within set limits and in a popular manner the renowned monuments (fortresses, monasteries, churches) that are preserved in Nakhichevan Autonomous SSR and to emphasize the architectural and historical significance of the famous towns and villages that played a major role in the political and cultural life of medieval Armenia.

Within the past eight to ten years we have had the opportunity to study on site all of the monuments described in this book. We have published articles about some of them in scholarly journals in the Armenian SSR. The photographs as well as the architectural details, topographical information, and the plans of most of the monuments are being published here for the first time.[13] All of the photographs, with only a few exceptions, were taken by us between 1975 and 1978 and show the present state of the monuments.

The text of this work is based on historical sources and our own research. We preferred to present the monuments according to their geographical locations in the historic districts. In separate sections we also cover famous scriptoria, bridges, and wall paintings.

Nakhichevan's district of Goght'n is a beautiful region that played a major role in the history of the Armenian people until the beginning of the twentieth century; Armenian music, art, writing, and literature thrived there. Writing about the epics and myths of the Armenian people, Movsēs Khorenats'i, the father of Armenian history, states that "the inhabitants of the wine-producing districts of Goght'n have lovingly preserved" the ancient traditions.[1] According to linguist E. Aghayan, the etymology of the word *Goght'n* is connected with the Proto-Indo-European roots *-gal* or *-ghel,* meaning "to call" or "to shout."[2] *Goght'n,* therefore, means "story," "song," or "epic." In Armenian historiography the district of Goght'n is variously named Goght'n, Goght'an (by Movsēs Khorenats'i), Goght'an tun [House of Goght'n] (by Koriwn, a fifth-century historian), and Goght'nastan (by T'owma Artsruni, a tenth-century historian). The Greek geographer Ptolemy calls it Golthēnē, the Latinized form of which is Colthene.

According to the historian Koriwn, Saint Mashtots' during his residence in Goght'n "was surrounded and ensnared with sad thoughts" and conceived the idea of creating an alphabet for Armenian.[3] Movsēs Khorenats'i testifies that since ancient times the Goght'nets'i ruled in Goght'n. He states that "the Goght'nets'is, I have found it said, . . . are truly branches of the Sisakan [family]. I do not know if they called the provinces for these men's names or whether they called the principalities after the name of the provinces."[4] Thirteenth-century historian Archbishop Step'anos Orbelean makes the same assertion.[5] The feudal principality of Goght'n as an inseparable part of historic Armenia comprised the territory of one of the major feudal families of ancient Armenia. The head of the household, bearing the title of "Lord of Goght'n," held the sixteenth place in the *Throne List,* which is a fifth-century document, and according to the Armenian *Military List* he supplied the royal armies with five hundred horsemen. [The *Throne List* is a list of the Armenian feudal families arranged in hierarchical rank. The *Military List* is a list of the feudal families and the number of knights each house supplied to the army.][6]

The information preserved in the Armenian Atlas [*Ashkharhats'oyts'*][7] of the seventh century points out that Goght'n was the thirty-third district of Vaspurakan. After the middle of the fifth century it probably fell under the domination of the Artsruni family. T'ovma Artsruni informs us that the district was a part of Vaspurakan until 737: "The district of Goght'n [was severed from Vaspurakan] in 737 when Saint Vahan, who was the son of Khosrov, lord of Goght'n, was executed by the Arabs."[8]

The district of Goght'n, which occupied the area of the present-day Ordubad region, was located in the southeastern part of Nakhichevan, on the left bank of the Arax River, at an altitude of 948 to 960 meters above sea level. According to the historical sources, the inhabitants of this district have occupied themselves with the cultivation of grapes and fruits and with different kinds of crafts since ancient times. In Armenian history Goght'n was better known as a wine-producing district, but was renowned for its grapes, pomegranates, peaches, and other fruits. The medieval architectural monuments, the ancient dwellings, towns, and villages located in the Goght'n valleys of Agulis, Orduar, Trunik', Vanand, Ts'ghna, Gilan, and Bist are integral parts of this ancient and beautiful land.

AGULIS

This famous, ancient town of Goght'n originally covered the area now occupied by the villages of Verin [Upper] and Nerk'in [Inner] Agulis. Historic Agulis ("Igulis," according to the local dialect) is located 2 to 2.5 kilometers to the east of Ordubad, the center of the district. Since ancient times the town has stretched over the entire area of a long valley surrounded by rocky hills and measuring 1 to 1.5 kilometers in width. Spread out over an area of 5 kilometers on the left and right banks of a mountain stream, ancient Agulis lay on the sides of sunburnt, barren, rocky hills. The city was divided into more than ten regions, the more noted of which were Vank', Verin get [Upper River], Nurijanents' mahla, Meydan, Khts'adzor, Verin t'agh [Upper quarter], and Nerk'in [Lower quarter]. Agulis had a population of eight thousand Armenian families (houses).

Agulis is located in a setting in which, over the course of history, many political and cultural events have taken place. According to historians, the town was for centuries considered the capital of the district of Goght'n and a center of cultural and political life. According to Ghewond Alishan,[9] the etymology of the word *Agulis* derives from the expression *Aygeōk' lik'* [full of vineyards]. Academician S. Eremian, however, traces it back to Oskiola.[10] The historian Movsēs Khorenats'i calls Agulis Oskioghay awan [the village of Oskioghay]. In an encyclical the eleventh-century catholicos Sargis calls the city Agulis, and in the middle of the seventeenth century Zak'aria of Agulis calls it Agulis, or Ak'ulis.[11] The city has also been called Oskē dzor [golden valley] because of the wealth of its inhabitants.[12] Two- and three-storied mansions hidden in ancient vineyards, 120 to 150 shops, rich stores, several religious and trade schools, more than seventeen fountains, pharmacies, bathhouses, bazaars, the rich library with its reading room, silk factories, tanneries, olive oil factories, inns and hotels, and twelve churches and monasteries of great architectural and artistic value enhanced the glory of Agulis with their exceptional beauty, splendor, and stateliness.

Research on the architectural monuments of Agulis and on questions concerning the plan and construction of the city shows that Agulis, like other medieval Armenian cities (Ani, Kars, Khlat', Kharberd), had a tripartite structure comprising a citadel, the city proper, and the suburbs. The houses in the city, built on open and elevated sites, were constructed according to specific architectural designs. Their portals and facades had beautiful architectural patterns and decorations on stone and wood. Their plans included many rooms. The houses, villas, and buildings in Agulis were surrounded with rich vineyards and tall outer walls (3 to 4 meters high) built with bricks and stones that gave the city a special look.

At the beginning of the nineteenth century, Mesrop T'aghiadian visited Agulis and wrote: "The buildings in Agulis are more exquisite than what I have seen until now; they are decorated with beautiful paintings."[13] Even at the beginning of the twentieth century, E. Lalayian, an archaeologist and ethnographer, wrote that the city had still retained its urban character and civilized state. "Here there are about ninety very beautiful stores with European commodities the likes of which one cannot find even in Ordubad. In every respect Agulis resembles a city and is even more advanced than a number of provincial towns such as Nakhichevan."[14] After visiting Agulis at the end of the nineteenth century, a Frenchwoman, Mrs. B. Chantre, wrote: "[Agulis] could be considered a center with intelligent, enlightened and rich people. . . . The Armenians call it 'Lesser Paris.'" She reports that the houses of the local inhabitants "are large buildings with extended wings to the right and the left. Along the entire width of their fronts are terraces that are covered. These doors open into the vestibules. The courtyards between the main buildings and the wings comprise gardens that are carefully and beautifully decorated with large fountains."[15] Wandering around Goght'n in 1914, the painter Martiros Sarian noted:

We approached a mountain pass on the side of which we noticed Agulis shining like a miniature beauty. That is one of the passes in the Lesser Caucasian range that descends down to the Arax River and cradles the city on a suitable spot on its side. The brook was not abundant, but instead there were many fountains which were carefully preserved by the townspeople as architectural landmarks. In the center of the city was St. T'ovma Church, with its beautiful wall paintings, which were painted by the Hovnat'anians. There were a series of smaller churches in Agulis that created harmony in the panorama of the city, which stands on an area that uniquely resembles a set of stairs.[16]

Agulis, considered one of the most advanced cities of Armenia in the sixteenth to eighteenth century, was for a long time engaged in business transactions with India, Persia, Italy, Russia, China, and other countries. According to the testimony of eyewitnesses, in the nineteenth century "Verin Agulis had a small but beautiful marketplace with approximately one hundred shops."[17] In his memoirs the famous Armenian writer and educator Perch Pŕoshian wrote: "Here [in the marketplace] the merchants of Agulis carry out their wholesale trade; the small shops in this marketplace have ties with the larger commercial firms of Russia and Europe."[18]

Agulis, which witnessed so many historical events, suffered from continuous Arab, Mongol, Turkish, and Persian attacks and invasions, forcing her inhabitants to migrate to other parts of the world. One of the horrible devastations that struck the city is known as "the holocaust of Agulis." In 1751 Azat Khan of Azerbaijan demanded from Melik' Esayi of Agulis a great amount of money and supplies for his army. When Esayi refused, the savage khan, in October of that year, ravaged and burned Agulis and its neighboring villages and towns.[19] Shattered and robbed of their possessions, the inhabitants left their ancestral homes; some migrated to Constantinople and Persia, others to India, Venice, Amsterdam, and Karabakh (Shushi), where they built a church for themselves.[20]

One of the reasons for the decline of Agulis was the pressure exerted by the Turkish and Persian rulers and the local *melik'*s. The unfavorable geographical setting of the city was another factor. Barren and rocky, the land could support very little vegetation, and what arable land existed was loamy and sandy. During heavy rainfall, the rainwater rushing down the slopes brought with it huge boulders and mud and the torrents washed away vegetation and good soil. Agulis and its inhabitants were frequently hit with rainstorms. History has recorded a number of floods, the worst of which occurred on July 26, 1872, and May 21, 1884. According to the written testimony of eyewitnesses of the 1884 storm, the hailstones that fell were as large as eggs! Unexpectedly the mountain stream swelled and the raging torrents of rainwater that rushed down the mountains caused large boulders to roll down the hills toward the city, destroying several houses, stores, shops, and bridges. It covered everything with silt, and several people drowned.[21] But despite such events, the people of Agulis did not abandon their ancient ancestral abode.

The historical monuments, monasteries, and churches of Agulis occupy a special place in the history of the local culture. Tradition assigns the founding of some of these (St. T'ovma, St. K'ristap'or, Mets Astuatsatsin) to the first century A.D.[22] From one end of the city to the other one can see the wonderful spectacle of the nine medieval churches (some of which are now damaged) and the Monastery of St. T'ovma. St. Step'anos Church is located in Verin t'agh'; a little below is the Monastery of St. T'ovma. To the southeast of this is St. Minas. The majestic St. K'ristap'or Church is located in the central quarter of the city and is called "Cathedral" because of its location. Approximately 160 meters south of St. K'ristap'or Church is St. Shmawon, and above it is St. Hovhannēs, which is located at the foot of a mountain. A little below this church is the Church of St. James of Nisibis, and on the side of a mountain in the eastern part of Agulis are the ruins of the monastic complex of Mets Astuatsatsin [The Great Mother of God]. St. Errordut'iwn

[Holy Trinity] and Amarayin [summer] churches still stand in Lower Agulis (or the Plain of Agulis). St. K'ristos Church is located outside the city at the base of Mount Gindar. All of the above monuments (with the exception of St. Minas Church, which had a wooden roof) and the Monastery of St. T'ovma were built of polished blocks of basalt and local stone. They have splendid reliefs and were skillfully designed by master architects.

In the vicinity of the city one can see the remains of a number of other churches and chapels and the vestiges of the outer walls that once protected the city. The monuments of Agulis, whether standing or in ruins, say a great deal about the architectural skills of the local inhabitants. Some of the monuments have been restored since the Middle Ages. Several others were renovated in the seventeenth and eighteenth centuries. The Monastery of St. T'ovma, St. K'ristap'or, St. Step'anos, St. Hovhannēs, and other monuments—with their thick walls, arches, beautiful *khach'k'ars* carved on slabs, and their unique harmony with nature—are considered among the masterpieces of medieval Armenian architecture. In a valley surrounded with barren rocks they rise high from the ground like plants of stone. The existence of so many complexes and monuments in a small city is remarkable. These structures are significant for their architectural solutions and features, and especially for their polygonal apses.

Among these monuments St. T'ovma is still in relatively good condition. It is architecturally the most beautiful complex in the district of Goght'n. Catholicos Abraham of Crete, an eighteenth-century author, describes this monastery as ''beautiful and wonderful to the eyes of the beholder.''[23] It is indeed a marvelous architectural monument. According to tradition and the long inscription of 1694 on the lintel of the western portal, the Monastery of St. T'ovma was founded by the Apostle Saint Bartholomew in the first century A.D. and was rebuilt a number of times during the centuries that followed. In published and unpublished sources the monastery has been mentioned since the beginning of the fourteenth century.

The renovation of the present church of the Monastery of St. T'ovma occurred in the seventeenth century. The monastery, located in the present-day Vank'i t'agh [quarter of the monastery] in Verin Agulis, was one of the important religious complexes in medieval Armenia. Like a number of other great monastic complexes from the Middle Ages (Khor Virap, Gnevank', the Great Her-

Fig. 1. The cupola of the church of the Monastery of St. T'ovma from the southwest.

Fig. 2. The plan of the church of the Monastery of St. T'ovma.

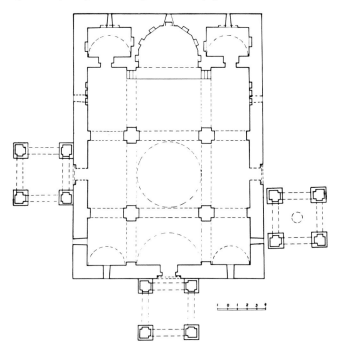

Fig. 3. The bell tower/chapel of the Monastery of St. T'ovma.

mitage of Tat'ew, the Hermitage of Lim, and Astapat's Karmir Vank'), this has a regular rectangular plan. The sanctuary is located in the center of the complex. Surrounding the church along the perimeter of the rectangular walls, which have six strong towers, are dwelling places and buildings of an economic and auxiliary nature.

The church, a domed basilica with four pillars, is built of polished blocks of basalt and red stone. The structure extends from east to west. On the east side are the main apse, which has a seven-sided exterior, and two vestries. The interior of the church is spacious and lofty (Figs. 1, 2). The cupola, with its twelve windows, rests on four thick cruciform pillars. The church has three portals, one each on the western, northern, and southern facades. These are decorated with ornamental bands, reliefs, and

inscriptions. During the seventeenth-century renovations, bell towers with two pillars made of polished stone were erected in front of the western and northern portals. Near the southern portal but slightly to the west another bell tower with four pillars was built (Fig. 3).

The spacious and bright interior was made more picturesque by the wall paintings executed by the noted painter and poet Naghash Hovnat'an of Shoṙot' in the 1680s.

Fig. 4. St. K'ristap'or Church from the south.

1 Bartholomew came to Armenia and first founded the
  Lord's house here. He named the place after the Apostle
  Saint Thomas

2 and established an episcopal throne, on which he placed
  his disciple Komsi as the overseer of this land,

3 which is the district of Goght'n. He turned over to him
  the chosen flock near Agulis and its renowned plain.

4 He also bequeathed to him Ts'ghna, Ṙamis, Bist, P'aṙaka;
  Buhrut and Tewi also became permanent possessions,

5 together with Shrju and Masrewan. He put on the list
  Aghahets'ik, to which he added Dastak and Vanand.

6 To these he added Trunis, Tnakert, Obovanis,
  K'aghak'ik, and the Anapat [hermitage] of Handamēj.
  He allotted [to the

7 monastery] Verin Getts'ik' and K'esh Erets'ik', Numnis,
  and Hordvat. When Saint Gregory [the Illuminator]
  came and saw the ordinance of the Apostle,

8 he confirmed it with his signature, and shielded it with
  anathemas. In the 305th year of Our Lord

9 the Illuminator arrived here and inscribed the original, of
  which the present inscription is a copy.

Besides enlivening the interplay between light and shadow, the niches and windows of St. T'ovma are inseparably connected to the religious function of the structure. The mysterious shadows cast by the arches that rest on thick pillars, and the wall paintings that receive their light from the windows, create a significant effect. The splendor of the western portal of the church is more noticeable than that of the others. In addition to the intricately carved decorative bands, reliefs, and wall paintings that surround it, there is also a lengthy inscription on its lintel that is of historical importance. Inscribed in the seventeenth century, it narrates in meter and rhyme the traditional story of the founding of St. T'ovma in the mid-first century and lists the names of the villages that were donated to the monastery, which served as the residence of the bishop of Goght'n. This inscription has been reprinted a number of times, but always with errors. Considering its importance for this study, in which it is cited several times, we present our own reading:

ST. K'RISTAP'OR CHURCH

Among the architectural monuments of Agulis this church occupies a unique place. It is still standing and is located in the central quarter of Verin Agulis (Fig. 4). Most of the villas and houses of Agulis's Verin t'agh lie to the north of this church. Opposite it, on the right bank of the river, the famous marketplace of Agulis was once located.

According to tradition, the Church of St. K'ristap'or was founded by the Apostle Saint Thaddeus in the first century. In the manuscripts the earliest mention of St. K'ristap'or is in the fifteenth century. The present structure, however, according to the inscriptions and the dependable information transmitted by Zak'aria of Agulis, was built in 1671–75 on the foundation of an older structure. Thirty or forty builders and masons from Vaspurakan participated in its construction, working under the guidance of "the great master mason of Moks."

St. K'ristap'or Church of Agulis is a domed structure with four pillars. It has a beautiful main apse, two vestries, a hall with a lofty interior and three portals, one on the western, one on the northern, and one on the southern elevations. Its cupola, which is built of brick, stands on four cruciform pillars. Under a tall arch above the lintel of the western portal, there is the carved image of the Mother of God bearing a crown and holding Jesus in her lap. This was commissioned by Zak'aria of Agulis at the time of the construction of the church. Arches decorated with reliefs encircle the other two portals as well; under each arch there is an ornament. The porch, now in ruins, was attached to the southern elevation of the church.

To the south of St. K'ristap'or there were a number of buildings, among which one can still see the remains of a vaulted caravanserai with a single-chamber nave.

ST. SHMAWON CHURCH

The other famous monument in Agulis is St. Shmawon, which lies in ruins today. This once-splendid domed basilican church with four pillars was standing until the 1920s (Fig. 5). At present one can see only the two pillars in front of the apse, the apse, and a part of the northern wall (Fig. 6). According to V. M. Sysoev,[24] St. Shmawon had three portals, in front of which there were twenty seventeenth- and eighteenth-century tombstones with inscriptions. Inside the church the arches were painted with plant motifs, and on the drum of the dome were images of four angels with their wings spread.

Founded in the Middle Ages, St. Shmawon was reno-

Fig. 5. St. Shmawon Church in the 1920s.

Fig. 6. St. Shmawon Church as it appears today.

Fig. 7. The plan of St. Hovhannēs Mkrtich' Church.

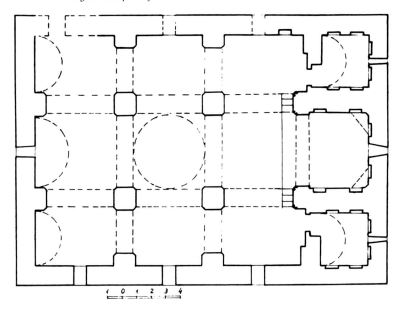

Fig. 8. St. Step'anos Church from the southeast.

vated in the seventeenth century. A bell tower stood at the corner of the roof to the west of the dome.

A scriptorium once operated at St. Shmawon Church. Only a few manuscripts copied there have survived. One of these is dated 1638. Another bears the statement: "This holy book [containing the writings] of Paul and Isaiah was bound by the unworthy presbyter Margar in the town of Agulis, at the gate of St. Shmawon Church, in the 1089th year of the Armenian Era [1640]."[25]

ST. HOVHANNĒS MKRTICH' [ST. JOHN THE BAPTIST] CHURCH

This church, now partly in ruins, played a major role in the cultural life of medieval Agulis. St. Hovhannēs is located in Nerk'in t'agh and is thought to have been the parish church of that neighborhood. The church (Fig. 7) structurally extends from east to west. At its eastern extremity is the main apse, which is polygonal on the exterior, and a pair of two-storied vestries. The only entrance to the main hall is on the side of the northwestern corner of the building. The eight-windowed dome stands on four thick octagonal pillars and is built of brick. The church and the auxiliary buildings were surrounded with a rectangular wall.

The present structure of St. Hovhannēs Church, according to literary sources and the inscription on the perimeter of the base of the cupola, was renovated in 1663. It was covered with gypsum and decorated with wall paintings in 1686. The cupola was built in 1703. The structure of St. Hovhannēs's five-sided apse in some ways reminds one of the main apse of the church of Karmir Vank' at Astapat.

ST. STEP'ANOS CHURCH

St. Step'anos Church in the Verin get quarter stands on a level site on the side of a mountain. There is very little information available on its history. The original structure was probably built in the twelfth or the thirteenth century and renovated in the seventeenth century. The church was once again renovated at the beginning of the twentieth century, but now it is in a semidilapidated state.

St. Step'anos Church (Fig. 8) is build of well-polished blocks of basalt and reddish stone. It is a domed basilican church with four pillars (Fig. 9) and two semicircular apses, one on each side of the main eastern apse. The western facades of all three are open and face the main hall. Under the apses are vestries with entrances from their bemas. The cupola of the church stands on cruciform pillars with rectangular bases.

St. Step'anos has three portals—one on the west, one on the north, and one on the south facade of the church. They are traced with striking decorative reliefs. At one time high reliefs were set in the tympanums of each portal, but these no longer exist. In front of the southern portal of the church was a bell tower with two pillars, now in ruins. The auxiliary communal structures of the monastic complex were surrounded by a rectangular outer wall. One can see only the remains of this today.

THE CHURCH OF ST. HAKOB HAYRAPET [ST. JAMES OF NISIBIS]

The Church of St. Hakob Hayrapet, within the perimeters of a rectangular outer wall, is still standing in the area called P'ok'r Blur [small hill] located in the Khts'adzor t'agh. This church (Fig. 10) is a domed hall

Fig. 9. The plan of St. Step'anos Church.

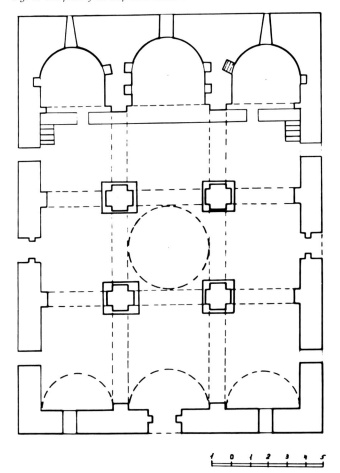

Fig. 10. The Church of St. Hakob Hayrapet.

with a single-chamber nave and is built of blocks of stone and baked bricks. It has a hall, a rectangular apse at its eastern extremity, and two portals, one on the west and the other on the south facades (Fig. 11). The cupola, built of brick, rises above the circular bay in between two pillars. The rectangular apse of St. Hakob Hayrapet Church has two stories. The entrance to the first story is from the northern corner of the bema, near the stairs that

Fig. 11. The plan of the Church of St. Hakob Hayrapet.

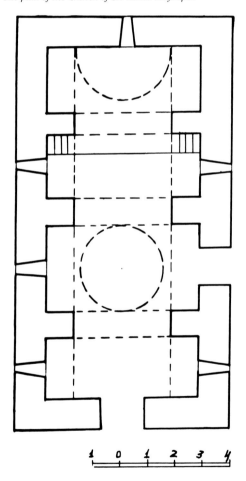

go up to the second story. According to the inscription in black paint on the perimeter of the cupola, the present structure of St. Hakob Hayrapet was renovated in six months' time in 1901. It is a monument with interesting architectural solutions.

METS ASTUATSATSIN

Mets [large] Astuatsatsin [Theotokos], or the complex of the Mets Anapat St. Astuatsatsni, is a magnificent group of monuments located 1.5 kilometers to the east of Agulis, on the side of a barren, sun-parched mountain. From there one can see the beautiful panorama of Lesser Agulis (or the Plain of Agulis) and that of the villages and fields along the Arax River. The epithet "Mets" [large] was given to this monastery in order to distinguish it from the other St. Astuatsatsin Church in the city. The church of Mets Astuatsatsin is part of a large architectural complex that includes a porch, a guesthouse, and ten to twelve other buildings that were all at one time surrounded with a high outer wall. The monastery also possessed a vineyard and a fountain. Most of the buildings and the outer wall are now in ruins, and the church is abandoned and dilapidated.

After investigating this complex and its vicinity, we came to the conclusion that this had been the site of an ancient pagan temple. According to the traditions of the natives of Agulis, the Apostle Thaddeus destroyed the idols of the pagan gods and founded a church there. During the ensuing centuries—almost to the end of the nineteenth century—statuettes of gods made out of clay and metal were frequently discovered there, according to the testimony of eyewitnesses, especially when renovations were in progress. E. Lalayian cites extensively from the diary of Tēr Hakob [Father James]:

In 1874, when Karapet Agha Shkhiants' of Shushi left Tabriz because of the cholera epidemic, he came to the Plain of Agulis and went on a pilgrimage to Mets Astuatsatsin. He donated one hundred pounds for the restoration of the complex and ordered Sargis Sarukhanbekov to oversee the work. At that time a wall divided the Church of Mets Astuatsatsin into two halls. In the middle of the wall there was a door that connected the outer hall with the inner. In the outer hall, right above the door there was an altar built of clay; access to it was possible through two stairways from both sides of the door. When the wall was torn down to restore the unity of the hall, idols made out of earthenware and cast iron were discovered inside the clay altar. Sarukhanbekov and his godfather Ōhannēs Makarov . . . fanatically threw these down on the stones and shattered them to pieces."[26]

ST. ERRORDUT'IWN AND AMARAYIN CHURCHES

St. Errordut'iwn, a domed church, rises in the northern quarter of Lesser Agulis. The Amarayin [summer] Church is attached to its north elevation (Fig. 12). The latter is a basilican church with two aisles and a nave. Its seven-sided main apse has on its left and right four-sided apses. The hall has six thick pillars that support the roof. In its present state the church's north, south, and west elevations are arcades that expose 60 percent of its elevation.

After examining the foundations of this building and its architectural structure, we were convinced that the earlier church preceding the present one was built in the ninth century. Subsequently, in the seventeenth century it was rebuilt with bricks and was converted into an open hall-type church where the liturgical services were performed during the summer months, thus the epithet Amarayin [summer]. The colophon of a synaxarium copied at this complex reveals that the name of the basilican church was St. Nshan, and that of the domed basilica, which is now called St. Errordut'iwn, was St. Step'anos. The colophon of another synaxarium, which is now in the Holy Trinity Armenian Church of Fresno, California, states:

I the contemptible Mahdasi [a person who has gone to Jerusalem on pilgrimage] Azaria, received this synax-

Fig. 12. Amarayin Church.

arium . . . and gave it to the churches that are called Erek' Khorani [three altars], St. Nshan and St. Minas, which protect and guard this town called Dasht [Plain of Agulis]. . . . If with the help of God they [re]build St. Minas Church and wish to take this book there, let them do so without any complaint. But should anyone try to take this away from the above two churches, he shall be anathematized by God and all of His saints. Amen.[27]

According to the same colophon, the synaxarium "was copied and completed by the unwise priest Ep'rem . . . in the 1139th year of the Armenian Era [1690] . . . in the village called the Plain of Agulis, under the protection of the St. Step'anos Church, which is called Erek' Khorani, and St. Nshan Church, which is called St. Minas."[28]

The domed St. Step'anos Church, which is also known as Erek' Khorani and St. Errordut'iwn, has four pillars and is built of polished blocks of sandstone and bricks. The apse of the church is polygonal on the exterior with five sides (Fig. 13). The four pillars of the hall

Fig. 13. The plan of St. Step'anos and Amarayin churches.

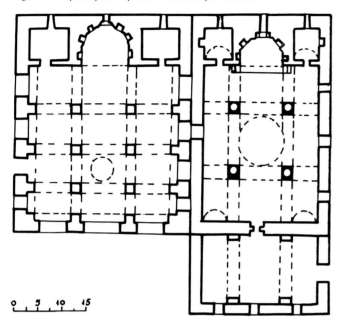

0   5   10   15

are almost circular. On the flat roof of the structure there is a beautiful cupola with an eight-sided drum built of brick. In front of the west elevation of the church there is a porch that, according to the inscriptions, was built in the seventeenth century when the church was being renovated. The St. Step'anos or St. Errordut'iwn and St. Nshan or Amarayin churches and the auxiliary buildings were enclosed in an extensive outer wall that is now in ruins.

Among the monuments of Agulis there are fountains built in the sixteenth to eighteenth century that are of great architectural interest. Many of these are vaulted structures built of polished blocks of stone and are still in use today. A. Araskhanian, a noted scholar who was born in Agulis, wrote with pride about these fountains: "In the entire Caucasus, I dare say in the entire world, one will be

unable to find such good fountains in such a small area as in Agulis, the heart of Goght'n. And what measures they have taken in order to preserve them! What a system of underground waterways and wells. . . . It's a marvel. But my heart longs for the Snasents' Fountain. Remember it. It's outside the village, on the road to the distant vineyards."[29]

Zak'aria of Agulis said of this fountain: "They called the Snasents Fountain 'Three Springs.' Two of the sources of the fountain had dried up. Thereupon a native of Agulis, a man called Khōjints' T'uman, drilled water from another source of the same fountain. The flow of the water was an inch wide. He brought the water to his vineyard in the 1111th year of the Armenian era [1662]."[30] In 1611 Melik' Melk'um of Agulis built two fountains, one in front of his house and the other in Meydan t'agh, near the house of Melik' Aghawel.[31] The merchant Nurihad, also a native of Agulis, had still another fountain built in Verin t'agh. It was named Nurunts' Fountain.[32]

We know from Zak'aria of Agulis that among the numerous fountains at the monasteries and churches and in the city proper Shambi or Shabi Fountain was renowned for the abundance of its waters. Every year the clergy and the people of Agulis gathered there to celebrate the ceremony of the Blessing of Water (on the occasion of the feast of the Baptism of Christ).[33]

The historic importance of the monuments of Agulis are such that any study on the medieval monastic complexes of Armenia would be incomplete without them.

MESROPAWAN

Historic Mesropawan (Masrewan) is the present-day village of Nasrvaz in the region of Ordubad and is situated on the skirt of a beautiful mountain range. It may have been inhabited by man since prehistoric times. The enchanting mountains and hills covered with vegetation

and the picturesque old vineyards, tall poplars, and walnut trees rising on the banks of running brooks offer a
delightful panorama.

The name Mesropawan [town of Mesrop] is derived
from Saint Mesrop Mashtots', the inventor of the Armenian alphabet, who lived there for many years. Mounts
Tapanasar (or Nawasar), Kïnakoch', ''Galis em, Galis
em,'' and other mountains that surround Mesropawan
appear in the ancient legends of the Armenian people.[34]
In the 1970s the mysteries of Tapanasar have been the
focus of scientific discussion: a series of petroglyphs discovered there are similar to those of Siwnik' and the
Mountains of Gegham. Mount Kïnakoch' is also of interest. At its foot there is a natural cavern that still bears
the name of Mashtots'. According to tradition, this is
where Mesrop Mashtots' and his pupils lived for about
seventeen years,[35] until the founding of a monastery.

Mesropawan is also known for its archaeological sites
and architectural monuments. Near the village one can
still see the ruins of ancient fortresses, buildings, gravestones, and *khach'k'ars* from the ninth to the fifteenth
century and later. The Monastery of St. Grigor, a famous
monument that was later renamed for Saint Mesrop
Mashtots', is situated on a small, level area in the western part of the village. According to tradition, in A.D. 456
Prince Shabit of Goght'n built the church of the monastery that preceded the present structure. Through the
centuries the rectangular outer walls of the monastery,
its porch, and the buildings adjacent to these have been
destroyed. Today the only monument that remains is the
church, which is in a semidilapidated state. It is a small,
domed structure extending from east to west and consists of a hall, which has four pillars, a main apse, and
two vestries—all enclosed in a rectangular perimeter
(Fig. 14). A large cupola with eight windows rises above
the four pillars. There used to be a small bell tower to the
left of the cupola and a porch that was attached to the
western elevation of the church. The latter had four pillars and its north and south elevations formed arcades.

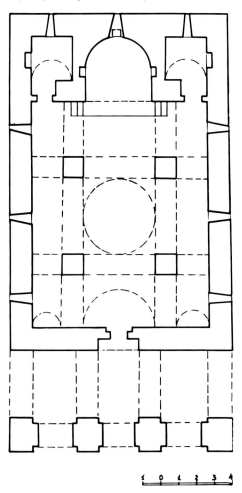

Fig. 14. The plan of St. Grigor or St. Mesrop Mashtots' Church.

The arches rested on the pillars and the squinches in the
western wall of the church.

According to the inscriptions on the walls, the church
was renovated in the fifteenth century and again in the
seventeenth. The most recent renovation was made at
the end of the nineteenth century.

THE CITY OF GIRAN

The ruins of this medieval city are located on the left bank of the Gilan (historic Giran) River 3 kilometers to the northeast of the present-day village of Verin Aza. Giran is geographically situated in the central part of the district of Goght'n and occupies an area larger than 12 square kilometers. There is very little information available on the historical background of this city. Confusing the site of Giran with that of the town of Azat, which occupied the area of the present-day villages of Verin and Nerk'in Aza and Der, certain nineteenth-century ethnographers identified the city as Azat-Giran, considering the two towns one and the same.[36] Azat and Giran, however, were two separate cities and were mentioned as such in Catholicos Khach'ik I's encyclical of 976.[37] The information given by the fourteenth-century historian Ḥamd Allāh Qazvīnī about the location of the city of Azat corroborates this fact.[38] According to Qazvīnī, Azat was well known among the cities of Goght'n for the cultivation of wheat, cotton, and grapes and for the manufacture of wine. The author of the *Life of Vahan of Goght'n* (eighth century) states that before the Arab conquests, the Persians called this town Azat Cheran. Subsequently, the Persians and later the Arabs identified the entire district of Goght'n by that name.

The ruins of the city of Giran reveal that it lost its significance in the middle of the sixteenth century. It was completely abandoned sometime after the seventeenth century and then fell into ruin. What remained of the city quickly disappeared, since after 1829 the inhabitants of the nearby villages began to make use of the stones of the ruined buildings. Today the city is entirely destroyed and the site leveled.

Giran attracted the attention of the scholarly world at the beginning of the twentieth century. But, unfortunately, until recently the site had been unexplored. In the early 1920s S. Ter-Avetisian surveyed and partially excavated the ruins of the city; his article is to this day the only study on Giran.[39]

Historic Giran was spread out in small glens around a citadel perched on the peak of a steep rock that dominates its surroundings. The archaic features of its numerous buildings, inns, and walls and the great variety of the excavated pottery and other items indicate that Giran was founded in the early Middle Ages and that between the seventh and tenth centuries it thrived politically and culturally. The layout of the city suggests that it consisted of three sections: the citadel, the *shahastan* [the city proper], and the suburbs. It was surrounded with strong outer walls.

The citadel, located in the eastern part of the city, covers an area more than 1 kilometer long and 500 to 600 meters wide. It is protected not only by the natural impregnability of the place but also by strong outer walls. Inside the walls one can see the traces of more than ten buildings and the ruins of a princely palace in which three wells are dug into the rock. The largest of these has three compartments, with the middle one the largest and deepest. Stone steps connect the other two compartments to the middle one.

From its elevated location the citadel of Giran dominates the city and its vicinity and the entire district of Goght'n, including the dwellings on both banks of the Arax River from old Julfa to the city of Ordubad. Its position is ideal for observing the strategic points of these areas.

ORDUAR

This city, now the center of the region of the same name, is historically known as Orduar, Ordvar, and Ort'var; foreign (that is, non-Armenian) sources call it Ortupat or Ordubad. The town is located in the eastern part of the district and in the past it was one of the best-known villages of Goght'n. It is spread out in a large valley, 2 to 7 kilometers wide, through which the Orduar River flows. Mountains and rich green vineyards surround the city, giving it an exceptional charm. According to historians and medieval travelers, Orduar was noted for its grapes, pomegranates, figs, and other fruits. From antiquity the town was also known for its silk, its architectural monuments, and its history. According to the information given in the *Kavkazskogo kalendaria* (1852), until the mid-nineteenth century there were approximately twelve thousand houses in Orduar. Some of these, which are now in ruins, stand in the vineyards to the north of the present-day town.

Today one can still see in the northern part of Ordubad the remains of the citadel of the older city, which is built on a rock about 50 to 60 meters high and occupies a large area. From our survey of the citadel and its vicinity it appears that historic Orduar was in fact located around the walls of the citadel and on the site of the older quarters of the present-day town. In the vineyards, on the squares, in front of buildings, and around private houses stand Oriental plane trees, the only surviving witnesses of the city's historic past. Some of these trees have been around for as long as twelve hundred years.[40]

The large number of Oriental plane trees in Orduar is not accidental. In the pre-Christian period the Armenians loved trees of this type and believed they were holy. According to historical sources, sacred groves of plane and oak trees were situated near the pagan temples of ancient Armenia. From the rustling of their branches and leaves the priests predicted the future. These same sources testify that the district of Goght'n put up the longest and the most unyielding struggle against the spread of the Christian faith, and her inhabitants persevered in their traditional idolatry. It was not accidental that Saint Mesrop Mashtots' resided in that district and with the help of his pupils undertook missionary work in such areas where the pagan temples were apparently still functioning. The plane trees of modern Ordubad are probably the scions of trees that stood near the ancient temples. The position of the present-day trees that have survived and their distribution in the different parts of the city suggest that they were originally planted.

Among the hundreds of plane trees in modern Or-dubad there was at Sar-Shahar Square in the central quarter of the city a huge, tall tree considered the patriarch of the plane trees of Goght'n. Noted naturalist Professor Pettsol'd came to Goght'n in person to study the plane trees of Ordubad and wrote: "At Ordubad one can see the largest known plane trees. I measured one of them [the one at Sar-Shahar—A.A.]. Its leaves were unfortunately damaged by lightning, and in its trunk there was a large cavity." The Russian historian I. Ozarovskii called this the "giant plane tree"[41] and noted that the diameter of the trunk measured twenty arshins. Nineteenth-century traveler and surveyor I. Shopen confused this tree with a baobab, referring to it as the "most ancient baobab."[42] The tree was very tall, robust, and impressive. Because of age and natural disasters such as lightning, a cavity of 5 square meters has formed in its trunk. According to Chantre,[43] a shoemaker's shop was located in this cavity and in it twenty-three people could sit comfortably. The circumference of the trunk of this tree was amazingly large, and it had a diameter of 18 meters. According to specialists, it was over twenty-five hundred years old.

Between the tenth and eighteenth centuries a series of palaces, monasteries, churches, bridges, caravanserai, markets, and other buildings of high architectural quality were built in Ordubad. Most of these have been destroyed. The Russian church, which was built with the contribution of Araskhanian of Agulis, is a beautiful structure. Of the Armenian monuments only St. Step'anos Church has survived, and it is in a semidilapidated state. Located on the grounds of the ancient citadel in the northern part of the historic city, this church was preceded by a structure built at about the end of the thirteenth century and renovated on a number of occasions. The present building, which has four pillars, two vestries, an apse, and a hall, is from the seventeenth century (Fig. 15). Its roof rested on the four pillars. Its only entrance is on the northern facade, facing the city. Today the cupola, the entire roof, and the upper parts of the walls are destroyed. One can still see the remains of

Fig. 15. The plan of St. Step'anos Church.

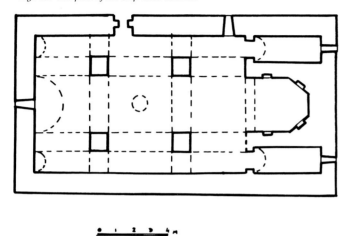

wall paintings on the white background of the interior. In the northern and southern walls of the apse there are secret passageways through which stone stairways ascend to the chambers above the ceilings of the vestries and in the upper sides of the apse. A porch [*zhamatun*] is attached to the south facade of the church. This large structure is also in ruins now.

GANDZAK

A beautiful but not a very deep valley extends to the northeast of Ordubad. The historic village of Gandzak, or Gandza, which is 4 to 5 kilometers from the city of Ordubad, is situated on the upper course of a river that flows through this valley. Our survey of the area of Gandzak and its vicinity indicates that the village existed since ancient times and possessed a number of architectural monuments. According to the statistics of 1927, 665 people lived there. At the time of the archaeological expeditions of E. Lalayian[44] at the end of the nineteenth century and that of V. Sysoev in 1927,[45] the ancient

church of Gandzak, about which the sources unfortunately say nothing, was still standing in a semidilapidated state. The church is located in the center of the village and is now completely in ruins. At the time of Sysoev's survey, only its east facade and a part of the northern elevation had survived. The polygonal apse had an almost square plan (3.10 by 3.90 meters). Ghewond Alishan has published one of the inscriptions from the church of Gandzak; it is a short text dated 1577.[46]

ANAPAT

On the right bank of a brook 2 kilometers below Gandzak is the historic village of Anapat, which is mentioned in the seventeenth-century inscription on the lintel of the western portal of the church of the Monastery of St. T'ovma in Agulis. Only a few of the monuments of this once large and famous city have survived. According to I. Shopen, Anapat and its monuments were destroyed at the time of Nadir Shah. Shopen mentions the village church and says that there were over two hundred ruined houses.[47] According to the historical sources, Anapat was known in the Middle Ages for its church, bridge, and other architectural monuments. This information is corroborated by the ruins of the city.

Ghewond Alishan notes that Anapat, "formerly a large and a populous town . . . has a ruined church named St. Step'anos; it is built of unpolished stone. In it there are *khach'k'ars* and a stone baptismal font."[48] At the end of the nineteenth century E. Lalayian noted: "Here also there are a large church, which is entirely in ruins, a small chapel, and a large cemetery on the slanting side of the valley."[49] The historical information on Anapat and its monuments is very scanty. Our guess is that St. Step'anos Church was founded in the Middle Ages and was renovated several times. The monument was probably destroyed at the end of the eighteenth century.

We know of a seventeenth-century gospel that was

copied there. Its colophon states: "I, Gulkhandan, wife of Khoja Ghuli of Anapat, who received this holy gospel, bought it with possessions that were rightfully mine. . . . [This book] was completed on September 10, 1671, and I donated it to the Church of St. Step'an Nakhavkay [St. Stephen the Protomartyr] in the village of Anapat, which lies within the limits of Urtuar."[50] This vellum manuscript was decorated with the miniature images of the four evangelists, canon tables, marginal ornamentation, and fantastic birds.

The cemetery of Anapat is also of interest, although most of the tombstones in it have decayed or been removed or are effaced.

HANDAMĒJ

The historic village of Handamēj, or Andamēj, which is about 2 kilometers to the northwest of Ordubad, lies in the midst of green vineyards. In the famous inscription at the Monastery of St. T'ovma in Agulis, this village is mentioned as a place of habitation in the district of Goght'n. It is considered a suburb of the city of Ordubad and is divided into two villages, Upper Handamēj and Inner Handamēj. The village church, now in ruins, stands in the center of Inner Handamēj. The colophon of a gospel copied in 1684 in the village of Kits' in Geghouadzor near Tat'ew was written at Handamēj.[51] Formerly this gospel was kept at the church of Nor T'agh in Shushi,[52] but now it is in the United States. The colophon states: "This holy gospel, which had been taken captive by the Muslims, is again in memory of Tsatur son of Siran of Andamēj. Siranch'an liberated the gospel and gave it to St. Astuatsatsin Church of Andamēj. . . . Remember Tsatur and his mother, Eghisap'et'. . . . This was written on September 15, 1796."[53] It is clear from the testimony of this colophon that the church of Handamēj was called St. Astuatsatsin.

At the end of the nineteenth century, when St. Astuatsatsin Church was still standing, E. Lalayian wrote that "the church was a very clean building. It was a vaulted structure and there were beautiful rooms nearby."[54] In 1927, at the time of V. Sysoev's survey, this church was already in ruins. According to Sysoev's description,[55] the monument was a domed basilican church with a rectangular plan and four pillars; its lower measurements were 17 by 10 meters and its entrances were located on the western and southern facades. The apse, which was 5 meters wide, had seven sides and niches. The four pillars of the hall (1.04 meters) were square. There were vestries on both sides of the apse. From the northern vestry there was a special passageway leading down to the area below the apse, where there was a secret chamber that was built like a well. The interior of the church was covered with white plaster. On the blue background of the vault of the apse there were stars painted green. Its tall cupola was round inside and octagonal on the exterior. It was covered with a pyramidal roof. Inside the church, in the bay between the pillars, there were tombstones with dates, one of which was 1571. Our guess is that St. Astuatsatsin Church of Handamēj was built in the seventeenth century on the foundations of an earlier church. The new structure was still standing until the 1930s.

RAMIS

There is very little information available on the ancient village of Ramis, or Ramik', and its monuments. Ramis, which is in the region of Ordubad and still bears the same name, is situated on an elevated site in the mountains of Zangezur. It is 2,000 meters above sea level. The village was built in the uppermost part of the Ts'ghna Valley, one of the deepest valleys in Goght'n. The view is striking, since the village is surrounded with tall peaks covered with greenery. In the valley below Ramis one can see the historic villages of Goght'n: Mazra, Ustup or Stupi, and Ts'ghna, the largest village in the area.

The ruins in and around Ramis indicate that the origins of the village date back to a time before the birth of Christ. The ruins and the extant domestic, commercial, and religious buildings in the village, which is spread out on the sides of mountains, and the large cemetery bear witness that over two hundred Armenian families lived there. Now there are only seven Armenian families (fourteen people) residing in the village.

Today historic Ṙamis has a wretched and a dilapidated appearance.[56] The village lost its former energetic life decades ago. In the ruins around the village one can still see the remains of a number of chapels, water mills, and fortresses. The most famous and important monument in Ṙamis is the church, which is well preserved. It is located in the upper quarter of the village and dominates the entire panorama, since it is visible from a great distance. According to the natives, the church is called St. Astuatsatsin. The historical sources give no information either about the village or about the structure that preceded the present church. The latter has been mentioned in passing by M. P'ap'azian, Ghewond Alishan,

Fig. 16. St. Astuatsatsin Church from the southwest.

and E. Lalayian. V. M. Sysoev wrote a great deal on Ṙamis and its church in his work based on the survey of Nakhichevan Autonomous SSR in 1927.[57]

The only sources on St. Astuatsatsin of Ṙamis are the inscriptions from the church itself. It gives us authentic information on the reconstruction of the edifice in the seventeenth century. The stones of this church and those from neighboring buildings are cut in an archaic style that leads us to believe a pagan shrine stood there at an earlier period. The present-day church (Fig. 16) is built of polished blocks of basalt stone and granite. It has the plan of a basilican church with a nave and two aisles. The hall, the apse, and the vestries are located within a rectangular perimeter (Fig. 17). The monument has two entrances, one on the west facade and another on the south. The hall has two pairs of cruciform pillars, above which are the arches that support the gabled roof. The interior is elevated and bright. The apse is semicircular and has three niches. On both sides of the apse are two-storied vestries. The entrances to the second story are hidden in the niches in the walls of the first story. The apse and the vestries each receive their light from single windows on the eastern facade. The hall is illuminated through sets of three windows with wide, rectangular apertures located on the sides and the west facade. Four thick vertical supports divide the hall into a nave and two aisles. The arches that carry the vault rest on the central pillars and the engaged piers.

The architectural decor of St. Astuatsatsin Church indicates that the plain basalt walls of the structure that preceded it lacked ornamentation. The exterior appearance of the church was made considerably more expressive after the seventeenth-century reconstruction, when decorative bands were carved around the portals and beautiful *khach'k'ars* and high-relief friezes were set in the walls above the lintels and other areas. Subsequently, probably in the eighteenth century, the interior of the church was covered with plaster and wall paintings.

The inscriptions on the church state that the present

Fig. 17. The plan of St. Astuatsatsin Church.

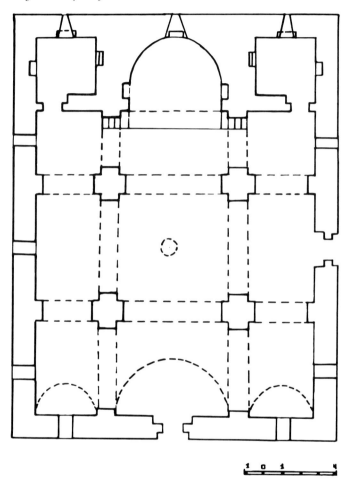

hundred tombstones from the fourteenth to the nineteenth century, is located on a hill in the northeastern quarter of Ṙamis. Most of the inscriptions on the tombstones are either effaced or partially covered by dirt.

About 4 to 4.5 kilometers down the valley toward the village of Mazra is the church of the Monastery of St. Sargis. It stands on the side of a mountain to the south of the valley and is on the road that goes down to Ts'ghna. The church, which is built of blocks of polished sandstone, is a small monument with a single-chamber nave and a wooden roof. Its plan is almost a square. At its eastern extremity it has a semicircular apse, but it lacks vestries. At present the roof and the upper parts of the walls are destroyed. The only entrance, which has a plain appearance, is on the north elevation. Above the portal there is a small *khach'k'ar.* On it, under the cross and on both sides of the arms, there is an inscription that is now effaced. In front of the west facade of the church there are a number of trees with thick trunks and the ruins of an older structure. A cold-water spring gushes out from beneath the church and flows along its west side for 2 to 2.5 meters.

STUPI

The historic village of Stupi, Ustupi or Ĕstupi, which is about 5 kilometers from Ṙamis, lies in a deep valley and is situated on the road to Ts'ghna. There are only a few facts known about Stupi's past. Our survey of the area shows that the village had a church and other buildings.

Stupi is first mentioned in eighteenth-century manuscripts. Petros the Deacon, a scribe who copied a manuscript at P'aṙaka in 1719, states: "Again in 1714 certain people from Ĕstup came and argued that the fields at the fountain of Smbat' were theirs. They raised much controversy."[58] In a letter dated June 25, 1725, sent by a mother from Ṙamis to her two sons, Paron Giram and Šahin, who were in Russia, there are references to the destruction of dwellings, oppression, and difficulties that

structure was built in 1677–78 through the efforts of Mahtesi Vardan, Nawasard, Awetis, and Anush, who were natives of Ṙamis. The renovation of the church according to the inscription on the upper part of the southeastern pier of the church was supervised by *"usta* [master] Murat."

The village cemetery, which contains more than six

the inhabitants of the villages of Goght'n suffered at the hands of the Persian khans and tax collectors. Stupi is also mentioned in this letter. The mother states: "It has been four months since the people of Ts'ghna, Ěstōpi, and K'uch', the ruined villages on our river, swarmed over with their children, families, cattle, and began staying in our village."[59]

TS'GHNA

Historic Ts'ghna is the present-day village of Ch'ananab in the region of Ordubad. It lies in the midst of ancient vineyards and is spread out in the valley of Ts'ghna along the right and left banks of a river. The antiquities in the vicinity of the village bear witness to the fact that the founders of Ts'ghna settled there many centuries ago. Since early times the village had schools, a theater, silk factories, and shops and was continuously inhabited by eight to nine hundred Armenian families.

Among the noted architectural monuments of Ts'ghna are St. Astuatsatsin Monastery and St. Sargis Church in the Tambri quarter.[60] The latter, which was renovated several times, was built in about the middle of the fifteenth century. St. Astuatsatsin Monastery of Ts'ghna, which is still standing, is an interesting monument of medieval Armenian architecture and, fortunately, is well preserved. Over the course of time the porch, the outer walls, the cells, and other buildings in the complex have been destroyed. Today only the church and the bell tower remain.

The church of St. Astuatsatsin Monastery of Ts'ghna is a large structure built of blocks of polished basalt and red stone. The complex was considered an important cultural center. According to epigraphical and literary sources, the present church was renovated at the end of the twelfth and in the course of the sixteenth and seventeenth centuries. The structure was rebuilt on the foundations of an ancient church. The present structure is a domed basilica consisting of a large, bright apse, two

vestries, and a hall (Fig. 18). Its striking cupola, which has eight windows, rises in the center of the cruciform roof and rests on four thick cruciform pillars. According to a traveler of 1691, St. Astuatsatsin Church was decorated with wall paintings that included images of Saint Gregory the Illuminator and Saint Silvester.[61]

A three-storied bell tower stands attached to the south facade of the church. Eight columns on the second and third stories carry the arches and rest on the first story, which has a rectangular structure (Fig. 19). On the southern side of the two pillars on the first level there are beautiful reliefs of the Mother of God and the crucifixion

Fig. 18. The plan of the church of St. Astuatsatsin Monastery.

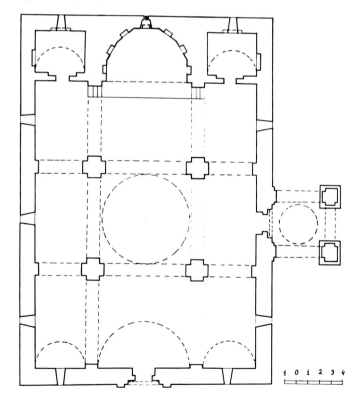

Fig. 19. The bell tower of the church of St. Astuatsatsin Monastery.

Fig. 20. A relief of the Mother of God on the bell tower of St. Astuatsatsin Church.

(Figs. 20–21). The church had another bell tower in front of its western portal, but it is now in ruins.

The beautiful semicircular ornamental bands that encircle the two portals, reliefs (Fig. 22), and inscriptions articulate the exterior parts of St. Astuatsatsin Church.

The decorative chain-like band carved around the entire structure joins the bands around the windows and portals, giving the church an exceptional splendor.

Between the fourteenth and seventeenth centuries, the Monastery of St. Astuatsatsin also had a school.

Fig. 21. *A relief of Christ on the bell tower of St. Astuatsatsin Church.*

Since the mid-nineteenth century the parochial school of Ts'ghna has been located in its courtyard. A number of manuscripts have been copied in the scriptorium of the school of Ts'ghna. Two of these are now preserved in the Matenadaran of Erevan (Mss. nos. 1184, 4175). These

have rich marginal decorations, canon tables, and uncials decorated as fantastic birds and flowers.

At a distance of about 1 kilometer from Ts'ghna lie the ruins of a medieval fortress with formidable walls.

MTS'GUN

About 3 kilometers south of Ts'ghna lie the ruins of a village in which a monument called Mizkunts' Vank' still stands. According to the testimony of Bishop T'ovma (seventeenth century), who was from the neighboring village of Vanand, the Armenians from his place of birth frequently went "to the wonderful district of Goght'n, to the Church of St. Step'anos, which is surnamed Mts'gun."[62]

According to the historical sources, this site corresponds to that of the ancient village of Mts'gun (Mzkun) and Mizkunts' Vank' is St. Step'anos Monastery. At the beginning of the eighteenth century, Catholicos Abraham of Crete passed through this village on his way to Julfa.[63] According to the inscription on the lintel above the northern portal of the church, St. Step'anos was most recently rebuilt in 1895. The church of St. Step'anos Monastery has a wooden roof. It consists of an apse, two vestries, and a hall. There are a number of ninth- to seventeenth-century *khach'k'ars* set into the walls of the church.

P'AŘAKA

The ancient village of P'aŕaka, one of the major places of habitation in Bstadzor or Gilan Valley, is spread out around a high hill. Tall mountains covered with greenery surround the village, and ravines that pierce their sides lend a special charm to the place.

Archaeological sites, ruined and still extant wine presses, water mills, the large cemetery, bridges, monasteries, and churches in the vicinity of P'aṙaka bear witness to the kind of life that existed in this ancient village. After examining the area of P'aṙaka and the antiquities in its vicinity, we are led to believe that the place was settled by people before the birth of Christ.

Unfortunately, the historical sources offer very little information on the history of P'aṙaka and its architectural monuments.[64] Some information, however, has been preserved in about ten manuscripts dating from the fifteenth to eighteenth century that were copied there and are well known to philologists. Two of these are now preserved in the Matenadaran of Erevan (Mss. nos. 7758, 8205). It is now clear from these manuscripts and the epigraphical sources that during the Middle Ages P'aṙaka was noted for the Hermitage of St. Gēorg of Dzoravank', St. Nshan, St. Eghia Margarē, St. Hakob Hayrapet, St. Shmawon, and St. Step'anos churches and monasteries, some of which are now in ruins. The churches of St. Shmawon and St. Hakob Hayrapet monasteries are still standing. These are seventeenth-century monuments with interesting architectural solutions.

St. Shmawon Church of P'aṙaka (Fig. 23) is a large basilica with a nave and two aisles. It is situated on a level area on top of a hill in the western part of the village. The building extends from east to west. A vaulted porch is attached to its west facade. The structure and the measurements of St. Shmawon are similar to that of St. Astuatsatsin Monastery of Bist, a basilican church with a nave and two aisles. Next to this basilica, St. Shmawon is the largest one in Nakhichevan.

St. Shmawon is built of polished blocks of local dark blue basalt and earth-colored and white stones. It is well preserved. The white stones on the outside of the church alternate with the earth-colored ones, breaking up the exterior monotony. The main apse, the two-storied vestries on either side of it, and the high-ceilinged hall are arranged in a rectangular perimeter. There are two portals, one on the west facade and the other on the east. The gabled roof rests on arches that stand on four cru-

Fig. 22. The west portal of St. Astuatsatsin Church.

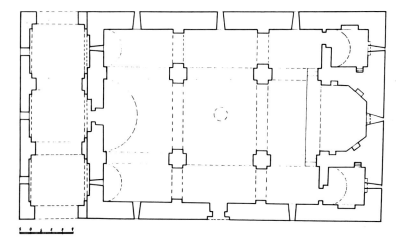

Fig. 23. The plan of St. Shmawon Church.

ciform pillars and divide the church into two aisles and a nave.

Considering the architectural characteristics of St. Shmawon, we can infer that the structure predating the present building was constructed in the twelfth century and was subsequently renovated several times. According to the inscription, now effaced, on the lintel of the southern portal, the present church was renovated in 1680 with the assistance of the clergy and the people of P'aṙaka. Attached to the western facade of St. Shmawon and extending from north to south there is a rectangular porch that has arcades on its northern and southern facades. This building was constructed in the seventeenth century.

Among the architectural monuments of P'aṙaka, St. Hakob Hayrapet Monastery stands out for its beauty. It is located in a small glen about 1 kilometer northwest of the village and stands on level ground that abuts the side of a mountain (Figs. 24–27). Ghewond Alishan, based on a few sources, notes that this "monastery was either

Fig. 25. The church of St. Hakob Hayrapet Monastery from the north.

Fig. 24. A general view of St. Hakob Hayrapet Monastery from the west.

built or renovated at the beginning of the eighteenth century by the inhabitants, who named it St. Hakovb Hayrapet [after Saint James of Nisibis]."[65] Today, of the entire complex, which was originally surrounded by a rectangular outer wall, only the church remains. In the course of time the porch, which was attached to the western facade of the church, the refectory, the outer walls, and the remaining buildings were all destroyed.

The church of St. Hakob Hayrapet is built of polished blocks of basalt and reddish and white stone. It is a domed basilica with four pillars (Fig. 28). Its only portal is on the west facade. The main apse, the two two-storied vestries, and the hall are enclosed within a rectangular perimeter. A cupola built of stones and with twelve windows stands on four cruciform pillars. Its roof is covered with bricks. In the interior, the areas between the pillars and the squinches were covered with reliefs. Now only two of these remain, one of which represents the head of a ram.

The exterior of the church of St. Hakob Hayrapet Monastery is particularly attractive (Figs. 19–21). Besides being in harmony with its environment, the use of white stones on the exterior and the reliefs decorating the sides of the windows lend the church a charming air. It also has striking *khach'k'ars* and reliefs on its walls. Two high arches above the portal that are decorated with ornamented bands make the western facade especially fascinating (Fig. 22).

According to a nine-line inscription on the tympanum of the portal, the renovation of the church, which was realized with the assistance of the clergy and the people of P'aṙaka, lasted for ten years, from 1691 to 1701. The porch on the western facade of the church had four pillars and extended along the entire width of the western elevation. In 1703 the cupola of St. Hakob Hayrapet was destroyed by lightning,[66] but it was later restored.

BOHRUT

The historic village of Bohrut (or Buhrut, or Bekhrut) is about 3 to 4 kilometers down the valley from P'aṙaka and is surrounded by woods. Information on the past of this ancient village and its monuments is sparse. The remains of an earlier village predating the present hamlet reveal that because it was situated on one of the local transit routes, Bohrut grew considerably during the Middle Ages.

Bohrut is mentioned as a place of renown in the important inscription on the western portal of the Mon-

Fig. 26. The church of St. Hakob Hayrapet Monastery from the south.

astery of St. T'ovma in Agulis. The village is also mentioned in a manuscript copied at P'aṙaka in 1719 by the deacon Petros, son of Łatam,[67] and in a letter written in 1725 by a mother from Ṙamis.[68] Among the well-known historical monuments of Bohrut are its beautiful bridge and the ancient church. The latter is in ruins and only a section of the bridge remains. According to our source, the church of Bohrut was still standing in 1873, but we have no description of its appearance.[69]

Like the merchants of P'aṙaka, Julfa, Shoṙot', and Agulis, since ancient times the natives of Bohrut traveled to different lands for commercial transactions. Eighteenth-century sources have recorded a touching event involving the patriotism of a certain Sahak, a seventeen-year-old native of Bohrut. According to the testimony of contemporaries, Sahak lived with his relatives in the

Fig. 27. The west facade of the church of St. Hakob Hayrapet Monastery.

Fig. 28. The plan of St. Hakob Hayrapet Monastery.

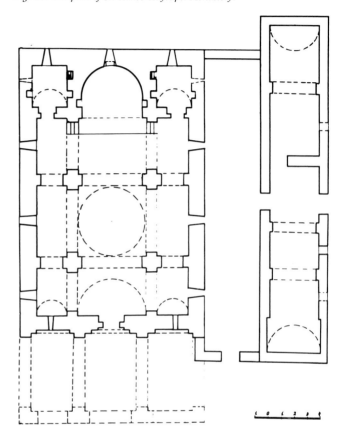

Crimea, where he preoccupied himself with commercial enterprises. Near one of the towns on the Crimean shore the Muslims seized Sahak and gave him the option of death or conversion to Islam. The Bohrut youth bravely resisted the temptation of living as a traitor to his faith and nation and instead offered himself as a sacrifice. Vrt'anēs Vardapet, who was an eyewitness to the event, notes (Matenadaran Ms. no. 7397, p. 639, recto and verso) that the Muslims tore apart the flesh from his body with iron tongs; they shred his body with swords and flayed him like a lamb. A contemporary chronicler wrote with pride about the patriotism of Sahak: "On October 17, 1715, the holy martyr Sahak was executed for the Glory of Christ the Blessed One. Amen. In the middle of winter he appeared like a blossoming rose and his wonderful fragrance filled the entire universe. Good tidings to you, O land of Goght'n; rejoice that you possess goodly roots and blessed branches. Rejoice, O land of Crimea, that a valuable gem, who had fled the Orient, lay at rest in you."[70] In one of the manuscripts that he copied, Step'anos of Cafa wrote as follows: "O blessed youth, where did you learn the great art of [spiritual] warfare? Where were you bound? Where are you headed for? The mention of death makes us shudder; instead of milk, you drank the cup of death."[71]

BGHEW

The historic village of Bghew, now called Bilav, which is 4 to 5 kilometers down the valley from Bohrut, is located on the bank of the Gilan River. The village occupies a large area. Our survey of its older buildings reveals that people lived there from ancient times. Through the centuries the older monuments have been destroyed, and the literary sources have preserved no information on them. Besides the church, there was a bridge with several arches that stood over the Gilan River in front of the village; only insignificant vestiges of its pier remain now.

Bghew was mentioned by the seventeenth-century historian Aṙak'el of Tabriz. Describing the topography of the upper course of a tributary of the Gilan River that intercepts the road from Shoṙot' to Ts'ghna, the historian notes that the brook "comes from Norakert and goes to Bĕghewi."[72]

NAWUSH (NAVISH)

The historic village of Nawush, or Navish, is now uninhabited and in ruins. It is located 7 to 8 kilometers to the north of P'aṙaka and is near the village of Tewi, from which it is about 4 kilometers. Nawush is situated on the slope of one of the valleys of Bstadzor. The sources say nothing on its history or the circumstances of its desertion. From the ruins and the cemetary one can surmise that the Armenians left there after the 1630s. Nawush

was known in the Middle Ages for the Hermitage of St. Step'anos, St. Astuatsatsin Church, and more. Unfortunately only one of these monuments, the Hermitage of St. Step'anos, survives, and even that is now abandoned and covered with bushes and grass (Fig. 29).

In the manuscripts St. Step'anos is best known as a hermitage, but occasionally it is also referred to as a monastery. From this hermitage, which is built on an elevated site near the village before which the Nawush River flows in a glen, one can see the splendid panorama of the middle course of the Bstadzor basin, which is surrounded with mountains covered with verdure in the spring. The plan of the St. Step'anos complex is a replica of seventeenth-century monastic structures. The church stands in the center of a rectangular outer wall. Near the walls there are buildings of an economic, commercial, and auxiliary nature. These, as well as the walls of the complex, were ruined at the end of the eighteenth century.[73] The only monuments in the complex that are still standing are the church and the porch. The church, like those of St. Grigor Lusaworich' Monastery of Shoṙot' and the Hermitage of St. Nshan or Kopatap' of Bist, is a

Fig. 29. The church of St. Step'anos Monastery from the northwest.

basilica with a nave and two aisles and two pairs of supports. It is built of polished blocks of black stone and basalt and has a rectangular plan (Fig. 30) that comprises a hall, an apse, and two vestries. The only portal is located on the western facade. The arches and the gabled roof rest on the two pillars and the engaged piers. Like a number of other churches in Nakhichevan, this church also has secret chambers; their entrances are hidden inside the niches of the apse and the vestries. On the tympanum of the church there is a long inscription stating that the present building of St. Step'anos was renovated in 1677 with the support of the people of the village of Tewi. A small vaulted porch stands before the portal of the church. It was probably built at the time of the renovation of the church in 1677.

In the early eighteenth century, on his way from

Fig. 30. The plan of St. Step'anos Monastery.

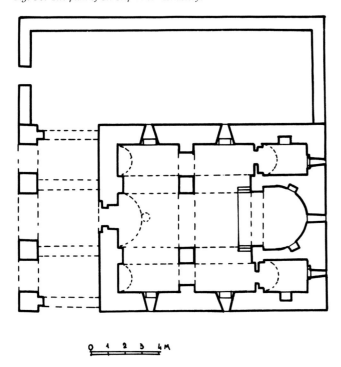

P'aṙaka to Bist, Catholicos Abraham of Crete visited the Hermitage of Nawush. At that time the village was already abandoned and desolate, and the hermitage had "only seven hermits. I went to see them as well as the monastery, and on the same day continued my journey to the great village of Bist."[74]

The literary sources say nothing about the founding and the past history of the earlier structure that predates the present church. However, the presence of fifteenth-century *khach'k'ars* in the apse of the church and the old masonry of the stones used in the structure and in the nearby ruins reveals that the hermitage probably was founded between the eleventh and twelfth centuries. One of the oldest sources on the Hermitage of St. Step'anos is a gospel copied in Bist in 1489 that was restored here. In the colophon of this gospel one reads: "Remember the monk Khach'atur who bound this holy gospel. . . . This holy gospel was renovated at the Hermitage of St. Step'anos of Nawish, St. Astuatsatsin, and the other saints."[75] There is also the testimony of a colophon in a synaxarium—its date and place are unknown—which states that two of the three monks who received the book were from Tewi and lived in the Hermitage of St. Step'anos. The scribe writing the colophon begs the reader to remember "especially those who received [the gospel], the celibate priest Lord Azariē from the village of Bĕst and a member of the congregation of the well-known Monastery of St. Nshan, and also Tēr Hakob and Tēr Hohan from the village of Tewi, who are of the congregation of St. Step'anos Monastery."[76] This manuscript has 529 pages and is decorated with marginal ornaments and embellished uncials that were probably executed by the illuminator Sargis, who copied the manuscript.

TEWI

The road ascending the mountains to the north of P'aṙaka is a dangerous one; it passes along the edges of deep gorges and descends from the sides of precipices.

Suddenly from a slope one gets a glimpse of Tewi, spread out in a valley and surrounded by different species of ancient trees. This famous old village, which is mentioned in the inscription of St. T'ovma Monastery of Agulis, is also known as Tiwi, Dewi, and now as T'ivi.

Since ancient times the site of Tewi has been inhabited by people much involved with cultural activities and building monuments. Since the village was situated on one of the busy local highways and was within easy reach of the towns and villages of Bist, Mesropawan, Shoṙot[c], and P'aṙaka, it reached a considerably advanced stage of civilization, especially in the seventeenth century. The monk Gabriel, a native of Tewi, who wrote a colophon in the "Lives of the Egyptian Fathers," a manuscript that he copied in 1625, was not ashamed to admit that he was from this village: "I, the humble monk Gabriel, from the town of Tewi in the district of Goght'n, came to Ṙēmal in 1695."[77]

In the sources there is very little information of a descriptive or historical nature on Tewi and its monuments. Catholicos Abraham of Crete, who was visiting the villages of Ernjak and Goght'n, departed from P'aṙaka and went "to the village of Tewi, where there was a ruined monastery."[78] Abraham of Crete, Ghewond Alishan, E. Lalayian, and H. Oskian do not mention the name of the village church. The historian Aṙak'el of Tabriz informs us that "in 1533 they burned the monk Hayrapet, who was from the Monastery of Tewi."[79] E. Lalayian identified this hermitage with St. Step'anos of Nawish, near Tewi, and noted that "only the two pillars of the Armenian church are standing. There is also a *khach'k'ar* there that has the following inscription: 'In memory of the son of Hohan. In the year 1659.' "[80]

In the course of our research we were able to discover the name of the monastery of Tewi in a gospel copied in 1554. In 1650 this manuscript was donated to the church of Tewi. According to its colophon, "This holy gospel is in memory of Karapet and his wife Shahristan. . . . In 1650 it was donated to St. T'uma Church in our village of Tew. Remember."[81] Nothing has survived of the remains of the church of St. T'ovma Monas-

tery, which was described by E. Lalayian at the end of the nineteenth century. It is thus impossible to reconstruct the plan of the church. But we can be certain that this church was a large building. As for its date of construction, St. T'ovma Monastery must have been founded no later than the fifteenth century and was probably renovated in the middle of the seventeenth.

SHRJU (SRJU)

On the left side of the highway 4 to 5 kilometers to the southeast of Bist one can see the ruins of an old village, Shrju or Srju, on a hill in a deep valley. The sources do not provide any information on this village. From the ruins one can surmise that human habitation was established there in the early part of the Middle Ages. Shrju, where as many as sixty to eighty families may have lived, evidently was abandoned in the second half of the nineteenth century and is now desolate. For decades it served as the winter quarters of the herdsmen of the neighboring village of T'ivi (Tewi). Shrju is also mentioned in the inscription of St. T'ovma Monastery of Agulis.

Among the ruins of present-day Shrju the village church is still standing in a semidilapidated state. It is built on a level site on the side of a mountain to the northeast of the ancient village. This church, according to its plan, was a basilica with a nave and two aisles and was built of polished blocks of basalt and local stone (Fig. 31). It has four pillars and a portal on the west facade. The apse of the church is five-sided on the exterior with two-storied vestries on the left and right.

There is a porch attached to the western facade of the church, covering its entire width. Today this building is completely in ruins. The northern and southern facades of the porch, which had four pillars, were arcaded and open. The arches rested on the four pillars and the squinches in the western elevation of the church. The remains of a number of ruined buildings that were part of the complex are still visible in the vicinity of the church. These were surrounded by an outer wall.

Fig. 31. The plan of the Shrju village church.

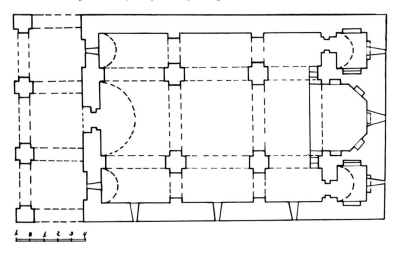

Fig. 32. The plan of St. Astuatsatsin Church.

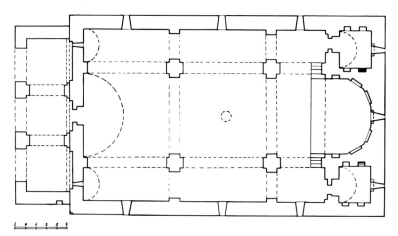

There is no information on Shrju or its church. Our guess is that the structure was renovated in the seventeenth century.

BIST

The historic village of Bist (Bust), or Pust, located 5 to 6 kilometers to the northwest of Mesropawan, is situated on a rocky promontory in Bstadzor Valley. To the north of Bist (which still bears the same name and is located in the present-day region of Ordubad) is the Gilan River and to the south the Mesropawan River (Nasrvaz River). On their banks rise tall poplars, walnut trees with thick trunks, and various other species of vegetation. The rich greenery adds to the beauty of the area.

Bist, where people have been living since ancient times, has been known to the historical sources since the thirteenth century. One can still see in its vicinity the ruins of early fortresses, cemeteries, chapels, water mills, and bridges. According to the colophons of fourteenth- to seventeenth-century manuscripts, Bist was known for St. Nshan Hermitage, St. Astuatsatsin Monastery, and St. Sargis Church; two of these are still standing. The Monastery of St. Astuatsatsin, situated in the northern part of the village, is one of the architectural monuments that is still extant. Catholicos Abraham of Crete, who visited Bist in the eighteenth century, called this sanctuary "a magnificent and a large church."[82] The church of St. Astuatsatsin is a basilica with a nave, two aisles, and four pillars. It was originally built in the twelfth or the thirteenth century. The present-day edifice was built by Alek'san Vardapet of Bist in 1687. Over the course of time the outer walls of the monastery, the school, the living quarters, and the buildings of economic significance were all destroyed. Attached to the western facade of the church is a graceful vaulted porch with two pillars. Its northern and southern facades are walled in. Today the only standing monument in the complex is the church. Its rectangular plan encloses within it a seven-sided apse, two vestries, and a hall (Fig. 32). It is built of polished blocks of basalt and reddish stone and was most recently renovated by the inhabitants of Bist in 1877. The exterior ornamentation of this magnificent church, with its high-ceilinged interior, is accentuated by the portal on the western facade, which is encircled by a decorative band.

The church of the Monastery of St. Astuatsatsin, where a number of manuscripts have been written, is one of the best-known medieval architectural monuments in Nakhichevan, and it is also the largest church in Nakhichevan.

The Hermitage of St. Nshan is another important monument in the cultural history of Bist (Figs. 33–34). It is located 1 kilometer to the north of the village. The hermitage, which is situated on a level site, was, according to tradition, founded at the end of the fifth century. It is a basilican church with one nave, two aisles, and two pairs of vertical supports. It has a five-sided apse and is surrounded by a rectangular outer wall. According to popular legend, Mesrop Mashtots', the inventor of the Armenian alphabet, who lived 4 to 5 kilometers from here, frequently visited the hermitage of Bist. Catholicos Abraham of Crete wrote about his visit to the Hermitage of St. Nshan: "I went to the monastery. It had the appearance of a dove and resembled the garden of Eden, being situated on an elevated site; for it was a place with well-watered gardens and fertile soil and clean healthy air. . . . I remained there for two days."[83] Attached to the southern front of the church is the arcaded porch with two pillars. The arches rest on the southern elevation of the church.

Between the thirteenth and seventeenth centuries this hermitage was considered one of the most famous religious and cultural centers of the district of Goght'n, and several manuscripts were copied there. Some of these are now preserved in the Matenadaran of Erevan. At the scriptorium of the Hermitage of St. Nshan, which was known as Kopatap', the scribe T'uma of Archēsh copied a manuscript in 1336. It is codex no. 6257 of the

Fig. 33. A general view of the Hermitage of St. Nshan or Kopatap' from the southwest.

Matenadaran of Erevan, a gospel, in which there are 193 marginal ornaments, 64 letters shaped like flowers, 71 letters shaped like birds, 22 letters shaped like animals, and 26 uncials with human shape. In the fifteenth century Mkrtich' illuminated a number of manuscripts in the scriptoria of Bist. Bist is also known for being the residence of Hakob the Scribe, surnamed Rabuni [teacher], a well-versed commentator on scriptural art and a pupil of Hovhannēs of Orotn. In 1407 the famous Armenian theologian Grigor of Tat'ew wrote his *K'arozgirk'* [book of sermons] at the request of Hakob of Bist. In the colophon of his book Grigor begs the reader to remember:

He who requested this book,
Hakob Rabun, my schoolmate
Who is from the house of Goght'n and a native of Bist.[84]

Fig. 34. The plan of the church of St. Nshan.

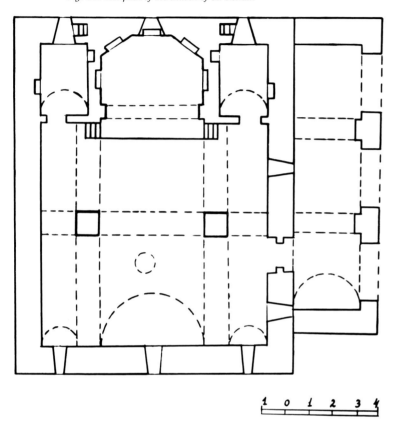

OGHOHI (AGHAHETS'IK)

The old Armenian village of Oghohi, or Aghahets'ik, the present-day village of Alahin, is situated on a craggy promontory in a deep valley in Bstadzor on the side of Mount T'awak'ali and is 4 to 5 kilometers northwest of Mesropawan and 2.5 kilometers northeast of Bist. It has been inhabited since ancient times. In 1827 Persian-Armenian families from Mazhanbar, Karabakh, and Salmast settled down there.

The historical sources have preserved only bits of information about Oghohi. In Step'anos Orbelean's *History*

of the House of Sisakan we come across the toponym Oghohi, or Ozohi, in his list of the villages of the district of Ernjak, which also includes Bist and its neighboring hamlets.[85] Our research shows that Oghohi is the present-day village of Alahi. Later, Oghohi was renamed Aghahets'ik and is mentioned as such in the famous seventeenth-century inscription at St. T'ovma Monastery in Agulis. Our survey of the vicinity of the village and its cemetery has shown that Armenians lived there ever since the early Middle Ages. Formerly the village was known for its bridge, St. Step'anos Church, and St. Khach' Monastery. Of these, St. Khach' is now in ruins and it has been converted into a chapel. Our survey of the ruins revealed that the monastery was an important complex. On its present site there was a church until the end of the nineteenth century. St. Khach', according to an inscription in St. Step'anos Church, possessed extensive estates in the seventeenth century.

St. Step'anos Church is located in the center of the village and is built with polished blocks of local grey stone. It is a domed basilican church with four pillars (Fig. 35), and its only entrance is located on the western facade. The cupola, the southern vestry, and most of the roof of the main hall were destroyed by the earthquake of 1930. There are dangerous cracks in the walls. Both the exterior and the interior of this church are simple and undecorated. The literary sources say nothing of the founding of the original structure and of subsequent renovations. According to dates on *khach'k'ars* set in the walls of the interior of the church, the edifice was renovated in the mid-seventeenth century. This church was most recently renovated in 1906 with the support of the villagers. The inscription commemorating this event is located above the arch of the portal.

NORAKERT (NIRGUD)

Nirgud, an old village in Goght'n, is located in the uppermost part of Bstadzor, in one of the upper zones of the Zangezur range. The village is situated in a deep

Fig. 35. The plan of St. Step'anos Church.

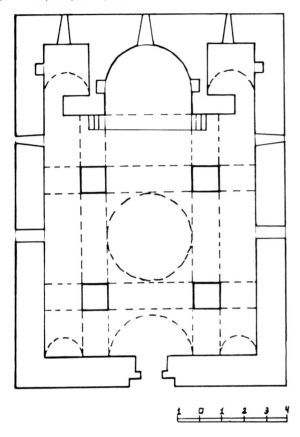

The church of Norakert, T'argmanch'ats Vank; the old fortress; and the cemetery are noteworthy among the monuments, indicating that there was life here between the fourteenth and eighteenth centuries. In the cemetery, which is located to the left of the road going to the village, there are fourteenth- and fifteenth-century tombstones and *khach'k'ars*. To the northeast of the village there is a mountain shaped like a pyramid. On its summit one can see the remains of walls. At an earlier period there may have been a fortress on this natural stronghold. The village church is now in a semidilapidated state. There is no information on its founding or the subsequent renovations. The church (Fig. 36), which is situated in the center of the village, is built of polished blocks of dark blue basalt and semipolished sandstone. Today a part of its southern roof and the roofs of the vestries are in ruins. The plan of this church (Fig. 37) is that of a basilica with one nave and two aisles. The structure has a semicircular apse, two vestries, and a hall. The roof of the church rests on four square pillars. There is one portal on the western facade. The vestries and the altar receive their light from long, narrow, arrow-like

Fig. 36. The church of T'argmanch'ats' Monastery from the southwest.

valley. The mountains surrounding it are covered with forests and different species of plants. There is no information in the sources about the history of this village. The village of Norakert is mentioned in the *History* of seventeenth-century historian Aṙak'el of Tabriz,[86] in connection with his description of the upper course of the brook that flows toward Bĕghew (modern Bilav) and intersects the road from Shoṙot' to Ts'ghna. This information and the topography of the historic villages of Goght'n give us a basis for identifying the present-day Nirgud with historic Norakert, also called Nor Giwt.

Fig. 37. The plan of the church of T'argmanch'ats' Monastery.

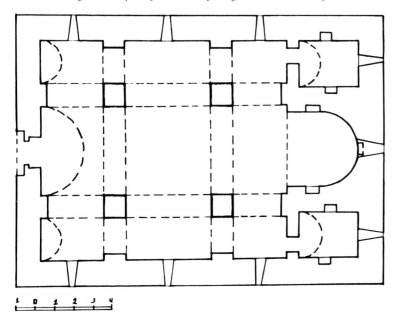

windows, and the hall is lighted by similar windows on the northern and southern walls and from a single window above the portal on the western facade.

The apse of the church, which is on the same plane as the hall—a trait of early medieval churches in Armenia—is also of interest. Both the interior and the exterior of the basilican church are simple and unadorned. The building technique leads us to suspect that the original structure was built at an earlier date and that it was renovated in the seventeenth or the eighteenth century, when restoration work was also done on other monuments in the neighboring villages. At the time of the renovation of the church large *khach'k'ars* covered with reliefs and inscriptions were used as lintels above the doors of the northern and southern vestries. These *khach'k'ars* have reliefs of crosses in an older, fourteenth-century style.

KHURS

The historic village of Khurs, or Khurst, which is spread out on the slope of a deep, wooded glen, is located about 4 kilometers down the valley from Norakert (toward Bist). It is not a large hamlet. The sources say nothing about Khurs, but our survey of the area reveals that Armenians lived there from ancient times until the beginning of the twentieth century. Even now one can still see the dilapidated Armenian church, a basilica with a nave and two aisles. No information is available on the name or the history of this church, which is built of local sandstone. Our survey of the structure reveals that the original building was erected at an early period.

ĔZNMER

About 3 to 4 kilometers below Khurs, to the east of the village of Oghohi, are the ruins of the historic village of Ĕznmer, or Aznamir. There is no information on the history of this village. The ruins of Ĕznmer, which was not a large village, and the partially effaced inscriptions on the moss-covered tombstones in the cemetery, show that this village had a long history. After the departure of the Armenians at the beginning of the nineteenth century, Ĕznmer was abandoned and reduced to ruins. One can still see the remains of the church.

In a manuscript copied in 1730 by the scribe Margar there is a list of the members of the congregation of St. T'ovma Monastery of Agulis. Among them is the name "Tēr Grigor of Ĕznmer."[87]

TRUNEATS' DZOR
(THE VALLEY OF TRUNIK')

Since ancient times Truneats' Dzor, or Vanandadzor, was famous in Goght'n for its villages and towns. In the Armenian historical sources the valley, known as Truneats' Dzor after Trunis or Tronis, which was located in the upper part of the valley, is acknowledged as an important place during the Middle Ages. The valley was also called Vanandadzor after Vanand, which is located in the central part of the valley. It was also occasionally called Dastaki Dzor after Dastak, the most remote village in the valley.

Truneats' Dzor, or Vanandadzor, which is quite deep, is situated between the valleys or Agulis and Ts'ghna. High mountains rise on both sides of the valley; those to the right are called Tsak k'ar, Spitak hogh, and Bazbar, and those to the left are Hars u P'esi, Mets k'ar, Hap'uk' k'ar, Tsiranak'ar, and Chalpast. A rivulet that rises in the glens of the Zangezur Mountains flows for 29 kilometers and empties into the Arax River. Its upper course is 3,400 meters above sea level. The upper course is called Truneats' get [Truneats' River],[88] the middle course Vanandi get [River of Vanand], and near the village of Dastak it is called Dastaki get [River of Dastak]. Located along the banks of the upper course of the river in Truneats' Dzor are fourteen to fifteen large and small villages 2 to 6 kilometers apart from one another that have several historical monuments. The extant and ruined architectural monuments in these villages and in their vicinities show beyond any doubt that there were people living there from prehistoric times on. The dwellings, churches, monasteries, fortresses, bridges, and other religious and nonreligious monuments bear witness to the active cultural and religious life in the region since pagan times. Unfortunately because of centuries of unrest the early monuments in the villages have been reduced to rubble. On the ruins of some of them new monuments have been erected. To this day the latter have not been surveyed and are known only from remarks in the works of Ghewond Alishan and E. Lalayian.[89] In his account of the results of the archaeological expedition of 1927 in Nakhichevan,[90] V. M. Sysoev published detailed reports on the monuments of Truneats' Dzor. Fortunately he provided information on certain monuments that are now in ruins.

BAZMAŘI

The historic village of Bazmaři, the present-day P'azmara, is located in the uppermost part of Truneats' Dzor and is spread out on the east bank of the Truneats' get. The village, which is not large, is situated in a very deep valley. The ruins in the northern part of Bazmaři are those of a small basilica with one nave and two aisles. The historical sources say nothing about this church, the ruins of which are badly deteriorated. There is also no information on the village. At the end of the nineteenth century it belonged to the Gēorgian family of K'aghak'ik.[91]

ST. KHACH' MONASTERY OF TRUNIK'

About 3 kilometers down the road from Bazmaři is St. Khach' [Holy Cross] Monastery, one of the most famous sites in Truneats' Dzor. The complex is situated on a small, level area on the road that goes down the valley along the east bank of the river. The monastery is spread out in a gorge in the upper part of the valley where the mountains almost meet. The site is striking-looking. About 20 to 25 meters west of the complex boulders rise precipitously on the sunburnt side of the mountain. The beautiful vineyard to the south of the complex gives the monastery a special charm. The vineyard, which belongs to the monastery, is full of trees with thick trunks. In the seventeenth century, T'ovma of Vanand, a noted figure in the history of Armenian letters, lived and worked there for many years. T'ovma frequently called himself "Bishop of St. Khach' Monastery of Goght'n, which is built on a suitable hill in Vanandadzor."[92] T'ovma always spoke with pride of this place and expressed his feelings in verse about pilgrimage to St. Khach':

Then they ascended to the Monastery of St. Khach'
Which is built in a peaceful place
At the peak of Truneats' Dzor.[93]

The monastic complex of St. Khach' included a church, a porch, and six to seven monastic buildings surrounded by a stone wall. Today the outer wall, the porch, and the other buildings are in ruins. The only standing structure within the complex is the church. The complex was planned around the church, which held the dominant position. The church is built of polished blocks of basalt and mostly with polished tuff-like stones (Fig. 38). It is a rectangular, vaulted structure with a nave and two aisles, an eastern apse, and two vestries, one on either side of the apse. Its only portal is located on the western facade. In the interior the longitudinal walls are intercepted by two engaged vertical supports that also bear the high, gabled roof of the church.

The monotonous exterior of St. Khach', which has a smooth, polished surface, is interrupted on the southern, northern, and eastern facades by narrow, rectangular windows and by the ornamental reliefs on the arch of the portal. The roof of the monument is built of polished square slabs that are cemented with lime. In 1859, after renovating the church, the leaders of Agulis had the roof of the church covered with tin. On the western section of the roof, a bell tower of medium height stands on six round columns. The western facade adds vitality to the

Fig. 38. The plan of Truneats' St. Khach' Monastery.

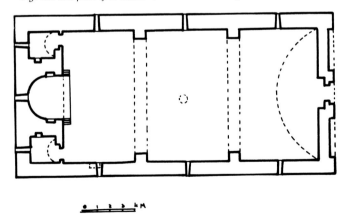

restrained exterior. Three niches divide the latter into sections. The portal is in the middle niche and has a rectangular opening encircled by entwining reliefs. Above the arch of the portal there is a large, rectangular window. At the level of the arches above the niches of the western facade, and in the spaces between them and on their sides, are four sills about 60 centimeters long. A little above the corners of these sills are 20-by-25-centimeter apertures. We think these sills and apertures were intended for supporting the weight of the arches of the porch. The porch, which covered the entire western elevation of the church, was probably destroyed before the mid-nineteenth century. The small number of inscribed sixteenth- to eighteenth-century tombstones in the porch have been moved away and have disappeared.

The historical sources testify that from the time of its founding St. Khach' Monastery was an active cultural center and a famed pilgrimage site. Since it was located near the villages of Nunis and K'aghak'ik, it was also occasionally called St. Khach' of Nunis or K'aghak'ik. A careful examination of the St. Khach' complex and of the ruins in its vicinity has convinced us that it was founded in about the twelfth century and was renovated several times. According to the inscription on the *khach'k'ar* above the lintel of the church's portal and the inscriptions on the five *khach'k'ars* set in the upper part of the south elevation, the present structure was renovated in 1687. In his 1870 catalog of the monasteries in the districts of Nakhichevan, M. Smbatian says: "St. Khach'avank' [Monastery of the Holy Cross], which is close to the village of K'aghak'ik, was built in 1687 and was renovated in 1859 by the magnates of Agulis."[94] M. Smbatian has evidently taken the date on the *khach'k'ar* above the portal of the church as the basis of his assumption about the date of the founding of the church. But his assumption is incorrect. The information in the historical sources refutes this conjecture. For example, in 1672, before the 1687 renovation of St. Khach', Zak'aria of Agulis and his relatives visited the monastery, and he noted in his diary: "On September 1, 1672, I, Zak'aria of

Agulis, brought my brother Shmawon's wife, who is from Erevan, his son and daughter, together with a penitent crowd, to St. Khach' of Trunik', where they offered their devotions and returned to Agulis."[95]

NUNIS, OBEWANIS

About 1 kilometer below St. Khach' is the historic village of Nunis, which is now called Unis. The ruins of the village and its vicinity reveal that it was not a large dwelling place. The village, which is called Nunis in the inscription on the western portal of the church of St. T'ovma Monastery in Agulis, probably had a church.

On the side of a high mountain about 6 to 7 kilometers north of Nunis one can still see the ruins of the historic village of Obewan, or Obewanis. The vestiges of this ancient village testify that seventy to eighty or more Armenian families lived there. This site is called Obovanis in the inscription of St. T'ovma Monastery of Agulis. There is very little information about it and its church. We know that the inhabitants of Obewanis received a gospel that was copied by the scribe Step'anos in 1488 in Ts'ghna. In the colophon of this manuscript is written:

> Now, the person who commissioned this holy gospel, which is the word of God, is the priest Abel, who spent much effort to have this copied in memory of his own soul and those of his parents—his father, the priest Mkrtich'; his mother, K'urik; his wife, Normelik'; Donia and Ahrik, his sons—the priest Esayi and his son the priest Abraham, and the priest Aharon and Trdat and the deacon Mkrtich' and Yob and Kostandianos, and all of his daughters, and the children of his paternal uncle— the priest Pawghos, and his brother Gorgik, who is the headman of the village, and the remaining landlords Khodabashkh and Ghambar, and the entire people, both old and young . . . who are in the service of the Church of St. Gēorg in the village of Yobēvank', which is in the district of Goght'n.[96]

From this context we learn that the church of Obewanis was called St. Gēorg and it had many priests, and that the headman of the village was Gorgik and the landlords were Khodabashkh and Ghambar.

In the ruins of Obewanis one can still see the remains of St. Gēorg Church. Inasmuch as it is possible to tell from its ruins, the church was built in the style of a vaulted hall with a single-chamber nave and it extends from east to west. It was not a large structure. The ruins of the monument and those in its vicinity lead us to believe that it was founded in the twelfth or the thirteenth century.

The ruins of the village of Obewanis and its cemetery suggest that the Armenian population abandoned this site toward the end of the eighteenth century. The village was completely deserted and ruined.

K'AGHAK'IK

The village of K'aghak'ik, which is about 1.5 to 2 kilometers below Nunis, lies on the west bank of the Truneats' River and presents a charming panorama. The beauty of the village is enhanced by the nineteenth-century stone houses that are surrounded with ancient vineyards and high trees. Some of these houses, among which are the two-storied family mansions of the Gēorgians and the Sant'urians, look like villas. According to tradition and the elderly inhabitants of Goght'n, a long time ago the wealthy people of Agulis founded this village as a summer residence for their families and relatives. At the end of the nineteenth century there were thirty-seven Armenian families (314 individuals), the descendants of the Gēorgian and the Sant'urian clans, living in K'aghak'ik.[97]

Among the noteworthy monuments of this village, which is also mentioned in the seventeenth-century inscription of St. T'ovma Monastery of Agulis, is its church. It is located on a level site in the northeastern section of the village and is built of polished blocks of sandstone in the style of a church with a single-chamber nave. At the time of its renovation flagstones were also used. The church has a rectangular plan with an eastern apse and two vestries. Its only portal is on the western facade. The vaulting is reinforced by means of arches that bear the roof, and it rests on two engaged vertical supports that are 20 centimeters wide and protrude 70 centimeters from the surface of the walls. The interior of the church is covered with plaster on which one can see the fragments of a sky-colored background wall painting. On both the northern and the southern elevations there are two windows. These are located at a lower elevation and have rectangular apertures.

The historical sources offer no information on the founding and renovation of the church of K'aghak'ik. According to the inscription on a *khach'k'ar* above the lintel of the portal, the church was either founded or renovated in 1441 by Agha Shain. The present-day structure provides proof that it was also renovated during the seventeenth and the nineteenth centuries. In front of the western facade of the church there was a porch that covered only a part of the western elevation. On its roof there stood a wooden bell tower.

About 200 to 250 meters to the north of K'aghak'ik, on a level area on the side of a mountain, one can see the remains of a small chapel with a wooden roof.

TRUNIK'

On the right slope of the valley 2 to 3 kilometers below K'aghak'ik is Trunik', or Truni, the most famous village or town in Truneats' Dzor. It is mentioned in the inscription of St. T'ovma Monastery of Agulis and is identical with the present-day village of Drnis (in the region of Ordubad), which has a spectacular view and is surrounded by lush vineyards. The name of this ancient village derives from that of the Truni feudal clan, and especially from Tur, the patriarch of that family. In his chapter "The Reign of Artashēs and the Rewarding of His Benefactors," historian Movsēs Khorenats'i speaks of the Truni family and notes: "In those same days he [Artashēs] also raised to princely rank the sons of Tur, fifteen young men, and called them Truni after their father's name—not because of any brave deed but merely because of the informing that their father had done from the king's house for Smbat; for he was a confidant of Eruand's and for that reason he had been put to death by him."[98]

The Urartean scholar B. Piotrovskii, in his article "On the Question of the Origin of the Armenian People," discusses the origin of the names of Armenian feudal clans and notes that "the most ancient Armenian feudal family names go farther back than the dates of the Armenian state and are connected with Urartu not only etymologically but also through their *-uni* ending, which is characteristic of Urartean. This accounts for the structure of the Arshakuni, Arsharuni, Mandakuni, Bznuni, Ŕshtuni ancient Armenian feudal family names."[99] The same is also applicable to the Truni feudal clan, which is mentioned with the fifth- to sixth-century Armenian feudal families. K. Basmajian, a scholar who studied the Urartean inscriptions, identified the toponym Trunik' with the place-name/family name Teriani, or Taruni, mentioned in the Urartean inscriptions.[100] These theories and the etymology proposed by Movsēs Khorenats'i lead us to believe that the Truni were descended from an ancient Armenian tribe that lived on the territory of Urartu, and later, during the formation of the Armenian people, they emerged as one of the feudal clans under the royal house.

It is clear from the above evidence that the Truni were of ancient origin. In the *Throne List* of the Armenian feudal lords, which was compiled in the fifth century, the Truni family, according to N. Adontz, held the fifty-third place and provided a detachment of three hundred horsemen to the royal army.[101] The village of Trunis, or Trunik', and its neighboring areas were probably the ancestral possessions of the Truni family. Unfortunately, to this day the historical role and the jurisdiction of this clan has not been studied. Ghewond Alishan alone notes that "the names of only a small number of lords and patriarchs of the Truni clan are mentioned. They are remembered with the gentry of Vaspurakan, since Goght'n was from time to time a part of that province. In the eighth-century rebellions against the Arabs, the Truni are mentioned among the leaders. Some of their cadets fell fighting at Archēsh. In the mid-ninth century, Vahram Truni is mentioned as a contemporary of Bugha, and in the early tenth century there is a reference to Yisē, the lord of Trunik' and son of Hōnowar."[102]

The ruins of buildings in the vicinity of Trunik' indicate that the village was an important center with churches, caravanserai, water mills, and other monuments of historical and architectural interest. Only fragments and ruins of the monuments of Trunik' have survived the ravages of time. In the present-day village one can still see the deteriorated building of the church of Trunik' and the chapel of St. Astuatsatsin, which is located in the northeastern part of the village. Near the chapel there is a rock with a few large and small crosses carved on it. Since early times the people of Trunik' have worshiped and honored this rock as a holy shrine. The church of Trunik' is now dilapidated and about to crumble. It is in the style of a basilican church with a nave and two aisles. Built of polished flagstones, its apse, vestries, and hall are all within the perimeter of a rectangular plan. The apse has five sides and five niches. The bema is considerably higher than the floor of the hall and has four steps. The interior is elevated and the plaster is painted white. The remains of the nineteenth-century wall paintings can be seen on the pendentives. The roof of the church rests on lancet-shaped arches that are supported by four pentagonal pillars.

The sources say nothing about the founding, renovation, or name of the church. The present structure was probably built (or renovated) in the seventeenth century over the ruins of the foundation of an older church. During the period of Persian domination, Trunik' and its neighboring villages were part of the jurisdiction of Khoja

Fat'hi-bek T'usi, which is verified by a deed issued in 1504. According to this, "The entire possession of twelve *dangs* [one-sixth] of all the possessions in the place called Dïnis, which is subject to Azad-Jiran, and the fields listed under that place, namely the village of Dïnis—3 *dangs;* the village of Danakert—2.5 *dangs;* the field of Sal—3 *dangs;* the field of Berdak—2 *dangs;* the field of the Vek'il possessions—2 *dangs,* with all the places that are subject or attached to them . . . belong to Khoja Fat'hi-bek T'usi . . . and are under his jurisdiction."[103]

TANAKERT

Tanakert lies 3 kilometers below Trunis, spread out on the side of the Tanaker Hill on the left bank of the Truneats' River. Rich vineyards and woods lie before the village. Its name is mentioned as Tnakert in the seventeenth-century inscription of St. T'ovma Monastery of Agulis and as Danakert in the Persian deed of 1504. The survey of extant and ruined monuments and buildings in the village shows that this site was inhabited from ancient times. Ghewond Alishan notes that "in the encyclical of the Monastery of Galatia the name of the village is written as Tōnakert, which seems to be the correct form. There is also a reference from the mid-seventeenth century to a certain benefactor, Aṙak'el son of Hovhannēs, a native of this place."[104]

Among the monuments of Tanakert, or Tōnakert, there are two well-known churches and a number of chapels, now in ruins. The sources say nothing about them. St. Astuatsatsin Church, which was built on an elevated site in the northeastern part of the village, is still standing. A colophon in the missal of St. Gēorg Church of Aprakunis offers the following information: "In memory of the presbyter Eghia of Masrvan in 1719, at the gate of St. Astuatsatsin Church of Tanakert."[105] After examining the church we learned that it was rebuilt from its foundation up in the seventeenth century and stands on the site of an older church.

St. Astuatsatsin is a domed basilican church with four pillars. It is built of flagstones and cobblestones. Its dome, roof, and the upper parts of the walls have been destroyed. The structure consists of a hall, an apse, and a pair of two-storied vestries. Its only portal is located on the western facade. The apse has four sides and receives light from a single window on the eastern wall. Each of the hall's four pillars has eight sides. The cupola was relatively low and had a drum with eight sides. Its roof was pyramidal in shape. The interior of St. Astuatsatsin was considerably elevated and illuminated. The plaster over the walls appears to have been painted several times. In the wall paintings of the earliest stratum, which were probably done in the seventeenth century, black is the prevailing color, whereas light blue stands out in the later strata. There was a porch attached to the southern elevation of the church, 5 meters wide and 11 meters long. This building is now in ruins.

Fig. 39. St. Hovhannēs Church from the east.

BERDAK

On the western bank of the river about 1 kilometer to the south of Tanakert and toward Vanand are the ruins of the village of Berdak; they do not occupy a large area. In the middle of the village there is a hill with a relatively flat summit, which is surrounded by vineyards and old ruins so that at first one may take it for a fortress. The people of Tanakert and the area traditionally called it Berdak [a small fortress].

Berdak is mentioned in a number of sixteenth-century Persian deeds. For example, in a deed issued in 1504 it was called a "field" and belonged to Khoja Fat'hi-bek T'usi.[106] In another deed, issued in 1575, Khoja Nubarshakh of Ordubad sold to Hovhannēs, son of K'iadkhuda K'ejmir of Agulis, "altogether forty *man* of arable land in the village called Berdak, which is one of the villages of Azat-Jiran (Nahia)."[107]

The only monument in Berdak that has been preserved is the semidilapidated St. Hovhannēs Church, which stands on the hill. This building (Fig. 39) is a vaulted structure with a single-chamber nave. Its dimensions are small, enclosing an apse and a hall (Fig. 40). It has only one portal, which is on the southern facade. The church is built of blocks of sandstone and evidently had a considerably elevated interior. The gabled roof of the building rested on arches supported by two pairs of engaged vertical supports. The roof, the upper parts of the walls, and other sections are now in ruins. There are a number of inscribed *khach'k'ars* from 1625 set into the walls. A short inscription near the entrance states that the church was most recently renovated in 1888.

There is a small, rectangular hall attached to the southern elevation of St. Hovhannēs. This structure, which probably served as an exterior vestry or a bell tower, is also in ruins today. From a survey of St. Hovhannēs and its vicinity it is possible to surmise that the present-day church was rebuilt in the seventeenth century on the foundation of an earlier church.

Fig. 40. The plan of St. Hovhannēs Church.

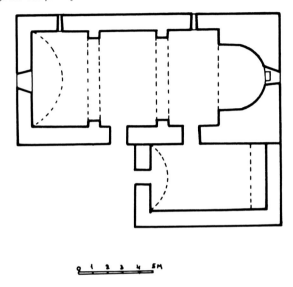

SAL, DISAR, VAGHAWER

The villages of Sal, Disar, and Vaghawer are located 2.5 to 3 kilometers below Tanakert and 1 to 2 kilometers apart from one another. They are not large. At present only the wretched vestiges of their ruined monuments remain. The most important of the three is the village of Disar, or Deghsar. There, one can still see the ruins of the village church and those of a bridge that was built over the Truneats River. The church of Disar, which stands on an elevated site in a central location, is a relatively small monument. The structure comprises a hall, an apse, and vestries; its portal is on the western facade. The apse is semicircular and has three niches.

Considering the presence of stones cut in an archaic style in the walls of the church of Disar, and taking into account the two *khach'k'ars* with effaced inscriptions set into the eastern elevation, we can surmise that the sanctuary was rebuilt in the seventeenth century on the foundation of an earlier church. On one of the stones of the bema there is the inscription "In the year 1900," which indicates that the church was once again renovated in that year. At that time the building was covered with a wooden roof that was supported by four wooden posts in the hall.

The bridge of Disar had a single arch; only its ruined pillars have survived. The structure was built of polished and semipolished blocks of sandstone.

VANAND

Vanand, which is the present-day village of the same name in the region of Ordubad, is located on the middle course of the Truneats' River about 2.5 to 3 kilometers below Disar. Since ancient times the people of Goght'n have had a special affection for this village and its fertile fields and vineyards. The earliest historical information on it dates back to the first century A.D. and subsequently to the period of Vahan of Goght'n (eighth century). The patriotic deeds of the inhabitants of Vanand are frequently cited by the seventeenth- and eighteenth-century sources.

According to folk etymology, the name Vanand derives from *Vank'n and* [the monastery is there]. Thirteenth-century historian Archbishop Step'anos Orbelean states that the Apostle Bartholomew entered the province of Siwnik' in the middle of the first century in order to preach the Christian faith: "He began to preach in the village of Ort'vat in the district of Arewik', in the kingdom of Bałk' and in Goght'n."[108] Then, after building the church of Teaṙněndaṙaj in Agulis, which lies at the eastern extreme of Goght'n, and appointing his pupil Kumsi bishop, Bartholomew "came to the village of Vanand, where one of his pupils, whose name was Lusik, died. They laid him to rest there and built a small chapel over him. . . . There was a pagan temple [in Vanand], which he destroyed and instead built a dark church, naming it after Saint Thomas. Many miracles took place there."[109] Step'anos Orbelean's information does not derive from legendary traditions passed on from one generation to the other, but rather is based on sources that tell of the origins of various extant and ruined monuments. Our survey of the area of Vanand revealed the truth of Orbelean's testimony—that this ancient and beautiful village indeed had "many signs" of antiquity.

Vanand was one of the earliest inhabited sites on which an altar and temple stood in pagan times. After the Christianization of Goght'n, several architectural monuments, such as monasteries, churches, bridges, caravanserai, and splendid palaces, were constructed. Vanand, with its huge, ancient Oriental plane trees and its thick-trunked plantains, is second only to Ordubad in the majesty of its trees. These trees are up to fifteen hundred years old and are the living witnesses of a remote past. The distribution of the plane trees in Vanand and Ordubad irrefutably point to the fact that they were planted by human hand. The present-day plane trees in Vanand may be the descendants of groves and woods that stood in front of or near the pagan temples. One of the most ancient plane trees in the village is located in its center. The altar or the temple mentioned by Step'anos Orbelean was perhaps located near that tree.

The Armenian historical sources mention Vanand especially in connection with the martyrdom of the eighth-century patriot Prince Vahan of Goght'n. From these sources[110] we learn that Vahan's father, Prince Khosrov of Goght'n, was among the princes whom the Arabs burned in 705 in the churches of Khram and Naxchawan. Vahan, who was four years old at the time, was taken to Damascus along with a number of other children captured from the various Armenian districts. In Syria he was forced to convert to Islam and was given the name Vahap. When the youth from Goght'n came of age and realized what had happened to him, he could no longer tolerate a life in exile. The desire to return home to his fatherland tortured Vahan, who spoke several

languages and held a position under the caliphate. Thirteenth-century Armenian poet Khach'atur Kech'aṙets'i describes Vahan's plight:

He remembered the covenant bequeathed to him by his
    countrymen,
And longed for his paternal land;
He asked for permission
to go to his native land, which was called Goght'n.

The news of his arrival reached his relatives;
They came forward to greet him.
They took with them the cross of Christ
And went forward to meet Vahan.

Seeing the Cross of the One Who loves mankind,
Vahan was in fear and turned his face aside.
He was struck with fear at the sight of the cross
And publicly shed many tears.

He remembered the precepts of the gospel,
And was struck with grief in his heart.
His soul was pricked
By the threat of the Last Judgment.

When the inhabitants of his district learned [of his arrival],
They all cried copiously, saying
"Don't be afraid, Son of Khosrov,
We shall beg our creator
Through the intercession of the Holy Mother of God
To absolve you of the original sin
While you are still in your youth."[111]

Vahan, who had received permission to depart on condition that he would return to Damascus, married the daughter of Prince Dawit' of Goght'n. But the Arab officials forced him to return to Damascus according to the stipulation of the agreement. Before his departure Vahan took leave of his relatives in Vayots' Dzor, and wishing to bid a last farewell to his native soil, he disguised himself and

Returned again out of his heart's desire
To the beautiful district of Goght'n;

He reached the village of Vanand,
Which is surrounded with vineyards.
He asked the guards for a bunch of grapes;
The latter recognized Vahan by sight
And notified many of his friends, saying
"It's our prince in disguise."
When Vahan heard this from several people
He departed disheartened.[112]

At Damascus the Arab caliph brought several charges against Vahan and ordered his officials not to allow him to return to Armenia. Vahan, however, who longed for his people and country, was never reconciled with the prospect of remaining in Damascus and serving the caliphate. The caliph, seeing that Vahan refused to forsake his Christian faith, decreed that he be beheaded. On March 12, 707, at the age of thirty-six, Vahan of Goght'n chose to be beheaded in Damascus rather than to forsake his faith, people, and fatherland. The following hymn was written in his memory:

More Astonishing

More astonishing to me
than the lyrics made for you,
more amazing than the music composed
for your death,
is the sound of the sobbing mourning
you, Lord Vahan, chosen of God.
Let me be inspired in that clear part
of my soul, to compose songs for you too,
but not songs that mourn;
Armies of angels celebrate with men
and women enlist by heaven.
They conquer death, with virginity, by warring,
by befriending the crucified creator who came of virgin
    birth.

Close friends, during their earthly lives
being martyrs, and with united souls
they went together to the battle
armed with faith and ready to resist.

Mighty armies, and their supports, weakened,
were vanquished by frail but armed women.
And the king of evil, decked in dazzling power
was shamed, being vanquished by virgins.

The pagans joined to dance in joy
around their single blazing jewel.
They traveled East and West to preach
about the vision that had enchanted them.

Earthly kings heard and were thrilled.
They led the search, the hunt for the secret greatness.
And although they promised to aid each other
in private they meant only to rob.

True fruit of Christ's vineyard,
clusters crushed by the heavenly vintner,
pressed into vats after hard toil,
they became the quaff of the immortal cup.

How prudent were they and the wise virgins
not to be overcome by sleep, or by sloth
but to stay awake and stay ready to join
the immortal groom's wedding entourage.[113]

Translated by Diana Der Hovanessian and
Marzbed Margossian

In its poetic style, imagery, and sentiments this hymn, which is traditionally ascribed to Khosroviduxt, the sister of Vahan, treats the valiant and patriotic young man as a hero and praises his martyrdom.

During the course of the seventeenth and eighteenth centuries Vanand was frequently mentioned in connection with the activities of Bishop T'ovmas, the philologist Ghukas, Matt'ēos, and others. According to our sources, T'ovmas of Vanand, a native of Vanand and a member of the Nurijanents' family, was the bishop of St. Khach' Monastery in Truneats' Dzor. Unable to pursue his scholarly interests in his ancestral land, he departed from his fatherland in the middle of the seventeenth century and settled in Amsterdam, where he undertook the task of printing Armenian books. Through his own private finances and with the help of his nephew, the philologist Ghukas, and his cousin Matt'ēos, he founded a printing press and published several books. The services of these men of Vanand and of their press, which functioned from 1685 to 1717, were especially distinguished by the publication of Movsēs Khorenats'i's *History of the Armenians* and of the *Ashkharhats'oyts'*, a seventh-century atlas of the world.[114]

Today very little remains of the architectural monuments of Vanand. The Monastery of St. T'ovma, which was founded in the middle of the first century by the Apostle Bartholomew, was renovated and restored on several occasions, including in the seventeenth century with the other monuments in Goght'n. It is not clear on what basis M. Smbatian maintained that it was "the year 450 [when] Matt'ēos of Vanand renovated [the monastery]."[115] Matt'ēos of Vanand, the nephew of Bishop T'ovmas of Vanand, could have renovated this monastery before his departure for Amsterdam, that is, before 1680–81.

St. T'ovma Monastery of Vanand, which is built in the style of a basilican church with four pillars, is located on an elevated site in the center of the village. At the end of the nineteenth century, E. Lalayian stated: "Its miserable ruins remain."[116] These were around until the 1930s. Taking into consideration these ruins and the description of V. Sysoev,[117] we can assume that the monument had large dimensions. Its roof rested on the four square pillars in the hall and on the arches of the opposite walls. The arches of the dome, like those on the pillars, were in the shape of lancets. The apse had five sides.

Besides the Monastery of St. T'ovma, there were other noted places of pilgrimage in Vanand at the beginning of the twentieth century. Among these were the chapel built over the tomb of Lusik, St. Khach' Monastery, and other monuments. In his 1870 catalog of the monasteries of Goght'n, M. Smbatian writes: "St. Khach' Monastery of Vanand, which is called Andzrewaber [that which induces rain], was built in 1457 by Bishop Petros; it was destroyed by the Persian inhabitants."[118] According to

Ghewond Alishan, T'ovmas of Vanand was "in Nicosia" in 1668, "and he narrated the story of the discovery of the Andzrewaber cross [the cross that induces rain], which had taken place in 1457, and he told the history of the monastery, which was completed in 1460."[119]

DIZA, AGHRI, KHOGHVANI

The historic villages of Diza, Aghri, and Khoghvani are located below Vanand, on an extensive expanse reaching the highway that connects Nakhichevan with Ordubad and Meghri. These are not large hamlets. Their churches and other monuments have been destroyed and are in ruins. The largest of these villages was Khoghvani, or Khoghuank', which is the village of Khanagha in the present-day region of Ordubad. Here one can still see the remains of a church, a bridge, and a caravanserai. Writing about the history of Khoghvani, Ghewond Alishan notes that "in Step'anos Orbelean's *History* the traditional name of the village is given as Khoghuank' in Vanandadzor.[120] At the beginning of the eleventh century, the lords of this place gave it to the episcopal see of Tat'ew."[121] The historic name of the village, Khoghvani, or Khoghuank', was preserved until the sixteenth century. Subsequently the name was changed to Khanagha; in the seventeenth century Zak'aria of Agulis identified the village as Khanagha. Tracing the distances on the highway running from Agulis to Erevan, Zak'aria writes: "The first *mandzil* is this: from Agulis to the bridge of Khanagha is one *aghach*, from Khanagha to Azatu Dēr one *aghach*."[122]

DASTAK

The most remote village in Truneats' Dzor is the historic hamlet of Dastak, located on the right side of the highway that connects Nakhichevan with Ordubad and Meghri, on the bank of the Arax River. Until 1879 there were sixty-two Armenian families living there. After that the inhabitants moved to Agulis and Shushi.[123] There is very little information available on this ancient Armenian village and its church. In the list of villages in the inscription of St. T'ovma Monastery of Agulis, the name of this village is given as Dastak. According to Ghewond Alishan's study, "A certain traveler mentions a beautiful square that was shaded by a plane tree under which there was a spring. The industry and the love of the natives for commercial enterprises in foreign lands is evident from a tombstone of 1724 at the Armenian church in the town of Livorno in Italy: 'This is the ark of rest for Khoja Beg's son Paghtasar of Dastak who reposed in Christ on November 29, 1173 [1724].'"[124]

A gospel discovered in the village of Chachurak (Chalay) near Akhaltskha and copied in 1552 was restored in the church of Dastak. In its colophon it is stated:

> This Holy Gospel, which is the Breath of God, was restored in the district of Goght'n, in the village called Dastak, at the church called St. Khoran, during the pontificate of the Archbishop Lord Grigor of the Monastery of St. T'ovma the Apostle. . . . I beg you to remember the unworthy, sinful, vain, iniquitous, despicable scribe Sargis, who is not worthy of the priestly rank. I am only a priest in name, but in deed I am vain. Pardon the shortcomings of this book, since the times were difficult. Shah Tahmasp overwhelmed us terribly and, taking us by force, bestowed on us various torments and severely tortured us with clubs and swords. For the love of God I tearfully restored this Gospel . . . in the 1001th year of the Armenian Era [1552].[125]

It is evident from the testimony of the scribe Sargis, who restored the gospel of 1552, that Dastak, which was located on a transit route, was frequently demolished and ravaged. As a result, almost nothing remains of its architectural monuments in the present-day village. At the time of E. Lalayian's and V. Sysoev's visit, St. Khoran Church of Dastak, located in the northern part of the village, was in a semidilapidated state. According to V. Sysoev's description,[126] St. Khoran Church of Dastak, whose dimensions were very large, was built in the style of a domed basilica with four pillars. The lower parts of the walls of the church were made of flagstones, and the upper parts of bricks; the latter were presumably added during the seventeenth-century renovation. This church, which has an almost square plan, consists of an apse with a five-sided exterior, two vestries, and a hall. The four pillars in the hall had eight sides and capitals that were decorated in an archaic style. The dome was built with bricks and the drum of the dome had eight sides.

Ernjak is an ancient district. The historic district, which encompassed the present-day region of Julfa, was spread out on the left bank of the Arax River, on the plains and slopes on the right and left banks of the Ernjak River, and on the side of lofty Mount Ōdzasar, which is considered a landmark. The sixteenth- and seventeenth-century travelers considered this beautiful mountain, about which myths have been constructed, comparable to Mount Montserrat in Spain.[1] Ōdzasar rises 2,360 meters above sea level.

Since ancient times Ernjak's favorable climate, rich vegetation, fertile plain, and natural security have made it an attractive dwelling place. Between the twelfth and sixteenth centuries Ernjak was known as a "beautiful land."[2] In the seventh century, Anania of Shirak mentions it as one of the districts of the Province of Siwnik'.[3] According to H. Achaṙian, the etymology of the name Ernjak, or Ernjnak, derives from the word *erinj*, "eryngium campestre."[4]

Over the course of history, the district of Ernjak, as well as its villages, hamlets, and towns, have gone through several periods of decline and revival, destruction and recovery. Time after time, the inhabitants have rebuilt their burnt and ruined abodes and architectural monuments. The district comprises a unique world of antiquities rich with architectural monuments. Each *khach'k'ar*, fragment of an arch or an ancient wall, church—be it extant or in ruins—and every Armenian character inscribed on stone tells the story of the region down through the centuries.

THE FORTRESS OF ERNJAK

Since ancient times numerous fortresses and castles have existed in Armenia. These were built on secure sites that made suitable dwelling places. The castle of Ernjak, or Erinjak, which was one of the most renowned fortresses of medieval Armenia, was constructed with great skill on one such secure site. Foreign tribes that invaded the Armenian plateau called the fortress Alinja, Alinjakhana, and other names.

The castle of Ernjak[5] was the administrative center of the district. The city of Ernjak grew up around the castle in the early Middle Ages. This city, which was spread out on the lowlands and small hills to the south of the castle, occupied an area more than 4 to 4.5 square kilometers. In the mid-nineteenth century, the previous inhabitants (Persians) of the present-day village of Khanagha, which is located in one corner of the medieval city, leveled to the ground the vestiges of the city. Today, besides some insignificant remains, the ruins are covered by earth. Ernjak flourished between the eighth and eleventh centuries, during which time its inhabitants attained an advanced level of civilization.

The fortress is mentioned by tenth-century sources as a princely castle. Hovhannēs of Draskhanakert and Step'anos of Tarōn (tenth century), Step'anos Orbelean (thirteenth century), and historians of subsequent periods refer to it in their works. According to Step'anos Orbelean, "The wife of one of the princes of Siwnik', whose name was Ernjik, built the impregnable fortress of Ernjak, and the fortress as well as the district were named after her. Ernjak was where they kept the treasury of the realm and the taxes."[6] It is clear from this information that the fortress was known as "the impregnable fortress of Ernjak," which served as a repository for the taxes collected from the province of Siwnik'.

The fortress of Ernjak is situated on the peak of a rocky mountain with a wide base that occupies a large area.[7] It rises on the bank of the Ernjak River. The mountain (Fig. 41), which rises to 1610 meters above sea level, divides into two peaks. Centuries ago, on small, level areas on the sides of these peaks, the people of Ernjak laid foundations by joining together pieces of rock and stone, and built a castle in order to protect themselves from the ravages and attacks of foreign invaders. The sides of the castle have endured the terrors of past centuries and bear their marks.

Two roads ascended to the fortress; one went up the northwestern side of the mountain and the other up the southeastern side. The latter was considered the main road. Inside the walls of the fortress there were several buildings. On the peak of the mountain, which faces northwest, there is a splendid royal palace that dominated the entire fortress and crowned the peak with its architectural composition, enhancing the natural beauty of the place and the overall view of the castle. Our survey of this palatial complex (Fig. 42) and the buildings in its vicinity shows that the castle had a handsome church, a waiting room, a hall, narrow corridors, a number of rooms for the servants, depots for military and economic purposes, and other buildings. Around the palace and the square there were a number of dwelling places, barracks, watchtowers, guardhouses, and over ten other buildings of various kinds, most of which are now in ruins. Similar structures can also be seen on the eastern peak of the mountain, where more than ten rows of fortifications, ruins of a tower, and the remains of watchtowers, arsenals, barracks, and dwelling places have survived.

Besides the natural security of the place, Ernjak is protected with strong, man-made fortifications. The builders skillfully used the crags of the mountain to secure the castle through outer walls, inner walls, and innermost walls on the side of the southeastern defile. On the northwestern side, where the princely palace stood, there were eight rows of walls. At the top of the fortress, on the northern side, there are nine wells, each one capable of holding 800 cubic meters of water. These form an interesting network: during precipitation, the rainwater was apparently gathered in these wells through numerous vein-like channels on the summit, which were joined to each other.

Fig. 41. General view of Ernjak.

The building technique used to construct the castle and the unique architectural principles employed in the nearby buildings testify that the fortress was founded in the Urartean period. Later, during the early Middle Ages, the princes of Siwnik' rebuilt it from its foundations,

Fig. 42. The plan of the palace.

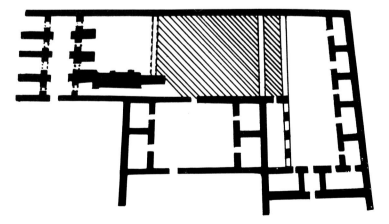

fortifying and beautifying it beyond its earlier state. As a famous medieval Armenian architectural complex, Ernjak is indeed an important site. It is amazing how the fortress and its natural surroundings blend in an unparalleled way. The view from Ernjak is enchanting: down below there is a long, wide valley; on the banks of the Ernjak River there are orchards, villages, plains, valleys, and boulders. In the distance one can see the outline of tall mountains and the white peak of Ararat. Ernjak is also remarkable for the artistic and architectural characteristics of its buildings. One can form a general idea about these from the descriptions in the literary sources. For example, the Spanish ambassador and chamberlain of King Henry III, Roy Gonzales di Clovijo, passed through the district of Ernjak in October 1405 and described the fortress: "This fortress is surrounded with walls and towers. In its immediate vicinity there are many vineyards and gardens and wheat fields. There are also many springs and grazing pastures for animals. These are located around the fortress and on the highlands above."[8]

In historical literature the fortress is first mentioned in connection with the events that took place in 909 when the Sadjid emir Yusuf attacked Ernjak, seizing King Smbat I of Armenia and torturing him. After laying siege to the fortress for a long time, Yusuf realized he could not conquer it. The tyrant brought King Smbat before the walls of the castle and ordered him to ask the Armenians to surrender. The king remained silent and urged the brave garrisons inside the fortress not to surrender. His punishment was torture and death on a cross. The historian Step'anos Orbelean puts this event in 913.[9]

After this, the sources say nothing about Ernjak until the invasion of the Tatars. At the end of the twelfth century it passed into the hands of the Orbelean feudal family of Siwnik' as their paternal realm. Thereafter, the fortress is mentioned in connection with Timur's siege in 1387 and that of his son Shahrukh in 1435, which lasted for thirteen years. According to certain sources, the first siege lasted for fifteen years, during which time there

were several interruptions. Grigor of Khlat' says of this siege:

> As for the fortress of Ernjak,
> Let me set aside the account of the events
> Which began to happen on the Easter holy days
> And continued until the Feast of the Holy Cross.
> They laid siege [to the fortress] with a large army but could
>   not harm it.
> Then they returned
> To the land from where they had come.
> The siege lasted for fifteen years;
> Only then did they seize it.[10]

After 1480 Ernjak occasionally passed from Ottoman into Persian hands. During the Russo-Persian War of 1826–27, the fortress was in Persian hands. After their defeat, the Persians deserted the place and it lay abandoned.

Since there are close parallels between the building techniques employed at Ernjak and Urartean buildings, we are inclined to see the Urartean verbal root *ere* in the archaic pronunciation of the name Ernjak and consider it a derivative of an Urartean toponym.

Thirteenth-century historian Step'anos Orbelean considers Ernjak the second most important castle in Siwnik', after Bałk'.

St. Gēorg Monastery of Ernjak

The ruins of this famous monastery are still visible on a hill that touches on the southern side of a tall mountain to the northeast of the fortress of Ernjak. The site and the location of the monastery were carefully chosen. From there one can see the old Julfa, the mountains of Persia, most of the villages on the banks of the Ernjak River, the spectacular Mount Ōdzasar, and the fortress of Ernjak. At one time the palaces and churches of the city of Ernjak, which are 1.5 to 2 kilometers below the monastery, must have added a special charm to the panorama.

The ruins of the Monastery of St. Gēorg reveal that this complex had a church, a porch, and other buildings, which were destroyed before the middle of the nineteenth century. Today only the semidilapidated church remains among the ruins. This structure is a vaulted hall with a single-chamber nave. It is built of semipolished and polished blocks of sandstone and lime mortar. The plan of the church includes a hall and a semicircular apse. It has two portals, one on the northern and the other on the western facade. A vestry is attached to the northern elevation and a porch stands in front of the western elevation.

According to M. Smbatian, who was there in July 1899, the name of the monastery was St. P'rkich', "which was later changed to St. Gēorg. It was the most ancient and uppermost monastery in the district of Ernjak, and was probably older than the early fifth-century translators. In 841 a church council met here and condemned Catholicos Hovhannēs V."[11] The survey of the complex of St. Gēorg Monastery and its vicinity indicates that the church must have been built by the ninth century; later it was renovated several times. Until 1940 the monastery served as a place of pilgrimage for the Armenians living nearby. Thirteenth-century historian Step'anos Orbelean knows the monastery by its present name, St. Gēorg, and states that it paid an annual tax of twelve *dahekans* to the Monastery of Tat'ew.[12]

Far to the south of the monastery there are the vestiges of an ancient cemetery where most of the tombstones have been removed and those remaining are effaced. Certain marred inscriptions on these tombstones indicate that the cemetery dates from the tenth to the twelfth centuries, and it probably belonged to the city of Ernjak. Under the outcropping of a rock 150 meters to the north of St. Gēorg Monastery one can see the remains of a chapel. In the 1860s, when A. Sedrakian visited there, he saw in this chapel a "tombstone that was cracked in the middle and had various reliefs. On one of its sides there were the following letters: *NGHĒ T'*

[in the year 1048]." The rest of the inscription seemed to be effaced. The nearby inhabitants traditionally call this site "hermit's tomb."[13]

THE CITY OF JULFA

Ancient Julfa, one of the towns of medieval Armenia, played a major role in Armenian life of the fifteenth and the sixteenth centuries.[14] The city experienced a period of revival, especially after the decline of Ani, the capital of Bagratid Armenia. The city was founded in the early Middle Ages and is recognized by Movsēs Khorenats'i and other historians as an important town. Armenian and non-Armenian sources refer to it as Julfa, Jugha, Jughay, Chogha, Ulfa, and other names.

Historic Julfa spread out over the lowlands near the present-day village of Julfa in the region of Julfa. It was situated on the bank of the Arax River, stretching out for over 1 kilometer from east to west and 400 to 500 meters from the river to the sides of the nearby mountains. The suburbs of the city were spread out on the opposite bank (modern Iranian side) of the Arax. Julfa was surrounded by the river in the south and a tall, wall-like mountain in the north; the narrow roadways entering the city from the east and the west were protected by a series of walls.

Since ancient times Julfa was a major point on the well-known commercial transit route that ran through ancient and medieval Armenia. Near the city there was a magnificent bridge built over the Arax River. Tradition attributes the construction of this architectural monument—the only parts of it that survive are its dilapidated pillars—and the caravanserai annexed to it to Alexander the Great. In 1605 Shah Abbas of Persia destroyed the bridge so that the Armenian inhabitants of Julfa and those of the plain of Ararat who had been driven to Persia would not consider returning home. But the major reason for his action was to make it difficult for the Ottoman forces to cross the river.

The historic sources testify that from as early as the

mid-thirteenth century commercial transactions and the crafts began to increase in the city. During the ensuing centuries commerce became the main pursuit of the inhabitants. In the period from the fifteenth to the seventeenth century, the merchants of Julfa, who called themselves "Khocha," became known for their riches and patriotic dedication to the establishment of printing plants. For centuries the enterprising and fearless merchants of Julfa frequented all the cities and commercial centers of the Orient and the Occident and established their companies. Their caravans had access to India (Madras, Calcutta), China, Persia, Italy (Venice), Vienna, Amsterdam, Constantinople, Moscow, Crimea, Astrakhan, even Java and the Philippines (Manila). The merchants introduced to the Egyptian and the Mediterranean markets spices, leather, wool, especially raw silk and other items.

Besides being experienced merchants, the inhabitants of Julfa were also skilled builders and art lovers. In their native town they erected hundreds of palatial villas, inns, and *khach'k'ars* with beautiful reliefs. During the fifteenth and sixteenth centuries, architecture, epigraphy, calligraphy, engraving, needlework, the cutting of precious stones, carpet weaving, and other crafts were greatly developed by the people of Julfa. The beautiful *khach'k'ars* in the cemetery, the seven churches and monasteries, the inns, the covered marketplace, which have reached us either in ruins or in a partially dilapidated state, were wonderful architectural structures. In his encyclical of 1511 Catholicos Grigor XI called Julfa "the town of Julfa which is protected by God," a statement that implies the prosperity of the city. Before the destruction of Julfa the English traveler Nipri (John Newbery?) visited the city on December 4, 1581, and noted that it had three thousand houses and a population of fifteen to twenty thousand people. But in 1590, according to the information given by another English traveler, John Cartwright, there were two thousand families in Julfa and a population of ten thousand.[15]

The socioeconomic and political life of this famous medieval city was regulated by a council of patriarchs or princes, at whose head stood the mayor. At the end of the nineteenth century, when most of the ruins of Julfa were still visible, H. Aṙak'elian visited the city and noted that "the houses are two-storied. . . . They are built not only on level ground but also on rocks and mountain sides. . . . A few are built on such craggy places that only roe deer can reach."[16] In 1912 Aram Vroyr, a man well acquainted with the material culture of Armenia, visited the ruins of Julfa and in his letter of April 4, 1912, to Nikolai Marr he pointed out that "Julfa is very interesting. It is a small replica of Ani and seems to be a rich repository of fourteenth- and fifteenth-century materials."[17]

After the fall of Ani, Julfa prospered because of its extensive commercial ties, but unexpectedly, it was destroyed. Shah Abbas I of Persia had visited the town and been amazed at its architectural monuments, opulence, and the creative spirit of the inhabitants. In 1604 the shah forced the entire population of Julfa and the inhabitants of the plain of Ararat to migrate to Persia. He settled them in the district of Peria, where he founded the town of New Julfa. The historians and eyewitnesses painfully described the destruction and burning of the prosperous city and its remarkable architectural monuments. In his elegy "Lament over Erevan and Julfa in the Land of Armenia," seventeenth-century poet Hovhannēs of Maku, who had witnessed the deportation of the people of Julfa, compared it to Paris:

> Alas, let me speak of Julfa, the pride of the Armenian nation,
> Which surpassed Paris of the French.

Another poet of the seventeenth century, Dawit' Geghamats'i, described in his elegy ("Lament over Julfa," according to Ghewond Alishan)[18] the ravaged state of the prosperous old city and deplored the destruction of the palaces and villas of the rich merchants and affluent natives:

The city of Julfa was built well;
Palaces and villas rose high
And were painted in different colors;
It was a marvel to look at.

In the song of a contemporary composer, which is preserved in a manuscript now in St. Amenap'rkich' Monastery of New Julfa, the deportation of the Armenians from the plain of Ararat is narrated with remorse:

Here . . . let me present Julfa as a witness,
Where instead of psalmody one hears the cries of the owls
   in the ruins,
And the splendid paintings on canvas for which you cared
Have been taken to Isfahan, where they have defiled them
   with the foul palm . . .[19]

After the destruction of Julfa at the beginning of the seventeenth century, the historians turned their attention to New Julfa, where the former inhabitants of Julfa founded new monasteries and built numerous beautiful villas, monuments, and *khach'k'ars,* as they had done in their former residence.

Very little remains of old Julfa today. After the devastation wrought by Shah Abbas, the city was in ruins. Only a few families returned from New Julfa to the ashes of their ancestral city. They first sought refuge in the closed marketplace, which was still extant, built a few houses, and restored those churches and monasteries that were still standing. Of the seven churches and monasteries, St. Amenap'rkich' Vank' and St. Gēorg and St. Astuatsatsin survive in a semidilapidated state. Besides these, St. Sargis and the church of Verin Kat'ank' were also important cultural centers.

St. Amenap'rkich' Monastery of Julfa is located on an elevated, level site near the old city. It was built in the ninth or the tenth century. The dilapidated complex, which is surrounded by an outer wall, comprises a small church, a porch, a refectory, and other auxiliary buildings with one or two stories. The church, which is located at the southeastern corner of the enclosed area, has a main apse, two vestries, and a portal on the western facade. It is a domed structure with a central plan and is built of polished and semipolished blocks of stone. The large, round dome has a pyramidal roof. The wide portal has a lancet-shaped arch, which is common in twelfth- and thirteenth-century Armenian monuments.

According to M. Smbatian, Paron Vahram founded St. Amenap'rkich' Church in 1271.[20] The literary sources, however, indicate that the church is older than that. For example, St. Amenap'rkich' is mentioned in the encyclical of Catholicos Khach'ik in connection with King Ashot Shahnshah's donation of lands in 976 to St. Step'anos Church of Darashamb.[21] Considering the architectural characteristics of the monument, we are inclined to believe that St. Amenap'rkich' Church was founded no later than the ninth or the tenth century.

Attached to the western elevation of the church is a small, vaulted porch with two pillars. Inside the outer walls of the monastic complex and near the northern and southern elevations of the church there are cells, a refectory, bakery, kitchen, and other buildings with cross-vaulted ceilings.

In the 1850s, the inhabitants of historic Julfa moved slightly to the east of the ruins of the old city and founded the present-day village of Julfa in the region of Julfa.

Old Julfa was especially well known for its *khach'k'ars,* most of which are now destroyed. At the end of the nineteenth century the construction of a railroad that cut through the city provided a pretext to destroy some of the *khach'k'ars* in the cemetery and certain ruined buildings. Ignorant contractors and engineers used the ruins of monuments as if they were rubble; in order to construct a railroad over 600 to 700 meters long, they took thousands of fifteenth- and sixteenth-century *khach'k'ars* and remains of other monuments. Since the seventeenth century, *khach'k'ars* from the cemetery and capitals with reliefs have been destroyed by people seeking treasures and gold.

The cemetery of Julfa is unique in the Caucasus for its size and the variety of its monuments; it is a real archaeological and architectural repository. After visiting it in 1914, the painter Martiros Sarian noted: "At Julfa we saw the renowned *khach'k'ars*. The railroad crossed through a forest of *khach'k'ars*. . . . The *khach'k'ars* amazed me with their unique artistic value, and the wonderful variety of their motifs. At the same time I was upset to hear that many of them had been destroyed during the construction of the railroad."[22]

The cemetery is spread out over three hills located to the west of the historic city. The ruins of the city lie between the Arax River and the natural wall formed by mountains. The *khach'k'ars*, as well as the capitals, with their beautiful reliefs, are very expressive and mysterious; they bear witness to the art and architecture of the Armenian people.

The cemetery has numerous *khach'k'ars* with lovely reliefs and ordinary tombstones shaped like cradles. In 1648 the traveler Alexander Rhodes, who was passing through Julfa, described the antiquities of the city, noting that there were about ten thousand well-preserved *khach'k'ars*.[23] This estimate seems correct, since in 1903–1904 the existence of more than five thousand *khach'k'ars* was noted. By 1915 there were over twenty-three hundred extant *khach'k'ars*. At present the cemetery has about two thousand *khach'k'ars* and capitals; some of these are still standing, whereas others are either in a semidilapidated state or are fallen. The *khach'k'ars* of Julfa (Figs. 43–46) come in many varieties and forms. They were built between the ninth and the seventeenth centuries. The builders for the most part used pink and yellowish liparite. The *khach'k'ars* of the ninth to the fifteenth century are simple in form and dimension. They have few reliefs and are similar to the ones in other parts of Armenia. But from the end of the fifteenth century the inhabitants of Julfa vied with one another to build more ornate and beautiful *khach'k'ars* to perpetuate the memory of their martyrs and to bequeath their story to posterity. This is probably why the people of Julfa intro-

Fig. 43. General view of the cemetery.

Fig. 44. A section of the cemetery.   *Fig. 45. Another view of the cemetery.*

duced innovations in the traditional form of *khach'k'ar* sculpture in the sixteenth and the seventeenth centuries. The latter are usually narrower and taller. The central area on the monument, with its cross relief, is deeper and the top has bands and arches in relief. On the lower part one would find the relief of horsemen and other scenes. The artistic sources of sixteenth- and seventeenth-century *khach'k'ar* sculpture in Julfa are traditional.[24]

But the style that the artisans of Julfa developed was local and confined to that town.

One of the characteristic features of the cemetery is the presence of large and small capitals with beautiful reliefs that depict domestic scenes. These, as well as inscriptions, geometric patterns, reliefs of plants, animals, domestic items, and tools, are of great importance for the study of medieval Armenian life. Among the sixteenth-

Fig. 46. Elaborately carved tombstones.

and seventeenth-century sculptors who built a number of beautiful monuments were Hayrapet, Grigor, and the master mason Israyēl.

The art and the subject matter of the *khach'k'ar* sculpture of Julfa represent a picturesque testimony of the fifteenth- to seventeenth-century life of the Armenian people. These monuments, which were created with great artistic skill and architectural taste, are important for the study of not only art and architecture in medieval Armenia but also for the development of urban life.

About 1 kilometer east of the ruins of Julfa are the ruins of the village of Jughayi Dasht (the Plain of Julfa), which has been known since the early part of this century for the Gulistan tomb.

ABRAKUNIS (APRAKUNIK')

The present-day village of Abrakunis, which is on the site of the village of the same name, is mentioned by thirteenth-century sources. According to tradition, the village's name derives from that of the Armenian patriarch Arbak. From ancient times the inhabitants of Abrakunis were preoccupied with agriculture, breeding of livestock, stonecutting, potterymaking, and other crafts.

Abrakunis is noted for its historical and architectural monuments, cemeteries, and other antiquities. St. Gēorg and St. Khach' churches and St. Karapet Monastery are well known to students of Armenian art. At present, only St. Karapet is extant. In the fourteenth century the School of Aprakunik' was established at St. Gēorg (tenth century) and St. Khach' (twelfth century) churches. In 1868, when St. Gēorg Church was being renovated, more than ten eleventh- and twelfth-century *khach'k'ars* (plaster statues) and several earthenware items were discovered among its foundations.[25] St. Karapet Monastery of Abrakunis is known for its architecture and history.[26] This complex, considered the spiritual and cultural center of the district of Ernjak from the fourteenth to the eighteenth centuries, is located to the right of the road that goes to the village of Abrakunis and stands on a tableland that rises on the western slope of a small valley 1 kilometer from the Ernjak River.

From a distance the monastery appears to the beholder to be an immense complex (Figs. 47–51), with its structural volume, building material, and location all blending harmoniously. The structure and the plan of the monastery make it one of the famous monuments of medieval Armenian architecture. According to historical and epigraphical sources, this monastery was founded in 1381 by Maghak'ia of Crimea, and the famed medieval thinkers Yovhannēs of Orotn and Grigor of Tat'ew, who were responsible for the transfer of the theological school of the district of Ernjak from St. Khach' Monastery to this newly founded complex, where they generated widespread cultural activities.

The monastery, which was renovated several times, is still standing, but it is completely abandoned. Today most of the buildings of the complex are destroyed (in the second half of the nineteenth century there were more than forty buildings here). At one time these structures served the needs of the monastic community. The major monument in the complex is the main church, which was one of the striking architectural structures of its time. St. Karapet Church is built of polished blocks of bluish basalt (Fig. 52) and is constructed in the style of a basilican church with four pillars. Its tall, majestic cupola, which is built of brick, has eight windows. The interior is spacious and bright. On either side of the large main apse there is two-storied vestry. The entrances to the upper levels of these can be reached from inside the main apse, in which five stone steps lead upstairs. The vestry on the right side on the first level has a secret subterranean chamber that can be reached by a stone stairway carved into the rock. Formerly, manuscripts and sacred relics were stored there. A passage from the stone stairway branches out and rises behind the apse; another passage goes down and merges with a tunnel underneath the first stories of the monastic buildings, which have two to four flights.

Through the centuries St. Karapet has been renovated on several occasions. The restoration of 1648–49, when the architect Dawit' Usta [master], a famous figure in the history of Armenian architecture, supervised the construction, is well known. The church and the entire complex were also renovated from their foundations up in 1653 with the blessings of Catholicos P'ilippos. Subse-

Fig. 47. A general view of St. Karapet Monastery and Mount Ōdzasar from the west.

quently, in 1656 restoration work was made possible through the efforts of Esayi Vardapet of Meghri and Ghazar of Chahuk. There were also other renovations made in later periods. The western facade of the church of St. Karapet, with its beautiful portal decorated with reliefs, *khach'k'ars*, and carved bands, enhances the expressiveness of the exterior, giving the edifice a special majesty.

In 1740 the interior of the church was covered with delicate and attractive paintings, about which there exists epigraphical and literary information. Even today one can see fragments (Figs. 100–102a-b) of the wall paintings of Harut'iwn and Hakob Hovnat'anian, two noted artists from Shoṙot' who were the sons of the painter Naghash Hovnat'an.

Attached to the southern elevation of the church of St. Karapet is the beautiful chapel of St. Step'anos, which has an apse on its eastern side. According to scholars, this church was constructed in about 1653–56. In 1714

Fig. 48. The church of St. Karapet Monastery from the east.

Fig. 49. The west facade of the church of St. Karapet Monastery.

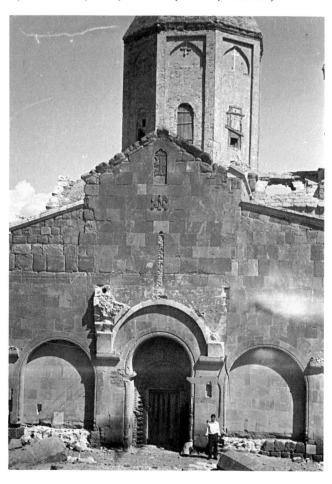

it was rebuilt by Khoja Ayvaz of Shoṙot'; this event is recorded in a long inscription in rhyme that is still extant.

St. Step'anos chapel is also built of polished blocks of bluish basalt stone and its only portal is on the western facade. On the roof of the chapel there is an attractive bell tower with a tall cupola standing on four columns. It was built in 1705 by Paron Aghamal, son of Aghajan of Nakhichevan. The bell tower was also renovated on a number of occasions; the cupola was destroyed in about 1915–20.

St. Karapet Monastery also had a handsome porch that occupied an area as wide as the church. The structure had four thick pillars; the arches rested on the pillars and the western elevation of the church. The pillars, three of which are now lying intact in front of the church, were built with massive eight-sided blocks of basalt stone, each block measuring 1.12 by 2.5 meters. There is no epigraphical or literary information on the

Fig. 50. An angle view of the west facade of the church of St. Karapet Monastery.

Fig. 51. St. Step'anos chapel/bell tower of St. Karapet Monastery.

construction of the porch. We are inclined to believe that it was built in about the middle of the fifteenth century and lasted until the beginning of the twentieth century, at which time it was entirely destroyed.

St. Karapet Monastery is surrounded by high walls that are built of stone, bricks, and lime mortar. Parts of the wall, especially the upper sections, are now in ruins. Inside the walls, in the northern, eastern, and western areas, there were cells for the monks and several other buildings. Some of these are now reduced to rubble, the rest are not sturdy and are near collapse.

To the east and north of the walls of the monastery one can see the monastic and village cemeteries where there are over one thousand tombstones dating from the fif-

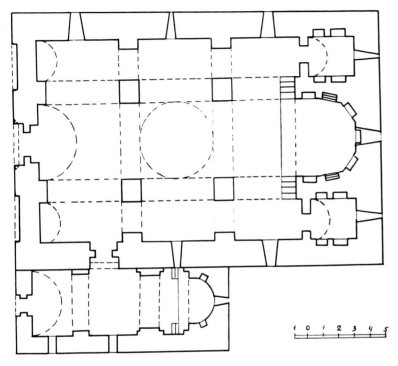

Fig. 52. The plan of the church of St. Karapet Monastery and St. Step'anos chapel.

teenth to the twentieth centuries. Despite a number of renovations and restorations, the architectural composition of St. Karapet Monastery of Abrakunis has remained basically intact. Even today it strikes the beholder as an interesting and impressive medieval monument.

APARANER

This ancient town in the district of Ernjak was located on the right bank of the Ernjak River, approximately 2 kilometers north of Abrakunis. Armenian and non-Armenian sources frequently mention the town and call it Aparaner, Aparan, or Aparank' [palace]. Medieval Aparaner, which is the present-day village of Bananiar in the region of Julfa, had an Armenian population of five to six hundred thousand families and occupied a large area within its fortified walls. The vestiges of some of the buildings, winepresses, and cemeteries of the earlier town can still be seen today in the vineyards and the fields surrounding the present-day village. Seventeenth-century traveler John Tavernier, who passed through Aparaner, wrote admiringly of it, stating that, with its delightful vineyards, fruit-bearing trees, and all the amenities of life, it was one of the most beautiful places in Asia.[27]

This town is mentioned in the *History* of Step'anos Orbelean[28] as Aparank' in the district of Ernjak. Beginning with the fourteenth century the historical sources speak about it frequently as the center of the Unitores [Armenians who converted to Catholicism]. According to the colophon of a manuscript copied by Mxit'ar of Aparan, the religious monuments of Aparaner were named after the "Holy Mother of God, Saint Stephen the Protomartyr, the Apostle Saint James and All Saints."[29] Unfortunately these monuments are now completely destroyed and razed to the ground. The sources do not give us any descriptive or historical information on them. There is only limited information about the All Saints Church, which was the seat of the Unitor diocesan bishop.[30]

The grandiose complex of the All Saints Church of Aparaner stood on a small hill in the central area of the old town. Until 1970 one could still see the vestiges of its ruins. Visiting Aparaner at the end of the nineteenth century, A. Sedrakian described the semidilapidated church: "The church is built of stones and lime mortar to the level of the arches. The arches and the roof are built of baked bricks. The vaulted church is divided into three chapels of which the middle one, with its four pillars, is the largest; each chapel has a cupola."[31] According to Ghewond Alishan, the roof and the cupolas were destroyed during the earthquake of 1848.

There were a number of beautiful *khach'k'ars* with

reliefs and tombstones with twelfth- to fourteenth-century inscriptions set in the walls of the apse and other parts of the church.[32] At ground level, probably under the apse, there was a secret closet carved in rock where vessels, ornaments, and other items were discovered in 1870.

On the basis of the inscriptions of the All Saints Church we think that the original structure was founded before the tenth or the eleventh century. On the foundations of this the Unitores built their diocesan church in the fourteenth century.

SALIT'AGH

The historic village of Salit'agh is located on the rocky western slope of Mount Ōdzasar and is near the town of Aparan, or Aparaner. It is situated on the left bank of the Ernjak River. According to tradition, this village was a suburb of the town of Aparan, and since it stood on wide slabs [*sal*], it was called Sali-t'agh [slab quarter], and it still bears the same name.

Salit'agh is first mentioned in a colophon of 1383–84 written inside a little decoration in a codex of Thomas Aquinas's *Summa Theologica,* part three, ''Treatise on the Incarnation,'' which was copied by Friar Hovhannēs in Nakhichevan: ''In the 833rd year of the Armenian Era [1384], Friar Sarsun Tērunakan, a father confessor, was hanged.''[33] Our survey of the vicinity of Salit'agh reveals that the village, which was founded at a very early date, had a church, a cemetery with *khach'k'ars,* a bridge, and other monuments. These were destroyed over the course of time. The proselytizing of the Unitores annoyed the inhabitants of Salit'agh and the other villages in the district of Ernjak.

According to A. Sedrakian's information, which dates back to the 1860s, and other data from 1873,[34] the church of Salit'agh was in ruins and only the remains of the foundation walls could be seen. The ancient cemetery, where only insignificant tombstones remain, is located on an elevated site in the northern section of the village. In his brief description A. Sedrakian notes that ''the cemetery of the unfortunate Armenians was full of numerous *khach'k'ars,* most of which were destroyed by the inhabitants of the village in order to pave the way for a newly opened waterway.''[35]

NORASHĒN

The village of Norashēn (Norakert), which bears the same name as the region, is located on the right bank of the Ernjak River and on the eastern side of Mount Bolu sar. The present-day village is spread below the side, whereas the old village was for the most part located on the side of the mountain and in the valley to the north. Our survey of the area of Norashēn and its cemetery shows beyond any doubt that the village was founded in the early Middle Ages and that stonecutting, pottery, and various other professions reached an advanced stage of development between the twelfth and seventeenth centuries. Considering the prosperity of the village, Kozma Rabuni, a renowned scribe and painter from Norashēn, called it ''the town of Norashēnik'' in a manuscript he copied there in 1668 (Matenadaran, Ms. no. 3817).

Norashēn is also known for its architectural monuments: the magnificent St. Astuatsatsin Monastery, St. Hovhannēs Church, the bridge over the Ernjak River, and other buildings.[36] Unfortunately only St. Astuatsatsin Monastery has survived the ravages of time. Its church and porch are still standing in a relatively well-preserved state.

St. Astuatsatsin Monastery, which was founded in the ninth or tenth century, is located in the central quarter of the village at a distance of 80 to 90 meters from the village cemetery, which lies on the side of the mountain. The monastic buildings, the cells to the west and east of the church, and the outer walls of the monastery are destroyed.

St. Astuatsatsin Church is a magnificent basilican

structure with a nave and two aisles, a spacious apse, two vestries, and a hall. The high gabled roof of the church rests on four pillars and engaged piers. A small four-sided bell tower stands on the center of the roof. The church has two portals, one on the western and the other on the southern facade. The western portal, which has beautiful reliefs and pilasters covered with spherical-shaped crowns, opens onto a porch that has four pillars.

According to the inscriptions on the portals and the exterior and interior walls of the church, the church was renovated between the fifteenth and seventeenth centuries. On different parts of the whitewashed interior walls one can see traces of effaced paintings. The porch is of particular interest; on the fronts of the four pillars that support the arches there are the reliefs of the four evangelists, the Mother of God, and decorations, most of which are now effaced. These were executed upon the order of Hovhannēs Vardapet and the couple Uhan and Nazlu.

VERIN [UPPER] ANKUZIK'

To the northeast of the fortress of Ernjak there lies a long, deep valley surrounded by tall peaks and precipices. It is variously called Ankuzadzor, Ěnkuzadzor, or Ankuzadzor [valley of walnuts]. On the hills and the slopes of this valley there have been since ancient times three villages: Verin [Upper], Mijin [Middle], and Nerk'in or Storin [Inner or Lower] Ankuzik's or Anzurs. According to thirteenth-century historian Step'anos Orbelean, one of these villages paid an annual tribute of twelve *dahekans* to the Monastery of Tat'ew.[37]

Verin Ankuzik', which is now uninhabited and in ruins, is located at the highest part of the valley. The village is situated on a beautiful hill. From its ruins one can assume that it was a sizable village with a large population. In the sources there is no information on Verin Ankuzik' and its monuments. In the ruins of the village one can still see the remains of a church. According to A.

Sedrakian, "It is a small but a magnificent church built of stone; the vaulted ceiling rests on engaged piers. It has an altar and two vestries and a portal on the western facade. The roof of the church has entirely caved in. On a stone set into the western facade there is an inscription: 'It was founded in 1168 [1719] during our Archbishop Lord Matt'ēos's tenure as prelate.'"[38]

To the west of Verin Ankuzik' is the large village cemetery, which has tombstones with inscriptions dating from the fifteenth to the eighteenth century. The data from the cemetery suggests that the Armenians left the village at the end of the eighteenth century.

MIJIN [MIDDLE] ANKUZIK'

This village, 2 kilometers down the valley from Verin Ankuzik', is uninhabited and in ruins. Its Armenian population abandoned it after the middle of the eighteenth century. The sources say nothing about the village church, which stands on an elevated site in the western part of the village and is entirely destroyed. The ruins of the church and a few tombstones to the south of the monument provide the necessary evidence to show that the edifice was founded at an early date and that it was relatively small. At a considerable distance to the east of the church is the large village cemetery, with its inscribed tombstones.

NERK'IN [INNER OR LOWER] ANKUZIK'

Nerk'in, or Storin Ankuzik', which is uninhabited and in ruins, is located at the lower part of Ankuzadzor, to the right of the highway that goes down to the fortress of Ernjak. From the large area occupied by the village it is possible to calculate that about 130 families lived there.

In the ruins of the northern part of the village there is a semidilapidated church built of polished blocks of sandstone and lime mortar; during the renovations of the seventeenth century bricks were also used. The monument has the plan of a basilican church with four pillars (Fig. 53), an apse, two vestries, and a hall. The apse is polygonal and its floor is on the same level as that of the hall. The ruins of a large building to the north of the church seem to be the remains of a refectory. The name of the church is unknown. On the structure one can see the traces of several renovations. The last one was done in the seventeenth century.

The large village cemetery, which has thirteenth- to eighteenth-century *khach'k'ars,* gravestones, and tombstones in the form of inscribed capitals, is located to the south of Nerk'in Ankuzik', immediately to the left of the road that goes to Verin and Mijin Ankuzik'.

KHOSHKASHĒN

The historic village of Khoshkashēn, or Khach'kashēn, is deserted, and since the 1950s it has been in ruins. The village is situated on the northeastern side of Mount Ōdzasar. The dwelling places and other buildings are perched like a vine on the rocky gray side of the high, sunburnt mountain.

From the ruins of Khoshkashēn-Khach'kashēn, the large old cemetery, and the surroundings one can tell that man had lived there since ancient times. H. Aṙak'elian identified this place with Khoshakunik', which is mentioned by Movsēs Khorenats'i: "It is mentioned during the time of Tigran I. It is known as being one of the five villages of the Unitores, which had 130 families or 700 people who received communion, 300 children, and a monastic congregation."[39]

During the Middle Ages and especially from the sixteenth to the eighteenth century, Khoshkashēn was one of the important centers of Ernjak and was noted for its historical monuments. According to the sources, this prosperous village was frequently raided by foreign marauders. For example, one of literary sources states that in 1598 a Turkish official entered the village with fifty

Fig. 53. The plan of the ruined church of Nerk'in Ankuziki.

horsemen and plundered it and its monastery.[40] The Turks beheaded the priest Matt'ēos with a sword as he was officiating the Divine Liturgy. Because of such ravages and destruction, the historical monuments of the village disappeared long ago. Today there is no descriptive or historical information available on them.

In the middle of the nineteenth century, St. Geghard Monastery of Khoshkashēn was, according to Ghewond Alishan, "almost uprooted from its foundations and changed into a garden."[41] According to the colophon of a gospel written in 1641, "On top of the mountain out-side the village there was a church named after the Apostle Thaddeus. Petik says that under his jurisdiction [in 1671] there were only seventy families of Armenians and he calls the church St. Step'anos Nakhavkay."[42] One of the manuscripts copied at this monastery is well known: "The Treasury of the Teachings of Christ. 1675. I, the cleric Tōnikean, copied [this] . . . in the village of Khōshkashēn in the Monastery of St. Step'anos . . . at the order of my superior Brother Dominicus son of Khōj."[43]

Unfortunately, not having excavated the present-day ruins of Khoshkashēn, it is impossible to give an approximate description of the monuments and their architectural characteristics, namely the Monastery of St. Geghard, and St. T'adē and St. Step'anos churches, which were still standing and functioning until the early part of the nineteenth century.

Because of its active role, St. Geghard Monastery, which was the seat of an Armenian Catholic bishop, occupied a special place among the monuments of Khoshkashēn. Between the sixteenth and seventeenth centuries a number of manuscripts were copied there. It had an active Catholic congregation. Augustine Bajets'i, a native of Ernjak, returning from the deportation imposed by Shah Abbas, wrote: "After these torments, I, a sinful man, went to the village of Khoshkashēn and lived in the Monastery of St. Geghard of Christ. There I served God for eight months."[44] Among the noted abbots of St. Geghard are Yovhannēs (1540), Mik'ayēl (1684), Andrēas (1696), Step'anos (1703), and Petros (1705).[45]

The people of Khoshkashēn were also known in the Middle Ages for their commercial activities and devotion to Armenian letters. In a manuscript there is mention made of a monk named Zak'aria of Khoshkashēn who went to Rome in 1568 to be near Archbishop Nikoghayos. Unable to return to his fatherland because of old age, he stayed in Italy and died in Florence. In 1570 Zak'aria copied *The Book of Hours According to the Order of St. Dominic,* in the colophon of which he noted: "This book was copied by Brother Zak'aria of Khoshkashēn in the city of Florence, which is protected by God . . . as a memorial for myself and my parents, my father, Nurijan, and my mother, Gilshat."[46] Father Movsēs of Khoshkashēn also visited Italy, and in the colophon of a manuscript he copied in 1628 he wrote: "In 1628, on the twenty-fourth day of June, on the feast of Saint John the Baptist, I entered Rome."[47] During his research, Ghewond Alishan saw a manuscript that was in one of the Italian libraries and was copied by "the worthless priest Father Yovhannēs of Khōshkashēn of the order of the Dominicans and from the province and district of Nakhichevan."[48]

Based on various sources Ghewond Alishan noted: "At the beginning of the eighteenth century certain merchants from Khoshkashēn, who were pious and rich, had religious books published in Italy and France, where they had gone."[49] Thus the sources testify that Khoja Azaria, son of Buniat' of Khoshkashēn, had a "Book of Hours" and prayerbooks printed in Venice in 1706. Sixty-four years later, in 1768, T'ovmas Isaverteants', at the age of sixty-four, had another book printed. In 1723 T'ovmas translated a missal.[50] According to Ghewond Alishan, T'ovma Isaverteants' was "a monk of the order of the Unitores, or the Dominicans of Armenia, who was wandering around in the west after the destruction or desertion of the monasteries of his order in Ernjak." Another native of Khoshkashēn, Yovhannēs, had a number of volumes printed in Marseilles. In the colophon of one of these he states: "I, Yovhannēs, son of Minas, had these meditative prayers printed as a memorial for myself and my parents."[51]

HIN [OLD] P'ORADASHT

There is very little information on this village in the historical sources. Like the village of Gagh, Hin P'or-

adasht, or P'aradasht, was built on the rocky side of a
lofty mountain range where level areas were cleared so
that dwellings and gardens could be built. This hamlet
was abandoned a long time ago and is uninhabited today. The ruins of the stone houses, the churches, various
other buildings, and the walls of the vineyards, which
are 2 to 3 meters high, and the extensive cemetery show
that this village existed since the early Middle Ages. The
area of the village could support ninety to one hundred
families. There is no information on its past history or the
circumstances surrounding its abandonment. But considering the dates of inscriptions in the cemeteries of
both Hin and Nor P'oradasht, we must assume that after
the mid-sixteenth century the inhabitants of the old village moved down to the level area at the foot of the
mountain probably because of unfavorable climatic conditions higher up.

One can still see the semidilapidated church in the
ruins of Hin P'oradasht. There is no information on the
name or date of the church. A. Sedrakian noted that
among the ruins of the village "there is a semidilapidated
vaulted church built of stones and lime mortar; according to native tradition, it was called "Franki [Latin]
church."[52] This edifice is built on an elevated site in the
center of the village. The structure is made of polished
blocks of light blue basalt and for the most part blocks of
sandstone. The besalt was used in the important joints,
corners of walls, edges of openings, on the walls of the
portal and the vestries. Today the entire roof of the
church, the second story of the vestry, the portal, and
the roof of the apse are all destroyed. The extant walls
are 2 to 2.5 meters high and are covered with vegetation
and bushes.

The monument is in the style of a vaulted hall (Fig.
54) with an apse on the eastern side. The portal is on the
western facade. On either side of the apse there are two-
storied vestries. The bema is 45 to 50 centimeters above
the floor of the hall. The apse and the vestries receive
their light from single windows located on the eastern

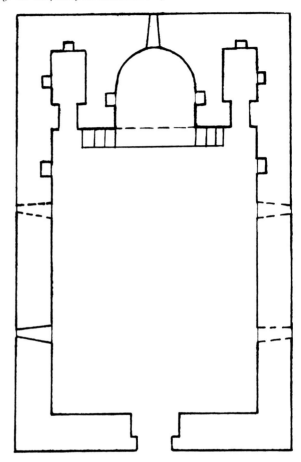

Fig. 54. The plan of the ruined church of Hin P'oradasht.

wall. The apse has two niches, whereas the vestries have
one each. No traces of windows can be seen on the walls
of the hall. Since the church is situated on slanted
ground, most of the northern elevation is used as a support. The vestries on the second floor have on their western facades fairly wide windows through which one can
look down at the hall. There are secret passageways from

the vestries to the hall. In the interior the apse and the vestries are covered with plaster and whitewashed. Because of seismic conditions, wooden beams have been placed in the walls of the church at the level of the ceiling of the vestry on the first floor. The walls of the church interior are smooth; there are no engaged piers. The interior and exterior walls of the church are undecorated.

The porch was attached to the western facade of the church. Only ruins remain of it today. On the basis of these one can assume that the porch covered the entire western elevation of the church and it had a rectangular plan. In the ruins and the vicinity of the church there are thirteenth- to seventeenth-century *khach'k'ars*, capitals with reliefs, and tombstones with human figures on them. According to inscriptions on *khach'k'ars*, the church was renovated in the seventeenth century.

The St. Step'anos monastic complex is located 4 to 5 kilometers north of Hin P'oradasht. It is situated on a stone platform over a level area on the southeastern slope of a deep valley. The complex consists of a church and twelve to fifteen auxiliary buildings that are attached to the outer walls and are located to the west, east, and south of the edifice. These are enclosed within rectangular walls 6 to 8 meters high. At present the entire roof and the upper parts of the church are destroyed. The buildings to the south and west of the church were already in ruins by the end of the last century, whereas certain ones to the east are still standing, though dilapidated. Most of the walls, which give the impression that they were intended for defensive purposes, are reduced to rubble.

St. Step'anos Church and the entire complex are built of polished stones that were brought from the mountain. In the seventeenth century, when the church was renovated, bricks were also used here and there on the exterior and interior sections of the upper rows of the walls. The church of St. Step'anos Monastery, which is located at the northwestern corner of the complex, is in the style of vaulted structures with a single nave (Fig. 55). The

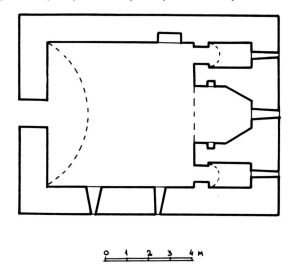

Fig. 55. The plan of the church of St. Step'anos Monastery.

0 1 2 3 4 M

apse has an exterior with five sides and is flanked by vaulted vestries. These, as well as the apse, receive their light from single windows on the eastern wall. The hall has two pairs of windows on the northern and southern walls.

The sources unfortunately have very little information to offer on St. Step'anos Monastery. According to M. Smbatian, this complex "was built by the Vardapet Maghak'ia of Crimea, one of the pupils of Yovhannēs of Orotn, in the year of the Lord 1385. It was renovated by Tēr Awag in 1560."[53] The source of M. Smbatian is unknown. Yet it is evident that in the fourteenth century and even earlier a religious center was functioning here. Tēr Awag built the outer walls of St. Step'anos and at the same time renovated the church. The *khach'k'ar* that attests to that event is still fixed a little above the portal of the church. A later inscription, which is now near the only portal of the complex (located on its eastern facade), states that Mughtasi Daniel, son of Sahak and Khupnikar, renovated the monastery and its outer walls in 1683.

Located at a distance of 250 to 300 meters down the valley to the northeast of the outer walls of St. Step'anos is the famous fountain of the monastery, called *Nahatak* [martyr]. Its waters flow directly from under two huge boulders that are attached to each other. Once a number of *khach'k'ars* stood near the fountain; only their fragments remain now. The cemetery of the monastery, which has only six tombstones today, is situated on a level area about 150 meters east of the complex. A number of *khach'k'ars* of the thirteenth to the fifteenth centuries stand along the road from the monastery to Hin P'oradasht.

NOR [NEW] P'ORADASHT

Nor P'oradasht is about 1 kilometer below Hin P'oradasht on a fertile plain below the side of a mountain range. By the 1950s the inhabitants of this village had moved to Erevan, and so nothing much remains of it today.

According to A. Sedrakian, St. Gēorg Church of Nor P'oradasht "was a small building built of ordinary stones and was covered with a wooden roof. It was situated in the center of the village. There was a small chapel called St. Eghia to the west of the village."[54] Among the present-day ruins of P'oradasht one can still see the remains of these two structures. We have no information on the dates of these buildings. St. Eghia Chapel, which is located on the peak of a hill, is a rectangular building constructed of flagstones. Its roof was slanted to one side and covered with wood.

St. Gēorg Church, which is located in the center of the village, is in bad condition. Its entire roof, southern wall, and second-story vestry are gone. The western facade is dilapidated and the roof of the apse could also collapse. St. Gēorg has a rectangular plan (Fig. 56) with an apse that is five-sided on the exterior. There are two-storied vestries on either side of the apse. Before the 1950s this church had been converted into a school and partitions

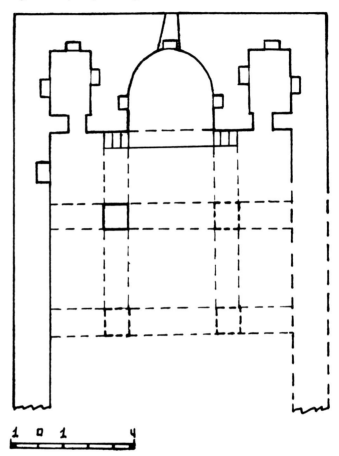

Fig. 56. The plan of St. Gēorg Church.

raised in the interior for making classrooms. The apse and the vestries receive light from single windows. The second-story vestries have wide windows on their western walls that open on the hall. In the niche of the northern wall, in front of the northern vestry, there is a *khach'k'ar* with reliefs. On its molding, inside the arches, there are three crosses on which one can see the building inscription, which states that the church was built in 1681.

The large cemetery of Nor P'oradasht is also of archaeological interest. It has over five hundred tombstones and capitals from the sixteenth to twentieth century that have reliefs bearing inscriptions.

SHOŘOT'

Shoŕot' (Shoŕod), now the village of Shoŕot' in the present-day region of Julfa, was one of the best-known villages of medieval Ernjak. It has been mentioned by the sources since the thirteenth century and was an important cultural center.[55] The ruins of its historical monuments and various other buildings bear witness to the high caliber of architectural talent and advanced commercial activities in Shoŕot'. From the fourteenth to the eighteenth century the merchants of Shoŕot' had commercial ties not only to the important trade centers of Armenia, but also to those of India, Italy, Russia, and

Fig. 57. St. Hakob Church from the southeast.

Holland. According to the historical sources, since ancient times the development of such crafts as pottery, weaving, dyeing, metallurgy, masonry, calligraphy, and painting reached an advanced stage in this town.

Shoŕot' is located in a valley called Zharazhur, the natural setting of which resembles a large, enchanting plain. Several small hills surround the village. The local lime, which is called *shoŕ jor*, has been used by the inhabitants as mortar for stone houses and as building material for water pipes and pottery. According to the older residents of the village, the place was named Shoŕot' (Shoŕod) because of the colorless lime covering the surface of the fields. The ruins of a number of cemeteries, monasteries, churches, winepresses, fortresses, fountains, and other buildings located in the vicinity of Shoŕot' testify to the bustling life of this medieval town, which was inhabited by an Armenian population of a few thousand. Most of the historic monuments of Shoŕot' were still standing, though in an unsturdy state, until the middle of the nineteenth century.[56] Among the architectural monuments of Shoŕot' there are six famous complexes—churches and monasteries—of which only three are still standing: St. Lusaworich' Monastery, the cathedral of St. Hakob, and St. Astuatsatsin. St. Hakob, which is a domed basilican church (Fig. 57), is architecturally significant. It is situated on a level, elevated area in the center of town. The outline of St. Hakob Church, with its magnificent exterior and its beautiful high-domed cupola, can be seen from far away. Its rectangular plan encloses a large apse, two vestries, and a hall (Fig. 58).

The present-day church of St. Hakob, which was originally built in the twelfth century, was renovated in the middle of the seventh century according to its building inscription. It is built mostly of polished blocks of basalt and grayish blue stone and bricks (the dome). The western facade, where the main portal of the church is located, is more impressive. Bands decorated with relief sculpture cover the rims of the portal (Fig. 59). The cupola, which was constructed in 1664, according to an inscription, is built of brick. It stands above the central bay and rises high on a cruciform roof, giving the interior of the church a special splendor and brightness. The cupola is almost as high as the hall. Its proportions and architectural details, according to the opinion of the architect Murad Hasrat'ian, are similar to those of the brick cuplola of St. Astuatsatsin Church of Mets T'agh of Meghri.[57]

A porch with a rectangular plan and four pillars was attached to the western facade of St. Yakob. It is a little narrower than the width of the church. This structure was built in the middle of the fifteenth century and was destroyed by an earthquake in 1841.[58]

St. Nshan Church was another famous monument that is now entirely destroyed; it is no more than a mound of stones. According to A. Sedrakian, this church "was a large and magnificent structure. Now one can only discern its western and southern stone walls, the foundations of the four piers and the altar. It also had a magnificent porch with two pillars. . . . On the interior surface of the tympanum of the southern portal there was the following inscription: 'In the year 1602 [1613]. This holy cross is in memory of Salur Bēg son of Hayrapet.' "[59] We are inclined to believe that St. Nshan was originally built at an earlier date and was renovated in the seventeenth century. It was still standing until the beginning of the nineteenth century.

St. Lusaworich' Monastery of Shoṙot' is by far the least well known of the three complexes. Over the course of time the auxiliary buildings in the monastery, its school, fountain, and the extensive outer walls have been reduced to rubble. At present the roof of the church is damaged and the southern wall has cracks. Because of these we could only take the measurements of the church and the porch. Our impressions of the remaining buildings are based on their ruins.

St. Lusaworich' Monastery (Fig. 60), which was one of the famous cultural centers of Shoṙot', is about 1 kilometer northeast of the village. It is situated on an elevated and extensive plateau to the right of a small valley that is slightly slanted toward the southwest. Historic Shoṙot', with its ruins and ancient fruit-bearing vine-

Fig. 58. The plan of St. Hakob Church.

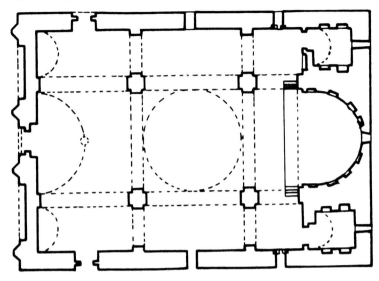

Fig. 59. West elevation entrance of St. Hakob Church.

Fig. 60. East elevation of St. Lusaworich' Monastery.

stands in almost the center of a rectangular area surrounded by outer walls. There is a porch attached to its western elevation. Both inside and outside the walls there were twenty-five to thirty auxiliary buildings, which were intended for the purposes of the monastic community. Now one can see only their vestiges.

The church of St. Lusaworich' Monastery is built of

Fig. 61. The plan of the church of St. Lusaworich' Monastery.

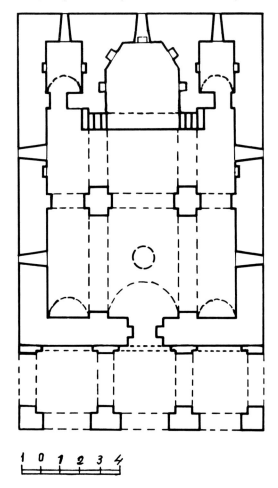

yards, lies before St. Lusaworich', which occupies more than four hectares.

The present-day complex of St. Lusaworich' was probably built during the early Middle Ages on the site of an earlier monastery. In the period from the sixteenth to the eighteenth centuries, this monastery was one of the greatest cultural centers in the district of Ernjak and possessed 51 *khalvars* (or *Kharvār*) of land. (One *kharvār* is equal to the load that a donkey can carry. As a measurement of land it probably is an area that can produce a donkey load).

According to the inscription on the bell tower, the monastery was renovated in 1708 by the people of Shoṙot' and Grigor Vardapet. Our survey shows that the complex was also renovated at the end of the eighteenth century and the middle of the nineteenth. The plan of the monastery is similar to those of the seventeenth- and eighteenth-century complexes in Armenia. The church polished blocks of basalt; yellowish stones similar to felsite were also used on the exterior. It is a basilican church with a rectangular plan and a gabled roof, and it consists of a hall, a five-sided apse, and two vestries (Fig. 61). The arches and the roof rest on pairs of cruciform pillars and engaged piers. The only portal is on the western facade. The porch covers the entire western elevation (Fig. 62). It is a structure with a rectangular plan and is in the style of porches with four pillars. It was probably built in the middle of the seventeenth century.

The church of St. Astuatsatsin Monastery, to the northwest of Shoŕot', is a monument with a single-chamber nave. It is still standing, but in damaged condition (Fig. 63). Its interior was covered with wall paint-

Fig. 63. The plan of the church of St. Astuatsatsin Monastery.

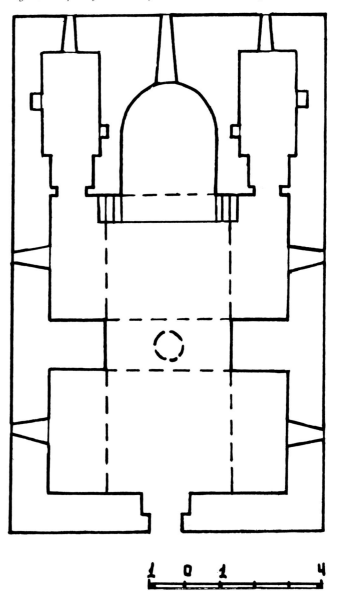

*Fig. 62. The porch of the church of St. Lusaworich' Monastery
    from the southwest.*

ings. The priest Vardan renovated the church and the complex in 1631 (Matenadaran, Ms. no. 3138, p. 275 recto and verso). The front of the bema is decorated with seventeenth-century *khach'k'ars* with beautiful reliefs.

In front of the western elevation of St. Astuatsatsin Church (Fig. 64) there was a porch, which is now leveled to its foundations. The cells of the monks and the other monastic buildings stood on the northern, southern, and western sides of the church. All of these are now in ruins. The cemetery lies 40 to 50 meters north of the monastery. To the south of the outer walls of the complex there was once a vineyard; very little remains of it now. One of the walnut trees in the vineyard is traditionally called "Margarit's tree"; it bears the name of a renowned seventeenth-century female scribe from Shorot'.

St. Step'anos Monastery is located on a mountain peak about 4 kilometers to the south of Shorot'. Its surroundings are exquisite and the panoramic view of Shorot' with its fields, ancient vineyards—called Suzut'—and the distant mountains are breathtaking. Today St. Step'anos looks like a chapel. This vaulted church with a single-chamber nave is built of sandstone, baked bricks, and lime mortar. Its portal is on the western facade, in front of which a two-storied structure had been erected, with its second story once used as a porch. This building is now in ruins. The vaulted ceiling of the chapel is in danger of caving in. The interior of the church receives light from the central opening in the roof and from a single rectangular window, 0.60 meters wide, in the southern wall. There are a number of sixteenth- and seventeenth-century *khach'k'ars* with beautiful reliefs that are set in the front of the small bema and in the interior eastern wall. But the most interesting feature of this monument is a *khach'k'ar* set in the front of the bema. It bears the date 926. The cross is carved on a small slab in fine relief. It was erected for the salvation of the souls of ten inhabitants of Shorot'.

St. Yakob, St. Astuatsatsin, and St. Lusaworich' churches are architecturally significant and important to the study of medieval Armenian architecture.

GAGH

Since ancient times a number of villages and towns have existed on the sides of Mount Ōdzasar, one of the highest, most beautiful peaks in the district of Ernjak. One of these ancient villages is historic Gagh, which is spread out on the rocky eastern side of Ōdzasar.[60] Gagh is the village of the same name in the present-day region of Julfa. Because of its impregnable location high up the mountain, the village played an important role in the history of the district and is known for its traditions, antiquities, and monuments. Nevertheless, the sources contain no information on its past or its approximately ten architectural monuments, of which only St. Grigor Lusaworich' Church is still standing. Gagh and her monuments have been mentioned in passing and are only briefly described in certain studies published at the end of the nineteenth century. Until now no attention has been paid to the village and its monuments.

Fig. 64. The east elevation of St. Astuatsatsin Church.

Considering the area occupied by historic Gagh and its ruins, we can state with certainty that man has been living there since ancient times. Beginning with the early Middle Ages, cultural life thrived in this village of over seven hundred Armenian families. After the invasions of Shah Abbas, Nadir Shah, and others, the Armenian inhabitants of Gagh migrated en masse to Izmir, Constantinople, and elsewhere.

At the beginning of the nineteenth century one could clearly discern the remains of more than seven hundred houses and other buildings all built in the same architectural style.[61] Even today, along the range of mountains that runs parallel to the village for over 2.5 kilometers there are two-storied houses, ruins of monuments, a number of winepresses, and the remains of water mills— all built by early inhabitants and still standing. The old cemetery of Gagh is of great interest for its over one thousand tombstones with fourteenth- to eighteenth-century inscriptions and reliefs depicting everyday life.

Northwest of Gagh, along the valley called K'arhezneri Dzor, which extends as far as the sides of Ōdzasar, one can see some monuments and the remains of water wells. St. Gayianē Chapel, the ruins of St. Hrip'simē and St. Nahatak churches, and St. Anapat Monastery are situated in the valley. The ruins of St. Eghia, St. Sargis, and other chapels and the remains of the fortress of Gagh can still be seen in the vicinity of the village. Renowned among the monuments of Gagh is the fountain of St. Hrip'simē Church. The water basin (4.5 by 3 meters) built in front of this had a vaulted ceiling. This fountain is called Gagh-Jarajur and is connected with the virgin Saint Hrip'simē, who had escaped Rome and sought refuge in Armenia. According to tradition, she hid in Gagh the holy relics that she brought with her and from this act comes the name of the village.[62] (*Gaghel* in colloquial Armenian means "to hide.")

Over the course of time, the ten or so architectural monuments of Gagh have been reduced to rubble, so it is impossible to describe them today. On the basis of the memory of the elderly inhabitants of Gagh and our sur-

vey of the ruins we can surmise that St. Hrip'simē and St. Nahatak churches were hall churches, whereas St. Anapat was a basilican church with four pillars.

St. Grigor Lusaworich' Monastery, which is still standing, was an important monument and a cultural center. It tells us a great deal about the architecture of early Gagh. St. Grigor (Figs. 65–66) is located in the central quarter of the village, which is on an elevated site on the rocky side of Mount Ōdzasar. This monastery was probably founded in the twelfth or the thirteenth century. There is no information on its original form or its renovation. The present structure was rebuilt in the sixteenth or the seventeenth century and was damaged by the earthquake of 1841.

The plan of St. Grigor Monastery of Gagh (Fig. 67) is similar to those of the traditional domed basilican churches of Goght'n and Ernjak. Four pillars and the exterior walls of the church support the cruciform roof.

Fig. 65. St. Grigor Lusaworich' Monastery from the southeast.

Fig. 66. The porch of St. Grigor Lusaworich' Monastery from the west.

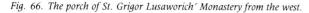

Fig. 67. The plan of St. Grigor Lusaworich' Monastery.

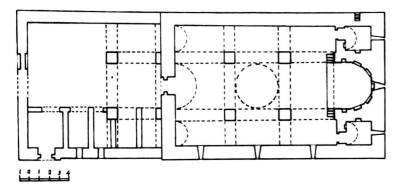

St. Grigor is built of blocks of basalt stone, light yellowish felsite, and bricks (the dome). The exterior of the church is plain. The western facade, where the only portal is located, has some architectural decoration. On both sides of the portal there are beautiful pilasters crowned with fine decorations. On either side of the entrance, set in the walls above the lintel and under the arch of the portal, are a number of splendid *khach'k'ars* and inscriptions. The seven-sided apse of the church has an elevated double row of niches that give it a special splendor. The second row of niches in the apse open in the direction of the first, which are, unlike those of the second row, lined up with pilasters decorated with arches. On both sides of the apse are two-storied vestries; access to the second story is possible only through secret, tunnel-like passageways characteristic of seventeenth-century monuments of Nakhichevan.

St. Grigor Church of Gagh, like the other famous monuments and churches in the district of Ernjak, was covered with wall paintings. The remains of these are preserved in the dome and on various areas on the walls. After the mid-nineteenth century, the interior of the building was covered with soot because of a fire that destroyed the items stored in the church. The wall paintings were entirely destroyed and only damaged traces of them remain. The porch of the church, which is attached to the western facade, has a rectangular plan and its arches rest on pairs of pillars and on the engaged piers that are attached to the western facade of the church; they are also supported by the northern and southern walls of the porch, which bear the vaulted ceiling as well.

SHAHKERT

Shahkert, which is the modern village of Ghazanch'i, is in the region of Julfa, and has been mentioned by the historical sources ever since the thirteenth century.[63]

Shahkert is spread out on one of the elevated plains

on the left bank of the Ernjak River and is surrounded by beautiful mountains and hills that are covered with rich greenery. To its west is the beautiful fortress of Ernjak; Mount Meghradzor lies to its south; and an impregnable fortress on a very high peak is to the north.

In ancient times, the historic town of Shahkert had an Armenian population of about fifteen hundred families. In the village there were over forty water mills, several factories, shops, and caravanserai.[64] From the fourteenth to the seventeenth century carpentry, the manufacture of arms, pottery, and coppersmithing (from which the name of the present-day village derives) were especially advanced among the inhabitants of Shahkert. Even now one can still see the ruins of the buildings and the remains of material culture around the town. But like the other villages and towns of Ernjak, Shahkert was not exempt from destruction and burning. Shahkert in particular suffered greatly from the endless invasions of Persian and Turkish oppressors; because of this, the village gradually went into decline and its inhabitants were dispersed to other places. Many of the townspeople settled in the city of Shushi, where they founded the Ghazanch'ets'ots' quarter and built a church.[65]

Today only a few monuments remain, among which are the Amenap'rkich' Monastery, the ruins of St. Hovhannēs Church, a lovely seventeenth-century bridge, the ruins of the fortress of Shahkert, the caravanserai, and the village of Berdik.

Amenap'rkich' Monastery is a large structure built of polished blocks of stone (Fig. 68). It is the most impressive building in Shahkert. Over the course of time the walls of the monastery, the porch, which was attached to the western elevation of the church, and the other auxiliary buildings have been destroyed. The only building still standing is the church, which is a basilica with a nave, two aisles, and four pillars. It consists of an apse, two vestries, and a hall. The church has only one portal, on the western facade. Set above the lintel of the portal is a small *khach'k'ar* with an inscription stating that the building was renovated in 1654. Its simple exte-

Fig. 68. Amenap'rkich Monastery from the west.

rior and the high-ceilinged interior give the church a special grandeur. There is a small bell tower on the roof.

Especially well known among the monuments of Shahkert is the fortress-castle, the ruins of which are on the steep peak of an impregnable mountain in the northern part of the village. From ancient times this site served the princes of Siwnik' as a castle and a fortress. It was renovated in the sixteenth and the seventeenth centuries by the nobility of Shahkert. According to historical sources, the castle was completely renovated in the eighteenth century by Hovhannēs Khandamirian, a native of Shahkert. During the restoration work, the fortress was enlarged and fortified with stronger walls and towers. Often, at times of difficulty, the inhabitants of Shahkert sought refuge there. The description of one of the heroic episodes connected with this fortress has been recorded in the annals of Armenian history. In 1750 five hundred patriots under the leadership of Hovhannēs Khandamirian rebelled against the oppressive rule of the local dynasts, and having sought refuge in the fortress, they initiated hostilities against the forces of Heydar Khan, lord of Nakhichevan. Grigor, Aghek'sandr Aghamalian, Mkrtich' Vardapet (the prior of St. Karapet Monastery of Aprakunis), and other natives of Shahkert were among the leaders of the rebellion.[66]

St. Hovhannēs Church, located in the center of the village, was reduced to ruins by the 1860s. According to A. Sedrakian, one could see "only the semidilapidated southern wall and the portal, while the rest of the building was gone . . . only on a stone that was set in one of the sides of the portal we found the date 1355."[67]

The medieval caravanserai of Shahkert, which were vaulted structures, were also of interest. In his time A. Sedrakian read the following statement on a *khach'k'ar* that stood near the ruins of one of these caravanserai: "I, Grigor, erected this cross [for the salvation] of my soul . . . in 1051."[68]

From information found in manuscripts we learn that calligraphy and other arts and crafts had reached an advanced stage of development in Shahkert. Unfortunately, only insignificant fragments of manuscripts copied there have survived. Today we cannot fully appreciate the work that was carried out by the scribes of Shahkert. There is a gospel known to us that was copied in the Monastery of Tat'ew in 1657–58(?) and was restored in Shahkert. In its colophon Mesrop Irits' [presbyter] states: "This gospel was repaired in the village of Shaghkert [*sic*] by the great sinner Mesrop Irits' at the request of the elderly priest Movsēs of Norashēn.[69]

BERDIK

The village of Berdik is now in ruins and uninhabited. It is situated on the left bank of the Ernjak River in the valley called Shah-beki, near Shahkert. From the ruins of the village one may surmise that it was one of the relatively large dwelling places in Ernjak, where approximately two hundred families might have lived.

The historical sources offer very little information on Berdik. Its Armenian inhabitants probably abandoned it at the end of the eighteenth century. Subsequently, the monuments and the buildings in the village fell into ruin and decayed. After the exodus of the Armenians, Persians lived there for a while, until the 1880s. Berdik, which was also called K'aratak [under the rock] because it was spread out at the foot of rocks, is first mentioned by Step'anos Orbelean as a locality in the district of Ernjak.[70] The village had a church called St. Step'anos, about which there is no information. The long colophon of a codex, a gospel copied in Berdik in 1497 and now in the Matenadaran of Erevan, states that at the end of the fifteenth century Berdik was administered by three headmen: Murat, K'amaraz, and Jomart, who were brothers and were "always kindled with the love of holy things. . . . They received this everlasting monument with great emotion as a consolation for themselves and as a hope for their salvation."[71] Following this the scribe Sargis Erets', the son of the headman Jomart, notes that he copied the manuscript "in 1497, during the patriarchate of Sargis and under the protection of St. Step'anos Church in the land of Ērnjak [*sic*], in the village of K'aratak, which is also called Berdik, during the prelacy of Lord Hovhannēs, the bishop of the district, during a period of confusion and grief when the tax collectors vexed the Christians of all the regions because of our sins."[72] Bishop Petros Aghamaleants' was also from this village. In his book *Astuadzanmanut'iwn* [Imitation of God], published in Calcutta in 1827, he writes: "Bishop Petros was born in 1743 in the town of Berdak [*sic*] in Ernjak, near the village of Shahkert. He was of the noble lineage of Aghamal Berdumeants'."[73]

T'EGHEAK

The historic Armenian village of T'egheak is the present-day T'eyvaz, which is 4.5 to 5 kilometers from the old town of Shahkert. It is situated on a plain in high, mountainous terrain. The village is first mentioned in Step'anos Orbelean's *History* as a place in the district of Ernjak.[74]

The literary sources have preserved insignificant bits of information on T'egheak. The survey of the area and its antiquities allow us to surmise that the village was established at a very early date and that sixty to seventy families may have lived there. Since the village was located on the busy highway that connected Nakhichevan with Aprakunis, Shahkert, and Zangezur, it reached an advanced level of development and its inhabitants were mainly preoccupied with commerce. The ruins of the historical and architectural monuments and the stone houses, with their stone fences, show beyond any doubt that between the thirteenth and eighteenth centuries special attention was paid to masonry and construction. Based on the data from the cemetery one can conclude that Armenians lived there until the 1850s. Only a few architectural monuments survive in T'egheak today. The cemetery is located in the eastern part of the village. Most of the tombstones that bear fourteenth- to eighteenth-century inscriptions are covered with moss and are either damaged or removed from their original sites. Of special interest among the monuments of T'egheak is its church, which is in a deteriorating state. This monument was a basilican church with four pillars, a nave, and two aisles. It is located in the center of the village and is built of polished blocks of stone. Its vestries are located on either side of the apse. The church has a bright, high-ceilinged interior. The sources say nothing about its date of construction, its name, or when it was renovated.

After the mid-nineteenth century, when the church was in a relatively better state, A. Sedrakian visited the village and described the church as ''a magnificent and beautiful structure . . . the roof has caved in at two places and the church has no inscriptions.''[75] Considering the architectural and archaeological evidence, one can say for sure that the original structure was founded during the eleventh or the twelfth century, and that it was completely renovated in the middle of the seventeenth century.

KZNUT

Historic Kznut is located on the immediate left side of the highway that connects Nakhichevan with Meghri and is 10 kilometers from Nakhichevan. This village, on the royal highway of ancient Armenia, is situated on an extensive fertile plain that reaches as far as the Nakhichevan River to the west, the mountains of Julfa to the south, the vicinity of the Khach'p'arakh and Arazin villages to the north and the east. Kznut, which is located at the crossroads of the ancient highway and the byway ascending to the villages in the district of Ernjak, has fallen into ruin on several occasions. The area that the village occupied reveals that between 250 and 280 families lived there. According to information from 1873, the village church was still standing then and 177 Armenian and 14 Azerbaijani families lived there.[76]

Unfortunately, there is little information on Kznut or its church, which has been in ruins for many decades. From conversations with elderly inhabitants of Kznut we have learned that the church was called St. Astuatsatsin. When this monument, which is a basilican church with a nave and two aisles, was renovated in the first decades of the nineteenth century, its roof was replaced with wood. The colophon of one of the gospels in this church states: ''This was written in 1660 at St. Astuatsatsin Church of the village of Gznut' [*sic*] in Ernjak. Under the images of the crucifix and the evangelist Matthew there were newly written cryptic characters, the decipherment of which is as follows: 'With one voice remember the sinful Zak'aria, who painted and bound this book.' ''[77] Unfortunately this information is not enough to lead us to believe that the painter and binder Zak'aria copied and illuminated this manuscript in Kznut.

ARAZIN

The historic village of Arazin lies 3 to 4 kilometers to the east of Kznut, on the road that goes to Abrakunis. Today there are almost no remaining monuments in this village. The extensive area occupied by Arazin is situated in a fertile plain, in the vicinity of which there are the remains of ancient and early medieval sites. In the nineteenth century, this village was inhabited by Armenians and had eight water mills,[78] a church,[79] and other monuments. Today one can see only their insignificant remains. The church of Arazin, which was located in the village, was a small, modest building.

K'R̄NA

This famous town is spread out in the fields on the southwestern side of Mount Ōdzasar and is located on the left bank of the Ernjak River. Our survey of the surroundings of the town showed that man settled here before the birth of Christ. During the Middle Ages it had four to five hundred Armenian families. Catholicos Mxit'ar I, surnamed Mxik (catholicos from 1341 to 1355) was from K'r̄na.

K'r̄na became well known when the Armenian Unitores founded a monastic congregation and a school there in 1330. From the fourteenth century on, K'r̄na and its school are frequently mentioned in Armenian and a number of non-Armenian sources in connection with the activities of the Armenian Catholics.

A number of historical sources testify that the congregation of the Unitores at K'r̄na and their school were founded in 1330 by Bartholomew, the bishop of the Catholic monastery in Maraghah, and Hovhannēs of K'r̄na, a graduate of the University of Gladzor, who were noted and authoritative figures in their time. The Unitores of K'r̄na subsequently established new congregations and schools in the city of Nakhichevan, in the villages and towns of Aparaner, Khoshkashēn, Salit'ar̄ (in

the district of Ernjak), Jahuk, Shahaponk', and Garagush (in the district of Jahuk). Like the Unitor congregations and schools in Tabriz, Maraghah, and Dehkharkan in Azerbaijan, the ones founded in the villages and towns of Nakhichevan were supposed to enhance the influence of Catholicism and the Vatican on the local inhabitants. For a while the activities of these centers were very detrimental for a segment of the Armenian people. The universities of Gladzor and Tat'ew and other schools put up a tremendous struggle against this religious orientation.

During the fourteenth and the fifteenth centuries the university of the Unitor congregation of K'r̄na played a positive and exceptional role in the development of Ar-

Fig. 69. The plan of St. Astuatsatsin Church.

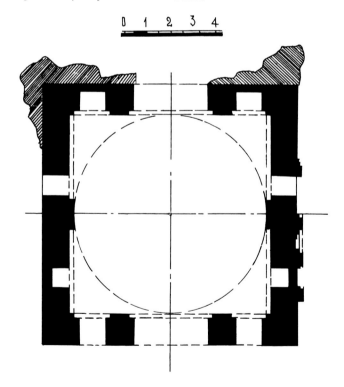

menian culture, especially by translating and copying the scientific and philosophical works of the thinkers and scientists of the ancient world. The University of K'ïna—where mathematics, philosophy, theology, grammar, foreign languages, calligraphy, natural sciences, and other subjects were taught—functioned at the now semidilapidated St. Astuatsatsin Church, which was attached to the Verin Vank' and was built in two months with the help of Gorg, the headman of K'ïna, and his wife, Elt'ik. There is proof that St. Astuatsatsin was erected on the foundations of an ancient ruined church. After 1740, when the Armenian congregation dispersed, St. Astuatsatsin was abandoned. In the nineteenth century, the local inhabitants dug inside the complex, where they discovered a secret chamber near the church and brought to light inscriptions, earthenware, and other items belonging to an older church. In 1899 M. Smbatian dug a ditch in front of the portal of St. Astuatsatsin and discovered a *khach'k'ar* with two arms that had the inscription "In the year 1191 this cross was erected to intercede for Gagik and his parents."[80]

St. Astuatsatsin Church, which was also called K'usaber by the local inhabitants, was a very large rectangular structure resembling a mausoleum (Fig. 69). Its foundations are built of polished and semipolished blocks of stone, and the rest of the structure is constructed of bricks. On the northern, western, and southern sides of the church there are various vaulted monastic buildings and monks' cells. The over twenty cells are now in a completely dilapidated state. The complex was enclosed within an outer wall. Today only insignificant remains of these exist. Between two hills to the east of the complex there was an ancient artificial lake that belonged to the monastery. It was damaged and has been without water for several decades. The ancient St. Hïrip'simē Monastery of K'ïna was about 600 to 700 meters to the southwest of St. Astuatsatsin. There is no information on the date of construction of this church, which was built before St. Astuatsatsin. One could still see the remains of the church in the 1970s.

The District of Nakhichevan (Nakhchawan)

The city of Nakhichevan, or Nakhchawan, the capital of the present-day Nakhichevan Autonomous SSR, is very well known in Armenian history. In Neolithic times the salt mine near the city was excavated by early man, who also left his marks at K'yul't'ap'a, a Chalcolithic dwelling place with several strata, and other ancient sites throughout the area occupied by the present city. After the early Middle Ages Nakhchawan was generally known as Nakhichevan.

According to legend, the name Nakhichevan is connected with the biblical myth of Noah, who is said to have first lodged here [*Nakh*, "First"; *ichevan*, "lodge"]. In non-Armenian sources and historical works Nakhichevan has different names: the Greeks called it Nachsuana; the Arabs Neshevi and Neshui; the Persians Nakhua, Nakhchevan, Nausha, and Naqshijahan; and the Turks Naqshijihan, which means "picture" or "ode of the world."[1]

According to Movsēs Khorenats'i, the possessions and the jurisdiction of the Mardpetuni clan, one of the major feudal families of ancient Armenia, extended from Atropatene to Chuash and Nakhchawan.[2] Thus the district of Nakhchawan was under the control of the Mardpetuni. This princely clan was in charge of the royal treasury and the harem. From several literary sources we know that there was enmity between the Mardpetuni and the princely clan of Vaspurakan that persisted until the fall of the Armenian Arsacid dynasty in the fifth century A.D. After that, the princely clan of the Mardpetuni disappeared from the historical scene and its possessions, including Nakhichevan, passed into the hands of the Artsruni family.[3] According to the seventh-century Armenian *Ashkharhats'oyts'* [World Atlas], Nakhichevan was the thirty-fourth district of the province of Vas-

purakan.[4] Ninth-century historian T'ovma Artsruni states that after burning the Armenian feudal lords in the churches of Nakhchawan and Khram in 705, the Arab governor Kashm (Kasim) separated Nakhchawan from Vaspurakan.[5] Subsequently, because of its convenient location and economic significance, Nakhichevan became a point of contention between the princes of Siwnik' and Vaspurakan. Consequently, from 705 to the beginning of the tenth century, this district occasionally passed from Artsruni hands to those of the Siwni, and then back again.

In ancient times Nakhichevan, which was situated on the crossroads of transit routes and major highways of the ancient world, became a noted center of social, political, and cultural activities. The surrounding villages and dwelling places around the city, which are spread out on the plain of Nakhichevan along the bank of the Arax River, made up a separate administrative unit. This district included all of the dwelling places in the present region of Nakhichevan, with the exception of some twelve villages located along the banks of the Nakhichevan River. These are all in the vicinity of the village of Jahr (Chahuk) and were historically part of the territory of the district of Chahuk.

THE CITY OF NAKHICHEVAN

According to Armenian and non-Armenian historians, from the early Middle Ages on Nakhichevan was well known as a center of crafts and commerce. It had a large population. During the early centuries of our era, Jews, Syrians, and Greeks, who had been brought here as captives by King Tigran II, lived side by side with the

Armenians. The sources tell of several major and minor historical events involving Nakhichevan.

The architectural monuments of the city, which are in ruins today, played a special role in the history and cultural life of Nakhichevan. Since the early Middle Ages the city was known for its fortress, which is mentioned by Movsēs Khorenats'i[6] and P'awstos Buzand.[7] Unfortunately the historical sources say nothing about its appearance or date of construction. In the southeastern part of the present-day city one can still see the ruins of the walls of the old city, which encircled almost all of the area now occupied by the modern city. The old walls extended from the hill near the main road to the city and the Armenian-Russian cemetery all the way to the center of town, and encircled the area occupied by the old city from the east. There were additional walls reaching as far as the borders of the historic village of Tambat (present T'mbul).

The remains of the walls of the city of Nakhichevan are more noticeable near the present-day park named after Sabir, which is in the vicinity of the tomb of Momina Khat'un (built in the twelfth century) and the old cemetery (now the Azerbaijani cemetery). Along the walls of the city, which are more than 3 to 4 kilometers long, there were important strategic points, namely the hill in the Armenian cemetery, Sabir Park, and the municipal cemetery, where one can see the remains of a number of watchtowers. In the municipal cemetery one can still see the ruins of late medieval walls and towers. Here there was a tomb attributed to Noah, now entirely in ruins. On the same hill, which is an important strategic site, there is also a tunnel 1.5 to 1.8 meters high at its main entrance. The latter occupies an area of 160 to 170 square meters, which is carved out of rock. One thousand people can easily be accommodated there. From the main entrance the tunnel runs under the entire city and branches off into a number of tunnels that run toward the walls and the Arax River. These tunnels are about 1.1 meters wide and 1.5 meters high. To provide fresh air to these tunnels, special ducts were built, two of which are still extant in the municipal cemetery. These ducts have circular openings with a diameter of 1 by 0.8 meters and are at a distance of 80 to 100 meters from each other. Unfortunately most of the tunnels were shut down a long time ago, so it is impossible to study their structure. Our survey in the 200-meter stretch near the main entrance leads us to conclude that these tunnels of Nakhichevan were built in the early Middle Ages and were used until the ninth or the tenth century.

The city of Nakhichevan was also known for its monasteries and churches. Thirteenth-century Flemish traveler William Rubruck, who visited Nakhichevan, testifies that "at one time there were eighty churches there, but now only two small ones remain, since the Saracenes have destroyed them."[8] Unfortunately none of the early architectural monuments of Nakhichevan remains. Today only a few thirteenth-, fourteenth- and fifteenth-century tombs and St. Gēorg Armenian Church are extant. According to tradition, Holy Trinity Church (St. Errordut'iwn) was one of the oldest architectural monuments in the city. It was a basilican church with four apses, a characteristic feature of early medieval Armenian architecture. It was in this church that the Arabs burned the Armenian feudal lords in 705. The church was especially noteworthy for its large size and height. It was built of polished blocks of basalt and local red tuff stone and firm lime mortar. The dome of the church was ruined by the earthquake of June 20, 1840, and the church itself was demolished in the summer of 1975 during urban redevelopment. M. Smbatian, who witnessed the restoration work of 1881–1900, wrote: "At the foundation level one could see the remains of burnt wood, reed, and also ashes of human bones from twelve hundred years ago. All of the inhabitants of Nakhichevan saw these and with grief they became acquainted with the tragedy that had happened in the city."[9]

Among the most ancient monuments of Nakhichevan was the crypt-chapel that was attributed to Noah. It was located in the old cemetery at the southern corner of the city. In 1881 the Russian scholar U. Nikitina noted that formerly there was a church above the crypt and that it was destroyed at a later date.[10] The British Mrs. Shants who visited the crypt of Noah noted that it was an eight-sided arcaded hall built with small bricks and that it was intended as a crypt under a church. The arch of the crypt was supported by a single central pier.[11] E. Lalayian gave additional information on the monument, underscoring the fact that "it was an eight-sided structure with a diameter of 10 feet. It was covered with a cupola and was supported by a central pillar. The doorway was low."[12] The crypt was destroyed several decades ago.

St. Gēorg Church of Nakhichevan was built in 1869 (Fig. 70) on the site of an earlier church. The exterior elevations of this domed basilican church are covered with polished red tuff from a quarry in the valley of Karmir Vank' of Astapat. These give the monument a beautiful appearance. The magnificent dome of the church, built of brick, stands on four pillars and is lo-

Fig. 70. St. Gēorg Church from the southeast.

cated in the center of the cruciform roof. Its exterior is simple; there are decorative reliefs only on the arch of the portal and the arches of the windows. According to an inscription in Armenian, Russian, and Arabic, the land on which St. Gēorg stands was donated by Ēksan Khan of Nakhichevan and the brick wall of the church (no longer extant) was built in 1888 by the inhabitants of the city.

After the Seljuk and Turkoman occupation of the region, Nakhichevan, with its dense Armenian population, became an administrative and economic center, since it was situated on a major, busy highway that was both strategically and economically important. But even before that, at the end of the thirteenth century, the historian Step'anos Orbelean considered this city the center of the province of Siwnik' and wrote that "Nakhichevan was the capital city" of that province.[13]

ASTAPAT

According to the historical sources Astapat was a noted town of Nakhichevan. According to tradition, the village bears the name Astapat because in 451, after the battle of Awarayr, the bodies of Vardan Mamikonean, the commander-in-chief of the Armenian armies, and of the heroes who were martyred with him were taken to the monastery in that village (the monastery was later renamed St. Vardan), and "here [*ast*] they were shrouded [*pat*]." Presumably at a later date the feudal lords of Maku transferred the bodies of the martyrs from Astapat to Maku, arguing that the heroes had fallen on the plain of Awarayr or Shawarshan, which is closer to their town.

Astapat is first mentioned by ninth-century historian T'ovma Artsruni in connection with the massacres of Nakhichevan and Khram in 705.[14] The town is then mentioned by Catholicos Khach'ik I in his encyclical of 976 and by thirteenth-century historian Step'anos Orbelean, and also by other later historians. The excavations of Bronze Age tombs in the vicinity of St. Step'anos or Karmir Vank' Monastery, an important architectural monument, brought to light archaeological data on Astapat as an ancient dwelling place.[15] In the Middle Ages this town was an appanage and had a large Armenian population. It was frequently ravaged during Persian (Safavid) domination and lost its former importance, becoming a small village. At the time of the invasions of Shah Abbas most of its population were driven to Persia. Subsequently, beginning with the middle of the nineteenth century, the remaining inhabitants dispersed and went to Astrakhan, Rostov on the Don, Krasnodar, Baku, and Erevan.

In the first half of the nineteenth century, Abbas Mirza, regent of Persia, transported the inhabitants of historic Astapat 3 kilometers to the north, where he founded a new village called T'azagiwgh. Heeding the advice of French architects, Abbas Mirza had a fortress built on the site of Astapat and named it after himself: Abbasabad. The fortress was conquered by the Russian army in 1827.

Since ancient times the inhabitants of Astapat were preoccupied with cultivation, viniculture, sericulture, pottery, commerce, calligraphy, and construction. The village was known for its fruit; the type of apple that grew there known as the "royal apple," was particularly famous. Seventeenth-century French traveler Jean Baptiste Tavernier testifies that Astapat was the only place in the world that exported the red roots of "Ronas" [madder], which were as famous as cochineal. With these, choice fabrics were dyed in India and Persia. Fifteenth-century traveler Joseph Barbario mentions the "silk of Astapat" and the fact that the village had great quantities of silkworms and many mulberry trees. Among the pottery factories of nineteenth-century Astapat that of the artistically inclined Hakob Vardapet Jalaliants' of Astapat was well known. Some of its products are now preserved in the Historical Museum of Erevan.

Astapat is also known for its beautiful architectural monuments—the St. Vardan, St. Pōghos ew Petros, St. Hovhannēs, and St. Step'anos (Karmir Vank') monasteries and churches. Unfortunately only Karmir Vank'

has survived. It is situated on the summit of a rocky hill near the town, which is about 60 meters above sea level. The monastery is built of polished blocks of stone.

Karmir Vank' is known by a number of other names.[16] Aṙak'el of Tabriz knows it as St. Step'anos Nakhavkay. It was called Karmir Vank' [red monastery] because the outer walls and some of the structures attached to them were built of red stone. Since it was built on a rock, it was also called K'arataki Vank' [monastery at the foot of a rock]. It is also known as Khndrakatar St. Step'anos and the Monastery of Astapat.

According to the literary sources, this complex was founded in the seventh century. In 976, when it was mentioned in the encyclical of Catholicos Khach'ik I, it was already very famous. Through the centuries Karmir Vank' was devastated and rebuilt several times. There is information on renovations of the thirteenth, fifteenth, sixteenth, seventeenth, and eighteenth centuries. The monastery suffered great damage during the invasions of Shah Abbas. As a result, it was renovated more than once in the seventeenth century. The complex was also damaged by the earthquake of 1841, after which it was renovated in about 1860. At the beginning of the twentieth century the monastery was deserted and started to fall apart. Because of neglect, the dome of the church, the upper sections of the walls, the southwestern section of the roof, the southern wall of the porch, the outer walls, watchtowers, dwelling places, and auxiliary buildings have all collapsed.

The only surviving monument of the Karmir Vank' complex is the semidilapidated church, a domed structure that extends from east to west. It has a five-sided apse, two vestries, and a hall (Fig. 71). The high-ceilinged cupola of the church stood on a square formed by the arches supported by two pairs of pillars and connecting the eastern pillars with the western wall of the apse. The only portal of the church was located on the western facade and opened onto the porch. The latter had a rectangular plan and two pillars. Using the slanted position of the church site, the builders constructed a lower level under the bema and the vestries that served

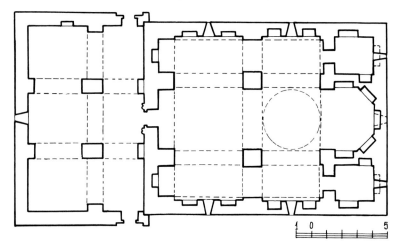

*Fig. 71. The plan of Karmir Vank' and its porch.
(Measurements by Murad Hasrat'ian.)*

as a hiding place where manuscripts and sacred utensils of the monastery were stored.

The exterior appearance of the church of the Monastery of Astapat is simple and modest. However, the only portal of the church is richly decorated. It repeats the patterns common to twelfth-, thirteenth-, and fourteenth-century portals. The ornamental reliefs on the tympanum, the pilasters were spherical columns, the two *khach'k'ars* set into the walls on both sides of the portal (the inscription on one bears the date 977)—all give the portal a magnificent appearance. The interior of the church is richly decorated with wall paintings that make the walls and the apse stand out.

Because of its architectural structure and construction techniques, the Monastery of Astapat is one of the important complexes of medieval Armenia.

St. Vardan Church of Astapat, where according to tradition the bodies of Vardan Mamikonean and his companions were wrapped in shrouds, was also a famous architectural monument. St. Vardan was situated to the north of the fortress of Abbasabad and was a magnificent

structure. According to Ghewond Alishan[17] and E. Lalayian,[18] it was a domed basilican church with four pillars. The lower parts of the walls were built of polished blocks of red stone and the upper parts of baked bricks. The dome had twelve beautiful windows. The apse was polygonal, and on either side of it there were two-storied vestries.

In addition to various reliefs, *khach'k'ars*, and ornaments, the interior of St. Vardan was covered with wall paintings. The apse was richly decorated with paintings. Painted at the corners of the arches of the square pillars were the faces of the four evangelists. The magnificent appearance of the church was enhanced by its portals, the most beautiful of which was the western. Above the arch of the western portal there is a relief of an event taken from the life of the Mother of God that is set in a frame. Above this, and also on the northern and southern sides of the portal, there are seventeenth-century *khach'k'ars* with beautiful reliefs and inscriptions. A number of *khach'k'ars* and inscribed stones decorate both sides of the arch of the portal. According to one of these, St. Vardan Church was renovated in 1655 with the support of Khoja Safar. An Italian architect correctly notes that the architectural style of the western portal of St. Vardan Church of Astapat reappears in a number of churches in Rome, but the latter are three times larger.[19]

In front of the western elevation of St. Vardan there was a porch with four pillars. From an inscription dating back to 1701 that is on one of the pillars of the porch, built of polished blocks of stone, one can tell that the building was either constructed or renovated in that year by Martiros Vardapet, the overseer of the church. Ghewond Alishan notes that "attached to St. Vardan Church and accessible from it is another, smaller church, which is named after the Holy Apostles Peter and Paul. It is a gabled structure built of red bricks."[20] Aside from what Alishan says, nothing is known about this church, which had a number of inscriptions from the fifteenth, sixteenth, and the seventeenth centuries.

St. Hovhannēs Monastery was once a famous monument and was known as a convent in the late Middle Ages. It was built of red stone and was located on the site of the fortress of Abbasabad. The regent Abbas Mirza had the monastery demolished in order to build the fortress. St. Hovhannēs Church had a porch and other buildings that were all enclosed within an outer wall.

KIUL-T'AP'A

Since the end of the nineteenth century this ancient village has been known as a famous archealogical site. The numerous remains of material culture discovered there belong to the different stages of agricultural development in Transcaucasia from the third to the first millennia B.C. This ancient dwelling place is hidden in a secure corner in the plain of Nakhichevan and is extremely significant to the study of the ancient culture of historical Armenia. The village of Kiul-T'ap'a [ash hill] and the ancient archaeological site nearby are located on the left bank of the lower course of the Nakhichevan River 8 kilometers northeast of the city of Nakhichevan. The depth of the cultural layer at this site is well over 32 meters and consists of four strata. The excavations of E. Lalayian[21] at the beginning of this century, those of O. Abibulaev[22] in 1951 and 1953, and those of modern archaeologists have brought to light many kinds of agricultural items, grinders, working tools, richly ornamented, colorful and unornamented pottery, and various other objects similar to those discovered at a number of other ancient sites in historic Armenia: Shēngawit', Garni, Shresh-blur, Shamiramalt'i, Elar, Göy T'ep'e, and in the ancient cultural centers on the territories of Abkhazia and Azerbaijan. The Chalcolithic layer in the second stratum at Kiul-T'ap'a has a depth of 8.30 meters and is related to the second stratum of Shēngawit'. It also shares a number of characteristics with the Chalcolithic of Göy T'ep'e in Iran (near Lake Urmia). Archaeologists also unearthed at Kiul-T'ap'a the reliefs of various animals (ox, horse), domestic and religious objects, and richly ornamented, colorful pottery. At a depth of 2.30 to 9.25 meters in the same stratum there were the remains of skeletons of large and small horned animals. It is interesting that the bones of the larger horned animals were at the bottom of the stratum and those of the smaller ones were at the top. In the lower strata there were the remains of dwellings, ovens, and storages. Some of the storage areas were used to hold seed, and on their floors there were the remains of cultivated soft wheat. The excavations at Kiul-T'ap'a revealed that agriculture and breeding of domestic animals were well developed in Nakhichevan in the pre-Christian era.

Beside the archaeological site there were also various architectural monuments at Kiul-T'ap'a that are now destroyed. According to the testimony of late medieval sources, the village was known for its St. Hrip'simē Church and a number of chapels. The chapels are now in ruins, but St. Hrip'simē is still standing. According to E. Lalayian, on the mound where the archaeological site is located "there was" before the excavations "a small fortress. But now there is an insignificant chapel built by the Armenian immigrants from Persia who thought that the relics of the Virgin Hrip'simē were buried under the hill. Later, however, they discovered the relics slightly to the southeast of the hill. They were in a tomb inside a ruined chapel located on the plain. They renovated this ordinary old chapel and set the relics in a silver reliquary, which they placed in the renovated edifice. The tomb was enclosed in the apse of the chapel."[23]

St. Hrip'simē of Kiul-T'ap'a, situated in the center of the village, is a basilican church with four pillars. The rectangular plan of the structure consists of a hall, an apse, and two vestries. Our survey of the church reveals that it was renovated several times. Seventeenth-century historian Arak'el of Tabriz testifies that a certain Awetik' from the town of Astapat, who was surnamed Alt'un, acquired with much trouble the relics of Saint Hrip'simē from the Catholic Armenians of Aparanner in the district of Ernjak. "He went to the city of Nakhch'uan near which there is a small village called K'ult'ap'a. Until then there was no church in the village. There he founded a church and placed the relics in the foundation of the church, and above it he built the sanctuary. And on the day of the consecration of the church he named it St. Hṙip'simē. Now there are some Armenian Christians in this village who belong to that church."[24]

ALIAPAT

This village is situated on the immediate left side of the Erevan-Nakhichevan highway, not far from the city of Nakhichevan, of which Aliapat is a northwestern suburb. According to statistical information from 1873, there were 58 families in this village,[25] and according to E. Lalayian, 103 Armenian families lived there in 1906.[26]

Fig. 72. St. Astuatsatsin Church from the east.

Aliapat is situated on the side of a hill near where the ancient highway approaches the city of Nakhichevan. On the extensive, flat top of that hill an entire complex of fortifications (or a citadel) was erected sometime before the birth of Christ. The ruins of these quickly began to fall apart in the eighteenth century. Now the new Armenian and Russian cemeteries, several living quarters, and other buildings occupy the area. We should note that the name Aliapat derives from the suffix -*apat*, which indicates place. According to the linguist P. Bedirian, *apat* was originally an adjective that meant "prosperous," "flourishing," "thriving," "inhabited."[27] The Armenian *apat* is from Pahlavi or Middle Persian.[28]

St. Astuatsatsin Church of Aliapat still stands today in the center of the village. It is built of flagstones and bricks and in the vital areas, of basalt. St. Astuatsatsin Church (Fig. 72) is a domed basilica with four pillars; it has two portals, one on the northern facade and the other on the south. The church was probably built in the nineteenth century on the foundations of an older church. Its structure and architecture—for example, its roof, the wide and elevated openings of the windows, the shape of its dome—are identical to that of St. Gēorg Church of Nakhichevan. The apse receives its light from two large adjacent windows in the eastern wall, and the hall receives it from sets of three similar windows in the southern, northern, and western walls. The slender polygonal dome of this monument, with its pyramidal cone, is built of brick and rises above the cruciform roof, giving it a beautiful appearance.

St. Astuatsatsin Church of Aliapat, according to a five-line inscription on a stone protruding from the wall above the arch of the southern portal was rebuilt with the support of the inhabitants of the village in 1887 in memory of their parents. A bell tower stands before the southern portal of the church. This structure has two pillars (Fig. 73) and is also built of brick. According to an eight-line inscription on a *khach'k'ar* set into the upper eastern side of the eastern pillar of the bell tower, it was built in 1854 with the support of Hakob's son Vardanian, who was a native of Aliapat. Formerly, the building to

Fig. 73. St. Astuatsatsin Church bell tower from the east.

the east of St. Astuatsatsin Church served as an Armenian parochial school.

KHRAM

Khram was one of the famous fortified cities of early medieval Armenia and was located within the confines of the district of Nakhichevan. It lay on the bank of the Arax River in the vicinity of the present village of Nehram, which is in the region of Nakhichevan. The modern Arabic name of the village derives from the Armenian Khram. Khram is only 16 to 17 kilometers from the city of Nakhichevan and 5 kilometers from Astapat. The historic city was situated in a narrow valley along the left bank of the Arax River. Because of this, Khram, which was spread out between the mountains and the Arax River, grew in size only longitudinally.

The Armenian historical sources since the time of Movsēs Khorenats'i have given trustworthy information on the topography and history of this famous fortress city. Movsēs Khorenats'i notes that Tigran I settled Anoysh, the sister of the wife of the Mede Azhtahak, and others in the villages to the east of "the large mountain" and in the appanages as far as the borders of the district of Goght'n. To these people "he [Tigran] also left three towns—Khram, Julfa, and Khorshakunik'; across the river he left the entire plain, at the top of which is Azhdanak, as far as the same fortress of Nakhchawan."[29]

At the time of the Arab domination, Khram was better known as a fortress. Seventh-century historian Sebēos notes that in 643−44 the fortress of Nakhchawan stubbornly resisted the invading Arabs, who when they could not conquer it instead marched against Khram. "They seized the fortress of Khram and put the inhabitants to the sword and took captive the women and children."[30] Thereafter Armenian historians speak about Khram with sorrow, especially in connection with the holocaust of the Armenian feudal lords in the churches of Nakhichevan and Khram in 705, which they call "the year of fire." In his *History of the Caucasian Albanians*, Movsēs Kaghankatuats'i (Daskhurants'i) gives the number of the feudals who were killed "in the year of fire": "Taking them to the town of Nakhichevan, he [the Arab general] incarcerated eight hundred men in the churches and burned them alive; in the same way he burned four hundred in Khram."[31]

The eighth-century Armenian historian Ghewond, who has detailed these historic events, notes that the Arab commander Kasim, acting on the order of the

Arab governor Mahmet, pretended to take an oath of allegiance:

> He summoned to the region of Nakhchawan the feudal lords of Armenia and their cavalry, telling them that they would be registered in the royal registry, receive their pay, and return. And in their simple way they trusted the deceitful words of the sneaky hunters and immediately came there. When they were assembled there, they were ordered to separate into two groups. Some were brought to the church of Nakhchawan and the rest were sent to the town of Khram, where they were shut in the church with guards keeping watch over them and planning to destroy them. They gathered those who were of noble status and released them, while those who were incarcerated inside the sanctuary were burned alive on the threshold of the divine altar.[32]

T'ovma Artsruni also wrote about this event in his *History* and noted that "through deceit [the Arab general] attracted the feudal lords of the land of Armenia. He burned all of them in the city of Nakhchawan and the town of Khram, which is below the Monastery of Astapat and is situated on the bank of the Eraskh [Arax] River.[33]

After the events of the seventh and eighth centuries, the sources are silent on the history of Khram until the thirteenth century. In his *Atlas of the World*, thirteenth-century historian Vardan Vardapet notes that "the city of Khram is now in ruins. It is located between Astapat and the Shamb valley along the bank of the Eraskh [Arax] River. The Church of Surb Step'anos Nakhavkay, which was renovated by Babgēn, is located there."[34] Seventeenth-century historian Aṙak'el of Tabriz writes that in 1605, after the deportation of the inhabitants of Julfa, a trunk was discovered in the ruins of that town. It contained holy relics and a parchment on which was written: "This is a part of the relics of Saint John the Baptist, which Saint Gregory the Illuminator brought to Armenia and placed in the city of Khram. Upon the destruction of the city in the Armenian year 421 [972] this

was brought to Julfa."[35] As Aṙak'el of Tabriz states, Khram in fact had a sad end toward the later part of the eleventh century and disappeared from the scene of history. Eighteenth-century Mekhitarist historian Mik'ayēl Ch'amch'ian, who gives a clear-cut account of the fall of Khram, states that in 972 "a large band of brigands attacked Vaspurakan and marched against the city of Khram, which is also called Shambidzor. They fell upon the inhabitants and sacked the city."[36]

At the end of the nineteenth century, when E. Lalayian was surveying and excavating in the area of Nakhichevan, he noticed that near the guardhouse of Nehram "there appear the remains of the former city of Khram . . . the foundations of a church and a number of tombs."[37] According to bits of information, the church of Khram was situated on a small dirt hill and was a magnificent structure. Almost nothing remains now of the ruins of historic Khram, since most of the area occupied by the ancient city was turned into fields and vineyards. But until the present day the local people refer to the area once occupied by the ancient city as "Dead City."

AZNABERD

Aznaberd is one of the old Armenian villages in the region of Nakhichevan and is the present-day Aznaberd, or Znaberd. It is situated at the southern foot of the Vayk' Mountains and is 35 kilometers northwest of the city of Nakhichevan. The village is surrounded by the K'armrawor, Giune, Mardak'ar, Karmir k'ar, and Apuner mountains and slopes. There is a level area extending from the village to the Arax River.

Since ancient times the Armenian population of this village have been preoccupied with agriculture, animal husbandry, and viniculture. Near Aznaberd one can still see the remains of cyclopean fortresses, villages, and Bronze Age dwellings. Aznaberd is also famous for its architectural monuments, among which are the Monastery of the Apostle Thomas [St. T'ovmayi Vank'], St. Grigor and St. Hovhannēs churches, and St. Hakob and St. Hrip'simē chapels.[38] Of these only St. Grigor and St. Hovhannēs are standing; the rest are in ruins. The churches of St. T'ovma Monastery, St. Hovhannēs, and St. Hrip'simē and St. Hakob chapels are vaulted halls that extend from east to west. They have semicircular apses and one portal each (Fig. 74). The original structures were built either in the ninth or the tenth century. The present-day buildings were erected on the foundations of these in the seventeenth century. Noteworthy among the ancient sites of Aznaberd is a hill called Ch'omad dar, on which the vaulted, single-naved St. Hovhannēs stands. The hill is located to the south of the village and looks like a stronghold. On its sides there are vineyards, old wells, and a part of Aznaberd. On the flat area on the peak of Ch'omad dar there were a number of buildings that were enclosed by outer walls. Unfortunately time has reduced these buildings and walls to rubble. Among the ruins and in the general vicinity of the hill one can see numerous shards of pottery. During our survey of 1976 we discovered abundant remains of painted but plain pottery dating from the tenth to the thirteenth century. In the present-day vineyards at the western foot of the hill the remains of a number of ancient fireplaces and various objects have been discovered. On the painted and ordinary pieces of pottery and jars there were several geometric designs and signs of potters characteristic of the artistic tradition of the Armenian plateau.

St. Grigor Church of Aznaberd, located in the center of the village, is a monument that attracts one's attention. According to its building inscription, it was rebuilt in the second half of the sixteenth century. It is a basilican church with a nave and two aisles and has a five-sided apse, two vestries, and a hall (Fig. 75). The church has two portals, one on the western facade and the other on the southern. The interior is covered with wall paintings (Figs. 103a–e).

Fig. 74. The plans of St. T'ovma Monastery (1), the Church of St. Hovhannēs (2), and the Church of St. Hakob (3).

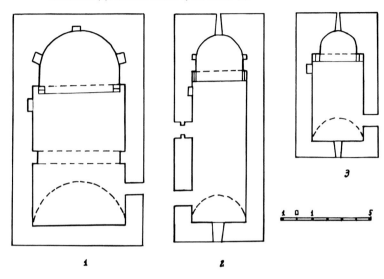

ARBA BERD (ARBA FORTRESS)

The ruins of Arba Berd are situated on the right bank of the Arp'a River near the village of Norashēn (the present Ulia-Norashen) on the historic plain of Sharur (the present-day region of Il'ich). This fortress is built on a circular peak that rises high in the northern part of an extensive plain that spreads out before the mountain pass of Arp'a.[39] Arba Berd was located on the famous crossroads of the transit highways that ascended from the plain of Arax to the basin of the Arp'a River. Consequently, the mountain pass of Arp'a, most of the plain of Sharur, the surrounding villages, and some of the commercial routes of ancient Armenia were placed under the protection of Arba Berd. On the mountain peak on which Arba Berd stands there is a level area of one hectare where in an earlier period there was a citadel with walls. One can also see the ruins of about fifty or sixty buildings on the other parts of the peak. These structures have rectangular plans.

Fig. 75. The plan of St. Grigor Church.
(Measurements by Murad Hasrat'ian.)

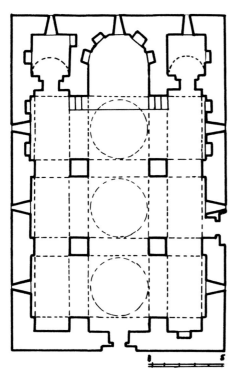

Fig. 76. Ruined tower of Arba Fortress.

The walls of Arba Berd are relatively well preserved. Certain sections are 20 to 30 meters long and 1 by 2.5 meters high. The foundation stones of the walls are 1.5 to 2.5 meters long and 1.5 meters high (average height). These large stones are not joined together with mortar. The fortress was made secure for defensive purposes by means of three sets of walls, at the corners of which there were towers and buttresses (Fig. 76). The construction technique at Arba reminds one in many ways that of the Urarteans. Arba was rebuilt in either the eighth or the seventh century B.C. according to a plan characteristic of the social stratification of the Urartean fortresses. From this point of view, the plan of the fortress, with its two parts, is very curious. The citadel was surrounded on all four sides by walls. Below them, on the lower sides of the mountain, there were multi-chambered buildings that were part of the fortress complex. These in turn were protected by outer walls. In the 1930s, in the central area of the structures of the citadel, the foundation of an architectural monument was discovered that is beyond doubt either a palace or a religious shrine.

The building technique at Arba Berd reveals that originally this fortress was a cyclopean monument of the second millennium B.C. and that it was rebuilt in the eighth century B.C. by the Urarteans, who used it for many years.

TAMBAT

Historic Tambat is the present-day village of T'mbul in the region of Nakhichevan and is located 5 to 6 kilometers from the city of Nakhichevan. Tambat, which was mentioned by the early medieval sources, was known in the late Middle Ages for its commercial ties with India, Italy, Russia, Syria, Persia, Turkey, and other lands. The palatial stone houses of the merchants of Tambat, with their special architectural designs, were filled with European furniture.

In the eighteenth and nineteenth centuries there were a number of workshops in Tambat: goldsmiths and potters. St. Hovhannēs Church of the village was a domed basilica with four pillars. It was rebuilt in the nineteenth century on the ruins of an earlier sanctuary. In 1868 a bilingual (Armenian and Russian) school was established there. The roof and the greater part of the walls of the church are now in ruins. Only the two-storied bell tower remains standing. It is a structure with four pillars that is attached to the western facade of the church and is built of brick.

ĒMKHANA

This village is located near the city of Nakhichevan. The village church, St. Minas, is the best known of its monuments. It is a basilican church with four pillars that was rebuilt in the nineteenth century, repeating the plan of St. Gēorg Church of Nakhichevan and St. Astuatsatsin Church of Aliapat.

The district of Chahuk (ancient Shahapunik'), which was considered the fourteenth district of medieval Siwnik',[1] is mentioned in the historical works of Sebēos, Anania Shirakats'i,[2] Step'anos Orbelean, Aṙak'el of Tabriz, and others. The historic district included all of the present-day region of Shahbuz and a part of the region of Nakhichevan. During the Middle Ages, especially between the twelfth and seventeenth centuries, this area was far away from the busy commercial routes. The only highway with any significance for the area was the main road between Nakhichevan and Siwnik'.

Chahuk-Shahapunik' is rich with historical and architectural monuments.[3] The majority of these monuments are today either in ruins or in a dilapidated state. The historic dwelling places in this district are situated in the bosom of mountains and on the banks of rivers. The Nakhichevan River flows almost through the middle of the district. The historic villages of the area are situated on its banks, on those of its tributaries—Kuk'i, Nors, Shahapunik', and other rivulets—and along the valleys. The historical and epigraphical information on this district and its dwellings and monuments is scant. During the period between the sixteenth and eighteenth centuries Chahuk was divided into two parts: Chahuk and Shahapunik'. The latter was occasionally separated from the rest and considered a distinct district.

According to epigraphical and historical sources, the district of Chahuk-Shahapunik' was the paternal domain of the P'roshid princes of Vayots' Dzor. The princes of the province of Siwnik' and Vayots' Dzor founded and later patronized most of the spiritual centers and architectural monuments in Chahuk.

CHAHUK BERD (CHAHUK FORTRESS)

The inhabitants of Chahuk call this place "the fortress of Ch'alkhan." It is a noted model for studying the techniques of ancient fortress construction. Chahuk Berd is located near the historic village of Pahest (present-day P'ayĕz), 22 kilometers northwest of the city of Nakhichevan.[4] The fortress stands on an impregnable mountain shaped like a pyramid and has a level area on the peak that is more than 50 hectares. The ancient fortified city was built on top of this peak and its citadel was situated in an inaccessible area. Thanks to its site the fortress prevailed over the major highways, the entire valley of the lower course of the Chahuk River, a part of the nearby artificial waterways, and the surrounding villages.

The ruins of the city walls, the dwellings, and certain other buildings are all that have survived from Chahuk Berd. The remains of the city walls, more than 550 meters long, are relatively well preserved. The walls protected the fortress from the north and the west, and the mountains enclosed it from the south and the east. In front of the northern walls of the fortress there is a plain that spreads over an area of about 20 hectares, along the circumference of which (1 to 1.5 kilometers) there were strong walls protecting the city from that side.

The construction technique of the walls and the special architectural solutions give us valuable information about the fortress. The northwestern wall (Fig. 77) of the citadel is important for the same reason. It is built in the unprotected zone between the two mountain ranges that surround the area of the citadel and separate it from the fortified city. Its foundation stones are 2 to 3 meters long and 0.6 to 1.1 meters high. The stones in the upper parts become smaller and smaller. The sandstone on top of the mountain has been used as building material. Polished stones of different size have been fit together without any mortar; they make for a sturdy wall. At equal intervals along the wall there is an entire series of reinforcements, and there were towers at the more important sections as well as near the two portals. With the exception of certain differences, the architecture and the building technique of the walls of Chahuk Berd remind one of those of the Bronze Age fortresses in the regions of Aragatsotn, the plain of Ararat, Amasia, and Ghukasyan.

THE TOWN OF CHAHUK

Chahuk, the center of the historic district of Chahuk, is the present-day village of Jahri in the region of Nakhichevan. It is situated on the left bank of the Nakhichevan River 15 kilometers northwest of the city of Nakhichevan. In ancient times the town[5] was known as an advanced provincial center where commerce and crafts such as dyeing and pottery flourished. In the late Middle Ages it was known for its parochial and girls' schools. The area occupied by historic Chahuk was 4 kilometers long and 2 kilometers wide, and a population of seven to eight hundred families lived there at any one time. According to the etymology of Ghazar Chahkets'i, Chahuk means *"chah* and *ĕmbon,* which is essentially 'beautiful' and 'very proper' because of the excellent site."[6]

Popular, secular architecture was also well advanced in this town. In its vicinity one can see the ruins of a number of buildings and fortresses from very early times and several ninth- to seventeenth-century Armenian cemeteries. Since ancient times Chahuk has had two churches, St. Shoghakat' and St. Hovhannēs Mkrtich'. Sometime during 1471–73 the Venetian traveler Joseph Barbaro passed through this town and wrote: "Ahead

Fig. 77. Ruins of Chahuk Fortress.

is Jagri [Cagri], the inhabitants of which are Armenians. . . . They have two monasteries . . . with fifty monks."[7]

St. Shoghakat' Church, which was built in 1325–30, was destroyed. St. Hovhannēs Church (Fig. 78) is still standing in the center of the town. It has an apse, vestries, and a hall. The portal is on the southern facade. On its roof there is a high cupola that rests on arches supported by four pillars. There is no information on the construction of this church. It was probably built in the twelfth or the thirteenth century and was rebuilt in the middle of the fifteenth, seventeenth, and nineteenth centuries. The scribe of a Bible copied in 1640 in Chahuk (Matenadaran, Ms. no. 6569, p. 471[r]) notes that St. Hovhannēs Church was rebuilt in the fifteenth century. "In 1640 we began to rebuild the church of Chahuk, which was dedicated to Saint Hovhannēs (Saint John), the Precursor of Christ. It was the fifth day of the month of April."

Fig. 78. St. Hovhannēs Church.

THE FORTRESS OF SHAHAPONK'

This early medieval fortress-castle, the present-day Kiand Shahbuz, is situated near the village of Shahapunik' in the historic district of Shahapunik'. According to Step'anos Orbelean, "the fortress of Shahapunik' was built by Shahap the Persian, and after him the valley was named "the Valley of Shahapawnits'. Because of a falling out [with the Persian court] he had come to the Siwni *nahapets* [the chiefs of feudal families]." According to tradition, Shahap [satrap], displeased with the Persian government, left Persia and came to the Siwini *nahapets*, who gave him land and the right to live in their native district of Chahuk. Here Shahap built an impregnable fortress, which was named Shahaponk'. Yet the etymology of the name Shahaponk' seems to be more ancient. Grigor Ghap'ants'ian notes that the word is of

Urartian origin.[8] Ararat Gharibian also believes that Shahaponk' has an ethnic origin.[9]

The ruins of the fortress of Shahaponk' (built in the sixth century) are located in the southwestern part of the present-day village of Kiand-Shahbuz. The citadel is on a pyramid-shaped rock that rises 300 to 350 meters and is 200 to 250 meters wide (Figs. 79–80). Access to the fortress from the outside is possible only through a road that passes over a mountain range 300 to 400 meters high. In the vicinity of the fortress and in the citadel one can see the remains of a number of buildings and walls and numerous fragments of pottery. Near the entrance of the fortress there is a round, man-made ditch carved 1.8 meters into the rock; according to tradition, it was originally 4 to 5 meters deep. At the top of the citadel there is the trace of a well carved into rock. It is 4.8 meters long, 3.5 meters wide, and more than 8 meters deep. Inside on its four sides there are two layers of walls, built of bricks and lime mortar so that the water would not drain out of it.

Over the course of history Shahaponk' has witnessed several events and changes. History has recorded the heroic battles at Shahaponk' in 1387 against the hordes of Timur. One of the active participants in these was Grigor of Tat'ew, the most renowned philosopher of late medieval Armenia, who wrote his *Book of Questions* on the hill of Shahaponk'. In the colophon of that book Grigor describes his stay at the fortress of the Pŕoshid princes "as a voluntary banishment in the stronghold of the fortress called Shahaponk'."[10] The siege of the fortress, which is compared with the days of the Last Judgment, lasted for three months. According to legend, the great philosopher personally went to Timur to persuade him to lift the siege and stop the bloodshed, and Timur complied with his wish. The fortress of Shahaponk' was still extant in the eighteenth century, after which it was completely abandoned and fell into ruin.

On the northwestern side of the fortress there is a fountain that gushes out from the bottom of the mountain. Near it there are the ruins of a chapel, among which one can see fragments of medieval *khach'k'ars* and shards. Several decades ago Garegin Hovsēp'ian deciphered an inscription from the chapel dated 1293: "In the year 742 [1293]. In the name of God, I, Lady Gohar, an unworthy spouse, erected this cross for Grgo [Grigor?] the priest of God."[11] About 300 to 400 meters below this chapel and down the side of the mountain as far as the river there are the ruins of the village of Shahapunik', or Shahapont'. Our survey of the historic village and its cemetery shows that almost two hundred Armenian families lived there. From the fourteenth to the seventeenth century this village was known as an Armenian Catholic center where St. Astuatsatsin Monastery was active as the seat of a bishop. The monastery is now completely in ruins. During the Middle Ages a number of manuscripts were copied there.

KUK'I

The historic village of Kuk'i, or Guk'i, is identical with the present-day village of Kiuki in the region of Shahbuz. We first run across the name of this place in the *History* of Step'anos Orbelean.[12] Kuk'i is one of the ancient Armenian villages in the district of Shahapunik'. In its vicinity there are prehistoric dwellings and remains of Bronze Age graves.

In the Middle Ages Kuk'i was a large village. According to information in manuscripts copied in the churches of Kuk'i, the village had a number of architectural monuments. The colophon of a manuscript copied in 1471 in the renowned St. Nshan Monastery of Kuk'i states that the village had the following churches: St. Hazarabiwrits's, St. Kat'oghikē, St. Nshan, St. Grigor, St. Step'anos, St. Astuatsatsin, St. Vardan. Unfortunately these monuments are now in ruins. Only St. Nshan Monastery is partially extant.

St. Nshan, or Hazarabiwrits', Monastery (the Armenians in the vicinity call it Hazarap'rkich' of Kuk'i) is on a level site on a beautiful plain about 800 meters to the

Fig. 79. The citadel of the fortress of Shahaponk'.

Fig. 80. The fort and citadel of the fortress of Shahaponk'.

north of the present-day village. Today it is in a semi-dilapidated state (Figs. 81–84). Its polished facing stones, the slabs on the roof, and the cornices have fallen. The vaults, the arches, and the roofs of the vestries on both sides of the main apse are all destroyed. The roof of the vaulted porch, which is attached to the western facade of the church, is also destroyed. In the Middle Ages Kuk'i was under the rule of the Pŕoshid princes of Vayots' Dzor, but the building activity began there in the early Middle Ages and acquired greater momentum in the twelfth and the thirteenth centuries. St. Nshan Monastery was founded in the middle of the thirteenth century and is an important architectural monument. The sanctuary of St. Nshan Monastery is a domed church with three apses. The plan of its exterior is rectangular, whereas that of the interior is cruciform. The church has four vestries and one portal on the western facade. The latter opens into a porch (Fig. 85).

Fig. 81. St. Nshan Monastery ruins.

Fig. 82. St. Nshan Monastery entrance.

The plan and the architecture of St. Nshan Monastery of Kuk'i differ from those of other monuments in Shahapunik' and the other districts of Nakhichevan. The porch comprises the extension of the church and was probably built at the beginning of the fourteenth century. In the interior there are no pillars and its plan is rectangular. Its roof rested on engaged piers.

To the west of the church there is a vaulted structure that was probably the library. This building, which has

Fig. 83. St. Nshan Monastery porch pilasters.

Fig. 84. St. Nshan Monastery water spring.

Fig. 85. The plan of St. Nshan Monastery.

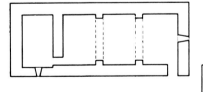

two sections, was built in the thirteenth century, at the time of the construction of the church.

During the course of centuries, the cells, the auxiliary buildings, and the walls that enclosed an area of more than 700 square meters were reduced to rubble. To the south of the church one can still see the remains of a vaulted fountain (Fig. 51) and to the northwest a ceme-

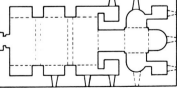

tery, which now contains about twenty tombstones, *khach'k'ars* from the twelfth to the sixteenth century.

ANUSHAWAN

Anushawan is located 6 kilometers below Kuk'i, on the right side of the Kuk'i River, but 5 kilometers toward the mountains. The historic village, which is the present-day Rameshin, is mentioned in the literary sources beginning from the thirteenth century.[13] Our survey of the vicinity of Anushawan shows that the village was an ancient Armenian settlement that had a medieval church and a number of chapels. The surviving tombstones in the Armenian cemetery of the village bear testimony to the migration of the Armenian population at about the end of the eighteenth century.

At present one can only see the ruins of the village church. The sources give no information on the name, the date of founding, or the destruction of this building. In a statistical document on Nakhichevan dating back to the beginning of the nineteenth century,[14] this church is registered as a ruined structure. Among the noteworthy monuments of Anushawan is the fortress called Anapat, which is located 2 kilometers north of the village and is on the summit of a hill about 200 meters high. From a strategic point of view it is a good, naturally secure site. The fortress has only one entrance.

ARMAWASHĒN

Historic Armawashēn is the present-day village of Nerk'in [Inner] Rameshin. It is located on the road to Kuk'i along the bank of the Kuk'i River. The literary sources say nothing about this village. From the ruins of the cemetery and the old buildings it is possible to tell that until the nineteenth century the population of the village consisted of about one hundred Armenian fami-

lies. There is no information on the church in the western part of the village, which was reduced to rubble long ago. On the bank of the river 1.5 to 2 kilometers below the village there was a village called Karmir Arotavayr [Red Pasture] now completely destroyed. In the cemetery of this village there are also a number of tombstones with Persian inscriptions. Opposite this village and on an elevated site on the left bank of the river there are the ruins of a chapel, in which there are two *khach'k'ars* from the twelfth and thirteenth centuries, as well as other fragments. The church of the village of Karmir Arotavayr probably stood on the site of this chapel.

SHAMEN

The historic village of Shamen, or Shamin, is the present-day Shada in the region of Shahbuz and is located 5 to 6 kilometers to the north of the village of Ōtsop' (Atsop'); it is situated in a valley on the upper course of the Saghuasonk' (Salasuz) River, which is a tributary of the Nakhichevan River. There is little information on this village; it is mentioned in the *History* of Step'anos Orbelean.[15] The remains of the village cemetery and the ruined buildings indicate that it was inhabited by Armenians and that there was a church there. About 2 kilometers down the valley, on an elevated level site to the right of the rivulet there is a famous monastic complex known as K'amu Khach' [the cross of the wind]. The monastery was originally called St. Khach' [holy cross]; it consisted of a church, a refectory, and a number of other buildings. In the course of time these buildings and the walls of the monastery were destroyed. The church alone has survived and is now in a semi-dilapidated state. Its entire roof and the upper parts of the walls and the pillars are ruined. It has the plan (Fig. 86) of a basilican church with four pillars. The church consists of a rectangular—almost square—apse, two vestries, and a hall. It has two portals, one on the north-

Fig. 86. The plan of St. Khach' Monastery.

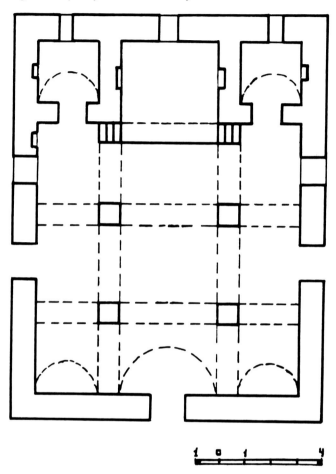

eral occasions. The last restoration was made in the second half of the nineteenth century with the support of Hambardzum P'irghalov of Ōtsop'.

ŌTSOP' (ATSOP')

The name Ōtsop', or Atsop' (also Metsop'), appears for the first time in the *History* of Step'anos Orbelean at the end of the thirteenth century. This village,[16] which is the present-day Badamlu (Nshut or Nshadzor), in the region of Shahbuz, is spread out on a concave depression situated between a level area and the sides of mountains. The present-day village was built on the ruins of the old one, but its boundaries spread out into the plain where they were ancient vineyards.

The ruins of a number of cemeteries, monuments, and two churches have survived in the vicinity of historic Ōtsop'. Among its most noted architectural monuments was St. Astuatsatsin Monastery, which was a major center in the Middle Ages. According to the colophon of a gospel copied there in 1292, the monastery had a large congregation and was the seat of an Armenian bishop.

St. Astuatsatsin Monastery is situated on the side of a high hill that lies to the northeast of the village and is 600 to 700 meters high. At present the only standing monument in the complex is the church, which is built of polished blocks of stone. The structure is a domed basilican church with four pillars (Fig. 87). It has an apse, two vestries, and a hall. There are two portals, one on the western facade and the other on the southern. The striking-looking dome rests on four square pillars. The drum of the dome is round and has eight windows not far above the base.

The porch of St. Astuatsatsin is attached to the western elevation of the church. It is now in ruins. The traces of its walls and engaged piers are visible only near the entrance of the church. The monastery was renovated on a number of occasions. There are bits of epigraphical and

ern facade and the other on the southern. The interior is covered with plaster and the windows have large rectangular openings.

The sources say nothing about the founding of Holy Cross Monastery. Nevertheless, one may surmise that religious life existed there beginning in the eleventh or the twelfth century. The complex was renovated on sev-

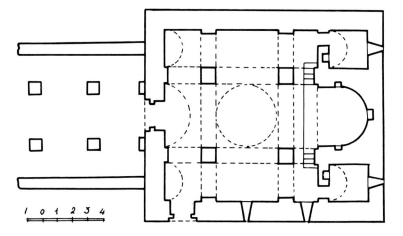

Fig. 87. The plan of St. Astuatsatsin Monastery.

literary information on the renovations. The original structure was erected in the twelfth century. The present church was rebuilt in 1610 and 1651–71. On the interior and exterior walls of the church and on the portals there are a number of reliefs, decorative bands, and inscriptions. To the east of the walls of the monastery and on the side of the mountain there is the monastic cemetery, with more than 150 tombstones *khach'k'ars* dating from the fourteenth to seventeenth centuries.

The other church of Ōtsop', which is called Zham [church] by the local inhabitants, is located in the northeastern quarter of the village. It is built of polished and half-polished blocks of stone. It is a vaulted structure with a single nave, an apse, vestries, and a hall. Its only portal is located on the western facade. The original roof rested on engaged piers that supported the vault. Now, as a result of renovations, the church has a flat roof.

There is no information on the date of construction of Zham of Ōtsop. The engaged piers with cornices in the shallow apse, the vestries, and on the portal indicate that it is an old vaulted structure built in the thirteenth or the fourteenth century. It was renovated during the period

between the sixteenth and eighteenth centuries. In the walls and in front of the western elevation there are tombstones and *khach'k'ars* from the fourteenth to the seventeenth century. About 15 to 20 meters to the northeast of the church there are four *khach'k'ars* with beautiful reliefs that are from the sixteenth and the seventeenth centuries.

AGARAK

This ancient village of Shahapunik', mentioned by the historical sources from the thirteenth century on, is now uninhabited and in ruins. The village is located on the right bank of the Shahapunik' rivulet 2 kilometers northeast of the present-day village of Kiulus (the historic K'yolk') in the region of Shahbuz. The historic Agarak lay on one of the mountain slopes in the valley of Shahapunik. From the village site it is possible to tell that Agarak was of medium size, with 100 to 120 families living there. The Armenian population of the village migrated from there between 1800 and 1810. Some of them settled in the village of Uz in Sisian. Later, Persians came to live in Agarak, and after their departure in 1825 the village was uninhabited and was reduced to ruins.

St. Khach' Monastery of Agarak, which is now in ruins, is situated on a hill in the northwestern part of the village. It stands on a level site on the slope of a mountain. From St. Khach' Monastery one can see almost all of the villages and towns in the district of Shahapunik'. In the immediate vicinity of the monastic church there are more than ten ruined buildings, which were surrounded by walls that formed a rectangular area. The only building in the complex that has survived is the church (Fig. 88), which is a vaulted hall. The original structure was built in the tenth or the eleventh century.

St. Khach' Church (Fig. 89) is a beautiful rectangular structure built of polished blocks of basalt stone. It has an apse, two vestries, and a hall. The only portal is located on the western facade in front of which there was an arcaded porch with a rectangular plan. The roof rested on the arches, which were supported by the engaged piers. According to historical information, the present-day church was rebuilt "by Shahan-Gagik in the year 1451 and was renovated by Lady Margarit in 1600."[17]

From the ruins of St. Khach' one can tell that it was a noted monastic complex and center during the Middle Ages and that it had a large congregation. Both the exterior and the interior of the church had a moderate amount of ornamentation.

The large ancient cemetery of Agarak, which is located near the ruins of the village and is 500 to 600 meters below the monastery, provides rich information about the history of the village. Among the two hundred and more tombstones there are some *khach'k'ar*s and monuments with reliefs dating back to an early period.

K'YOLK'

About 2 kilometers below Agarak lies the historic village of K'yolk', which is the present-day Kiulus. The historical sources mention K'yolk' from the thirteenth century on. The village is not large. In its vicinity there are a number of ruined historical and architectural monuments that bear testimony to the activity here during an earlier period.

In the Middle Ages K'yolk' was known for its churches, namely St. Arjakap, which is now in ruins, and St. Grigor. From the ruins of the first it is possible to tell that it was a large church with a number of auxiliary buildings. The sources say nothing about the date of its construction and the circumstances of its destruction. It was probably built in the thirteenth or the fourteenth century and was destroyed in the 1850s.

St. Grigor Church, which is still standing, is located in

Fig. 88. St. Khach' Monastery from the northwest.

the western part of the village on the main road. This is a basilican church with two aisles and a nave, an apse, two vestries, and a hall. It has two portals, one on the western facade and the other on the southern (Fig. 90). The structure is built of polished blocks of basalt and local sandstone. The original structure, which was probably built at an early date, was renovated in 1657 according to the inscriptions.

The architecture of the roof and the exterior of St. Grigor of K'yolk' is of interest. The sections of the roof produced by the arches that carry the roof and rest on the four pillars are not vaulted but instead have double layers of curvature. The curvature of the central vault rises 1 meter above the roof and gives the impression that there is a dome. Thus it does not have the structure of a ridged, or pitched, roof. We know that this dome-like structure is not characteristic of Armenian architec-

Fig. 89. The plan of St. Khach' Church.

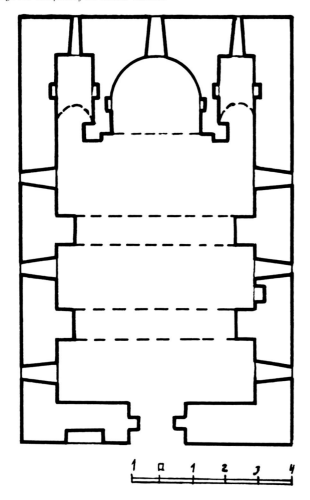

Fig. 90. The west portal of St. Grigor Church.

NORS (NORAGIWGH)

ture. It was used in the architecture of the churches built by the Persian-Armenian community of Isfaan (New Julfa). Among the monuments of Nakhichevan only three churches were constructed with similar roofs, namely the basilican churches of Aznaberd, Nors, and K'yolk'.

The ancient Noragiwgh in Shahapunik', which is the present-day Nors, is situated on an elevated jetty in a breathtaking valley. From the large area occupied by the village one may surmise that since ancient times more than seven hundred families have lived there at a time. During the eighteenth and nineteenth centuries a large part of the population of Nors migrated to Erevan and founded the quarter of Hin [Ancient] Nork'. Among the historical sources Step'anos Orbelean is the first to mention Nors, which he calls Noragiwgh [new village] and locates in the district of Chahuk.

Our survey of the architectural monuments in the vicinity of Nors reveals that man began living there sometime before the birth of Christ. The inscriptions on the buildings and the tombstones testify that since the middle of the twelfth century this, as well as the other villages of Shahapunik', were under the control of the Pŕoshid princes who built a number of monuments in Nors—fortresses, mills, *khach'k'ars,* and more. The ruins of some of these have survived. Among the better-known monuments of Nors were St. Khach' or Giwti Vank' Monastery, St. Errordut'iwn Church, and the fortress. St. Giwt Church, which was located in the eastern part of the village, is now completely in ruins. According to the inscription on the lintel of the portal of the church, the Pŕoshid prince Lianos built it in 1251 and donated to the monastery all of his ancestral lands and a water mill.

St. Errordut'iwn Church of Nors, which is a basilica with one nave and two aisles, is built of basalt and local reddish stone. On its eastern side the monument has a seven-sided apse, two vestries, and a hall (Fig. 91). It has two portals, one on the western facade and the other on the north. The roof of this church is similar to that of St. Grigor Church of K'yolk' and St. Grigor of Aznaberd.

Nothing is known about the original structure of St. Errordut'iwn Church. It was probably built no later than the fourteenth century and was renovated on a number of occasions. According to an inscription on a small *khach'k'ar* set in the tympanum of the western portal, the church was renovated in 1654. According to Ghewond Alishan, this monument was subsequently renovated in 1875 by the people and the clergy of Nors. St. Errordut'iwn Church, which is situated on an elevated site in the southern part of the village, is now in ruins. Its northern vestry is completely destroyed; a part of the northern wall of the church, the roof, and the

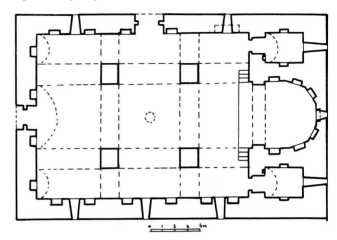

Fig. 91. The plan of St. Errordut'iwn Church.

other sections are badly damaged. In front of the western portal there is a large *khach'k'ar* with reliefs built by the Pŕoshids in the middle of the thirteenth century.

GOMER

The ancient historic Armenian village of Gomer, the present-day Giomur, is spread out on the scenic western foot of Mount Sarvard and lies along the Nakhichevan River and the road to Sisian. It is situated in the bosom of beautiful green hills and meadows 5 kilometers from the highway. From our survey of the site one can tell that man lived there even before the early Middle Ages. Between the twelfth and seventeenth centuries four hundred Armenian families lived in the village at any one time.

St. Grigor Church of Gomer, which is situated on an elevated site in the center of the village, is the only surviving monument. Because of its site the church dominates its surroundings. At a distance one can see the contour of the valley of the Nakhichevan River and the

Fig. 92. St. Astuatsatsin Church from the west.

Fig. 93. The east elevation of St. Astuatsatsin Church.

surrounding mountains. There is no information on the date of founding of St. Grigor Church, which has one nave and two aisles, two vestries, and a hall. The interior of the church is divided into one nave and two aisles because of two pairs of pillars on which the gabled roof rests. In 1696 a gospel was copied there and another one repaired: "In the village of Gomer in the Shahapunik' district of Nakhichevan, under the protection of St. Grigor . . ."[18]

St. Grigor has an elevated interior. It has two portals, one on the western facade and the other on the southern. Its external appearance is restrained, but the portals are decorated. In the walls on both sides of the western portal there are two splendid *khach'k'ars* with reliefs; they both are 2.2 meters high and 1 meter wide. The present structure was probably renovated in the middle of the seventeenth century.

In the vicinity of Gomer one can also see the remains of fortresses and ancient buildings and cemeteries. Among the other sites are Kapoyt Khaz, Anapat, and other chapels and holy places, and also the Shoṙ jur and T't'u jur spas.

KZHADZOR

The second village on the side of the majestic, green Mount Sarvard is the historic Armenian hamlet of Kzhadzor, or Kzhatsor. Around the village one can see the remains of a number of fortresses and a cemetery with 500 to 550 ancient tombstones. The most important monument in Kzhadzor is the church, which is located in the center of the village. The historical sources say nothing about its history or the founding of the church. The present-day structure (Figs. 92–93), which is still standing, was probably renovated at the beginning of the seventeenth century. The church has a nave and two aisles and an apse, two vestries, and a hall. It has two portals, one on the western facade and the other on the southern. From the colophon of a gospel written in

Shoṙot' in 1667 we learn that the church was named St. Astuatsatsin and that it had a large congregation. After the scribe had finished copying this gospel, "I, Lēli, daughter of Yovnis, promised to donate this holy gospel to St. Astuatsatsin in the village called Gĕzhaydzor. Read this and remember me."[19]

The basilican church of Kzhadzor does not have any decorative reliefs either on its interior or exterior walls. The only decorations are found on the frames of the windows and the arches of the portals.

On the hill in the cemetery there are the remains of a vaulted chapel, which has the plan of a hall-type church with a single nave. It is surrounded by a number of beautiful fifteenth- and sixteenth-century *khach'k'ars* and tombstones with reliefs. On the plain called Khach'i dzor one can see the remains of a town on a large area called Duk'an-Bazar, or Ch'arsu-Bazar, by the inhabitants of Kzhadzor. According to local tradition that was the site of an ancient Armenian town.

OP'IK' (BJNAGH)

This historic village is located on the upper course of the Nakhichevan River and below the Sisian pass, along the road that goes to Sisian. Op'ik', the present-day Bilanak in the region of Shahbuz, is a large village situated on the periphery of a forest in a green valley. It is mentioned in the *History* of thirteenth-century Armenian historian Step'anos Orbelean as a village within the borders of the district of Chahuk.[20] During the centuries that followed the name of the village was changed to Bjnagh, Karmalinovka, and Bich'anak.

The historical sources offer very little information on the past history of Op'ik'. About 3 to 4 kilometers north of the present village, in a forest across the river, there are the ruins of the village of Marni p'osht. According to tradition, the historic Op'ik' was originally located there. Besides the mass of ruins, one can still see there the remains of an ancient Armenian church whose architec-

tural style betrays its eleventh- or twelfth-century origin. In the 1960s, when barns were being built there, more than ten skeletons of cattle and items of archaeological interest were unearthed. Moreover, from the vicinity of the fountain on the road that goes to Sisian a number of Armenian tombstones and *khach'k'ars* were discovered. One of these has an inscription that bears the date 1084: "In 1084 we erected this as a memorial for Awag and Mariam."[21] From the antiquities around Op'ik' one can tell that the site of the village and the open areas in the forest were once Armenian villages and towns. It is not

Fig. 94. Hin tun or K'are tun.

known when Marni p'osht became uninhabited and when modern Bjnagh was established. We only know that in the second half of the seventeenth century this village was ruined and part of its inhabitants were put to the sword. Between 1750 and 1760 the Armenian inhabitants of Bjnagh abandoned the village. Subsequently, in the 1840s, the Molokans settled there and called it Karmalinovka. In 1919 they also migrated and some of them settled down in the region of Sevan in the Armenian SSR.

OLENI (K'OLAN)

About 5 to 6 kilometers down the valley below Op'ik' is the historic village of Oleni, which is located on the right bank of a river and is listed in Step'anos Orbelean's catalog of taxes as in the district of Chahuk.[22] Historic Oleni is the present-day village of K'olan in the region of Shahbuz. It is about 12 kilometers from the center of the district and is situated on the Nakhichevan-Sisian highway.

Oleni was a village of moderate size and had a church that was destroyed a long time ago. Two kilometers toward Bjnagh is the famed Hazarap'rkich' pilgrimage site where in the Middle Ages a large monastic complex stood. The complex was on the right side of the highway, situated on level ground under high-rising rocks. Besides the main church, the monastery had a number of other buildings, which were enclosed within outer walls. The complex is almost entirely destroyed today. The only discernible structures are the vestries of the church. There are also ruins of buildings and *khach'k'ars*. A gospel from 1696 was copied in the church of Gomer "by the prior Martiros Parontēr of Hazarap'rkich'."[23]

On a meadow called Bat'abat there are a number of dwelling sites. There is also an interesting monument there carved into rock[24]; it is called Hin tun [old house] or K'arē tun [stone house] (Fig. 94).

The Armenians have been acquainted with the art of calligraphy since ancient times. The history, art, culture, and entire experience of the Armenian people have been bequeathed to posterity by means of codices copied by Armenian scribes. Since antiquity the Armenians have shown great respect for the written word and especially to those responsible for the creation of books—scribes, illuminators, binders, manufacturers of parchment and paper, and patrons—all of whom bore the weight of a difficult but a rewarding task.

Between the fourteenth and eighteenth centuries, the scriptoria and art schools of medieval Nakhichevan played a significant role in the history of Armenian calligraphy and education and contributed to Armenian culture. That the art of calligraphy was practiced widely in the districts of Nakhichevan is apparent from the many Armenian manuscripts copied in that province. Besides religious and ecclesiastical books, such as gospels, synaxaria, and psalters, the majority of the manuscripts include the histories and works of Movsēs Khorenats'i, Eghishē, Mkhit'ar Gosh, Grigor Narekats'i, T'ovma Artsruni, Hovhannēs Orotnets'i, and Grigor Tat'ewats'i. These codices are not merely copies of texts, but beautiful works of art executed by scribes with linguistic and grammatical knowledge. They are richly decorated with miniatures.

The scriptoria of Nakhichevan have not escaped the tragic fate of the Armenian people. On several occasions they have been plundered and burned. That is why today we have little information on some of the libraries, scriptoria, and schools of Nakhichevan. Frequently the enemies took manuscripts ''captive'' and returned them, if at all, only after receiving large ransoms. The scribe of a damaged manuscript copied in the fortress of Ernjak in 1358 states with grief: ''The lawless Sat'lmish came to the fortress of Ernjak and destroyed many churches . . . many books were taken captive and brought to the fortress . . . with much effort and money I saved these books.''[1]

In spite of such problems, some of the manuscripts from the medieval scriptoria of Nakhichevan have been saved from destruction, fire, and natural decay and have reached us. They allow us to form an opinion on the development of art in the province of Nakhichevan. There are at present over 290 manuscripts from the scriptoria of Nakhichevan that are known to Armenists. About 140 of these are in the Mesrop Mashtots' Matenadaran of Erevan.[2]

From the extant manuscripts we can tell that the study of calligraphy in the medieval scriptoria of Nakhichevan had reached a high level and that a great deal of effort went into the art of illuminating and binding books. On numerous pages of vellum and paper, several illuminators, small fragments of whose original works have reached us, created decorations and miniatures. The historians of Armenian art know of more than twenty illuminators who were from the scriptoria of Nakhichevan. Their art is based on the traditions of Armenian miniature art. From the extant miniatures, wall paintings, and reliefs one can distinguish between the art schools of Agulis, old Julfa, Astapat, and Shorot'. In these schools special attention was paid to the art of binding. The majority of the manuscripts were bound in a traditional manner. Their covers are richly decorated with plant motifs, geometric designs, decorations, and religious pictures. Manuscripts no. 382 (thirteenth century, copied and bound in Astapat), no. 8567 (seventeenth century), no. 6846 (fifteenth century, copied in Agulis), no. 159

(fourteenth century, copied in Aprakunis), no. 6531 (fifteenth century, copied in Bist), nos. 5362, 7234, 9270, 10,386 (seventeenth century, copied in Shŏŕot'), and no. 8253 (seventeenth century, copied in Norashēn) of the Matenadaran of Erevan are interesting examples of the binder's art.

There were over thirty known scriptoria in Nakhichevan. Based on the extant manuscripts and epigraphical and historical sources, we shall give a brief catalog of the renowned scriptoria of Nakhichevan, which flourished from the fourteenth to the eighteenth century.

AGULIS

The better-known scriptoria and schools in Agulis were those of St. K'ristap'or Church and St. T'ovma Monastery. We have no specific information on the school of St. T'ovma Monastery, but it probably began to function in the middle of the twelfth century. Of the numerous manuscripts copied in this scriptorium only a few have reached us. These relics are from the fourteenth to the eighteenth century and are important examples of calligraphy, miniature art, and the binder's art. From these one can assume that in the scriptorium of St. T'ovma there were several scribes, illuminators, binders, commentators on the art of calligraphy, and original authors. Grigor of Narek's *Book of Lamentations,* which was copied at St. T'ovma in 1375 by the scribe Vardan, is a remarkable work of art.[3] The colophon of a manuscript possibly copied in the same scriptorium states: "This history book was copied . . . in 1432 by the sinful and artless scribe T'uma, who loves books."[4] During the fifteenth century the scribes Mat'ēos, Barsegh (who has a graceful hand), and several others copied a number of manuscripts at St. T'ovma.

Fifteen manuscripts copied at St. T'ovma between the sixteenth and eighteenth centuries are now preserved in the Matenadaran of Erevan (e.g., nos. 705, 497, 6819, 1157, 1836). These codices are decorated with marginal ornaments, decorations, canon tables, and miniatures.

Among the scribes and painters of this period were the monk Yovsēp', Sahak, Sargis, the monk Grigor, Ep'rem, the binder Azaria, Grigor, Pōghos, Step'anos—these last three were natives of Ts'ghna—and others. The school and scriptorium of St. T'ovma Monastery became well known, especially in the seventeenth century. The institution became one of the major cultural centers of late medieval Armenia, and its learned teachers, painters, and scribes succeeded in achieving excellence. Yet, the scriptoria of Agulis were frequently plundered and ravaged by barbaric invaders. One of these events is recorded in the colophon of a lectionary that was copied in 1477 and was repaired and rebound in 1663 at St. T'ovma Monastery of Agulis. The scribe writes about it with grief: "In 1789 Mustafa Khan came to Agulis and plundered the Monastery of St. T'ovma the Apostle. He seized the vessels, silverware, and the books of the church. . . . This lectionary was also taken captive by the infidels. It was brought to Dĕzmas, which is called Gharadagh. I, *tirats'u* [a person preparing to enter the priesthood] Petros, son of Gaspar, a native of Mizkit', bought it back for 3900 *shahi.*"[5]

During the seventeenth century Hovhannēs Vardapet, father of the poet-painter Naghash Hovnat'an of Shŏŕot', was a lecturer at the school of St. T'ovma. He and his son Naghash copied several manuscripts and illuminated them with miniatures while they were working in the scriptoria of the monasteries of Agulis and of their native Shŏŕot'. According to scholars,[6] after graduating from the school of St. T'ovma, Naghash Hovnat'an taught there and worked as a scribe. In the manuscripts that he copied he calls himself "I, the scribe Hovnat'an,' or "I, the clerk Hovnat'an'." Among his many paintings there are human images, natural scenes, flower motifs—all of which bear testimony to his artistic talent. Manuscript no. 3628 of the Matenadaran of Erevan, which he painted in the scriptorium of Agulis in 1682, is noteworthy. The decorative paintings on the cloth flyleaves in this codex also belong to Naghash Hovnat'an.

Among the renowned sixteenth- to eighteenth-century scribes and painters of Agulis are also the priest

Hovhannēs, Mkhit'ar, Mesrop, Ghazar the painter-priest, Mik'ayēl, and Ghukas Vardapet. According to the historical sources, in 1687 Khoja Giwlnazarean, son of Khoja Giwlnazar of Agulis, founded a press in his own house and printed the Book of Psalms, which he had translated into modern Armenian.[7] After the beginning of the seventeenth century, besides the school of St. T'ovma Monastery, a number of others were opened in Agulis. One of these was the noted school of the priest Andreas.[8] In the middle of the nineteenth century, and then in 1867, schools were founded for boys and girls through the efforts of the writer and educator Perch Pŕoshian.[9] There was also a trade school in Agulis where the talented novelists Perch Pŕoshian and Raffi taught. In the mid-nineteenth century, when most of the other cities in Armenia did not have libraries, Agulis had a reading room–library where people could find all of the Armenian and several of the Russian journals. The library was founded in the 1860s by Grigor Tēr-Mkrtch'ian, the son of the affluent Mkrtich' Tēr-Mkrtch'ian.

The manuscripts copied in the scriptoria and the schools of Agulis bear testimony to the fact that the academic level of the school of St. T'ovma was equal to those of the medieval Armenian theological schools, where the teaching of philosophy, mathematics, rhetoric, calligraphy, grammar, theology, painting, and other subjects was well advanced. According to the manuscripts, "the philosopher Hovhannēs"[10] was the director of the school of St. T'ovma in the second half of the fourteenth century; "the spiritual father and teacher Hakob"[11] was the director in the mid-sixteenth century, and "Barsegh the headmaster"[12] in the early sixteenth century. These men had the title "rabuni" [teacher].

APRAKUNIS

The school of Aprakunis emerged as a noted cultural center only toward the end of the fourteenth century. Until the founding of the famous school of St. Karapet Monastery, there were two schools in Aprakunis that were located in St. Gēorg Monastery and Verin or St. Khach' Monastery near the village. Among the teachers of these older schools were Grigor Vardapet and Sargis Vardapet, both of whom were from Aprakunis and had studied with Esayi Nch'ets'i, who was the head of the University of Glajor.[13]

Among the schools of Aprakunis the school of St. Karapet Monastery and its scriptorium were especially well known because of their cultural activities, influential role, and academic significance. Between the fourteenth and eighteenth centuries, this school was the foremost cultural and spiritual center of the district of Ernjak. Scholars have shown that after the construction of St. Karapet Monastery in 1381, through the efforts of such noted medieval figures as Maghak'ia of Crimea, Hovhannēs Orotnets'i, and Grigor Tat'ewats'i, the school of the St. Khach' Monastery of Aprakunis was transferred there.[14] The first director of the school of St. Karapet Monastery was Maghak'ia of Crimea (1381), and after 1382 Hovhannēs of Orotn who was succeeded by Grigor Tat'ewats'i. Subsequently, other famous rabunis and "vardapets" [doctors] supervised the school of Aprakunis.

Matt'ēos of Julfa, a well-known medieval scholar and a pupil of Hovhannēs of Orotn and Grigor of Tat'ew, taught at Aprakunis. In 1391 he composed one of his earliest works, *Commentary on the Gospel of Saint Luke,* at Aprakunis.[15]

Only a small segment of the rich production of the scriptorium of Aprakunis is now preserved in the Matenadaran of Erevan (e.g., nos. 95, 159, 2519, 1294, 2805, 2175, 3478). From these it is possible to tell that calligraphy and miniature painting had reached an advanced level in Aprakunis. Since the day of the founding of the school experienced scribes and miniature painters and men of talent gathered there. This is clear from the colophon of the scribe Hakob in the *Collection of the Works* of Grigor of Narek, Grigor Tghay, and others, which was copied there in 1386. After acknowledging the people who worked on the manuscript, the scribe begs: "Also remember our spiritual brethren, Hovhannēs who bound these holy books and Karapet who embellished them without compensation, and especially the goodly scions of the blessed root, the cleric Karapet, who is in the prime of youth, and his brother, the clerk Mkritch', who are both our pupils and who labored with us at great length by smoothing all of the flies in these holy books and by lineating them.''[16]

In the mid-seventeenth century the school of Aprakunis went through a period of revival under the supervision of Ghazar Vardapet and Esayi Vardapet of Meghri. In the colophon of a gospel written in 1649 the scribe states that he finished the work "in the hermitage of St. Karapet . . . in the district of Ernjak, during the prelacy of the industrious teacher Tēr Esayi.''[17] In the second half of the seventeenth century the school of St. Karapet was supervised by the rabunapet [chief rabuni] Mesrop Vardapet and others.[18]

Among the scribes and painters of the scriptorium of Aprakunis and clerk Astuatsatur, the binder Mat'ēos, the scribe T'at'ēos, and the monk Hovhannēs are well known. Based on the evidence in the manuscripts, one can assume that in the school of St. Karapet Monastery there was a special department of calligraphy where the pupils were taught to write, embellish, paint, and bind books.

SHOṘOT'

The tradition of this town emphasizes the preservation of the written word and cultural continuity. From early youth hundreds of natives of Shoṙot' engaged in the task of preserving the art of calligraphy and spreading literacy.

Calligraphy in Shoṙot' goes back to the time when Armenian writing was introduced into the region,[19] but unfortunately there are no surviving examples of the early works. Shoṙot' became better known as a cultural center during the sixteenth to the eighteenth centuries because of manuscripts that were copied there. About forty of these are now preserved in the Matenadaran of

Erevan. The well-known scriptoria of that period were the Anapat Kusanants' and St. Lusaworich' monasteries, and St. Astuatsatsin and St. Hakob churches, where the pupils were exposed to the commentaries and grammars of the most famous philosophers and grammarians of medieval Armenia and were trained in calligraphy, miniature painting, and other subjects.

There were also several women who occupied themselves with calligraphy, copying of manuscripts, and painting. The works of the nuns affiliated with the scriptorium of the Monastery of Kusanants' Anapat are especially worthy of attention, since they produced beautiful manuscripts. Among the scribes of this school are Shushan, Gohar, Margarit, Mariam, Eghisabet', and others. Between 1664 an 1666 Shushan, who was also a talented poet, copied the *Histories* of Movsēs Khorenats'i and Eghishē, the *Proverbs* of Solomon, and other books. In 1666 Shushan wrote in her colophon of the Proverbs that she finished copying the present manuscript with the help of someone else and that she undertook the task willingly, carrying it out with fervent love.[20]

Margarit, another famous and talented scribe, wrote in a manuscript that she copied in 1673: "I the wretched . . . Margarit am faithful, obedient, and compromising in name alone. . . . I copied this holy gospel with fervent love and hearty desire'' (Matenadaran of Erevan no. 7234). The scribe Gohar, who copied a number of manuscripts in 1667 and 1668, wrote in the *Prayerbook of Narekats'i* (Gregory of Narek's *Book of Lamentations*): "I the virgin Gohar desired to have and was the recipient of this spiritual book. I wrote this with fervent love.''[21] The colophons reveal that the female scribes of Shoṙot displayed a special devotion and dedication to the art of calligraphy.

Between the sixteenth and eighteenth centuries, the scriptoria and the schools of St. Lusaworich' Monastery and St. Astuatsatsin Church also played an important role. There are several manuscripts that were copied there by the expert clerks Bagarat, Militos, Sargis, Hovhannēs, Awag (seventeenth century), the scribes Mesrop and Hovhannēs (eighteenth century), and others. In the seventeenth century the clerk Hovnat'an (Naghash Hovnat'an), a poet and painter known for his miniatures, also copied and illuminated a number of manuscripts in the scriptoria of Shoṙot'. For several centuries the scribes of Shoṙot', the painters, and the binders diligently recreated numerous manuscripts and made a lasting contribution to Armenian calligraphy, art and culture.

Norashēn (Norakert)

The historical sources offer very little information on the scriptorium at Norashēn.[22] We assume that it started to function in the middle of the fourteenth century, since the oldest manuscript copied there is from that period. The scribe of this manuscript wrote "in the eight hundred and sixth year of the Armenian era [1357] in the village of Norakert in the district of Ernjak."[23] From manuscripts copied in Norashēn we learn that the scriptorium was located in St. Astuatsatsin Monastery.

The extant manuscripts from the scriptorium of Norashēn are mostly from the seventeenth century. Some of them are now preserved in the Matenadaran of Erevan (nos. 148, 1332, 1852, 3841, 7747, 8253, 3817). These manuscripts are embellished with marginal decorations, canon tables, and miniatures. Their bindings are made of printed linen. The decorations and bindings of these manuscripts were made with great expertise.

Among the well-known scribes, painters, and binders of Norashēn were the scribes Gawazan, Movsēs the priest, Hovhannēs, Alek'san, the clerk Baghdasar, the clerk Vardan the painter, the cleric Shmawon, and the scribe Kozma. From the colophon of Grigor of Tat'ew's *Girk' Harts'mants'* [Book of Questions]—which was commissioned and financed by the rabunapet Esayi of Karchewan, the prior of St. Karapet Monastery of Aprakunis, and was copied by the priest Ghazar and then by his son Alek'san—we learn that the scriptorium of St. Astuatsatsin Church of Norashēn was the alma mater of

a number of scribes and painters. Among the latter was Kosma, a well-versed and knowledgeable teacher about whom the scribe Alek'san wrote: "Kozma the scribe, from whom I learned my art and who worked very hard to write and illuminate this."[24]

Kozma of Norashēn was an expert calligrapher and miniaturist. Only a few manuscripts copied by him have reached us. A synaxarium that he copied in 1668 is now preserved in the Matenadaran of Erevan (no. 3817). In its colophon Kozma says that the copying was done "by a hand ephemeral like a flower and grass." In another manuscript that he copied in 1678, Kozma calls himself "unconsoled scribe Kozma of Norashēn."[25]

Old Julfa

The religious centers of this famous medieval city were also known for their scriptoria. Based on the testimony of the manuscripts copied in Julfa we can state with certainty that the scriptoria were located in the Amenap'rkich' Monastery, St. Astuatsatsin and St. Gēorg churches, and the Hermitage of St. Hovhannēs-Mkrtich'.

From manuscripts copied in Julfa we can assume that the art of calligraphy and its instruction were initiated in that town in the twelfth or the thirteenth century. The scriptoria remained active until the forced migration of the inhabitants to Persia, where after a short interruption the immigrants resumed their cultural activities in New Julfa.

Because of the destruction of libraries and scriptoria, especially at the time of the deportations at the beginning of the seventeenth century, very few manuscripts have been preserved and these are from the fourteenth to the seventeenth centuries. Some of these are now in the Matenadaran of Erevan. In 1286 the scribe Sargis copied in one of the scriptoria of Julfa the *Commentary on the Definition of the Offices and the Mystery of Prayers.*[26] In 1325 a lectionary was copied "by the unworthy priest

Khach'atur . . . in Julfa'';[27] a gospel "was copied in the year 1388 in the Amenap'rkich' Monastery of Julfa.''[28] During the course of the fifteenth to the seventeenth centuries, a number of manuscripts were copied in Julfa by the scribes Khach'atur of Khizan, Ṙestakēs, and Mariam (also an illumiantor), Mkrtich', Hakob of Julfa, and others.

The *Book of Sermons* of Grigor of Tat'ew, copied in 1456 in Julfa and illuminated by the scribe-illuminator Mariam, is worthy of attention for its 977 large leaves.[29] Luckily this singular example of miniature art of mid-fifteenth-century Julfa was saved from burning during the deportations organized by Shah Abbas and was taken from Ṙindigan to Gich'nigan, to Shahbulagh, to Mamuṙan—Armenian villages in the district of Charmahal province in Iran. As a result, a number of illuminated pages were removed from the manuscript. Finally the codex came into the hands of the bibliophile M. Tēr-Suk'iasian, a resident of the village of Mamuṙan. In the 1940s it was taken to the library of Ējmiatsin. On several pages of this manuscript and on the margins there are hundreds of miniatures, letters shaped like ornaments and birds and painted in various styles. They are executed with an artistic talent, subtlety, and poetical imagination that bear witness to Mariam's gift as an artist.

Mariam is the first known woman artist in the history of fifteenth-century Armenian art. Her work was inspired by the traditions of the art school of old Julfa. We see numerous parallels between the motifs in her artistic work, the miniature art of the school of Julfa, and the reliefs on the *khach'k'ars* in the famous cemetery of Julfa.

K'ṘNA

According to information in the manuscripts, after the construction of St. Astuatsatsin Church in 1330, through the activities of Bartholomew of Maraghah and Hovhannēs of K'ṙna, several renowned vardapets and rabunis gathered there and stimulated cultural life.[30] The scribes and binders who gathered around the scriptorium of St. Astuatsatsin Church copied translated texts, commentaries, theological and grammatical treatises, and other original works by the rabunis and vardapets of K'ṙna. During the fourteenth and fifteenth centuries, Hovhannēs of K'ṙna, Hakob of K'ṙna, Friar Dominicus of Salit'agh, Zak'aria, the binder Sahak of Van, and others copied several manuscripts.

The extant manuscripts from K'ṙna are now preserved in libraries in Erevan, Venice, Vienna, and elsewhere. They contain mostly unimportant religious works and dogmatic texts, for example, the *Book of Hours*, prayer books, and theological treatises translated for the members of the congregation of K'ṙna. Some manuscripts, however, contain important translations that were made in the school of K'ṙna, and despite the ban against the works of the Unitores, they found their way to the Armenian cultural and educational centers and schools, where they were used and studied.

Among the manuscripts produced at K'ṙna there are more than fifteen known translations. Through these the intellectuals of Armenia became acquainted with medieval Western thought. Thus the school of the Unitores at K'ṙna played a unique role in the history of fourteenth- and fifteenth-century Armenian culture.

Hakob of K'ṙna, who was educated in the schools of Siwnik', is an important figure in the history of the scriptorium of K'ṙna. Since he was a skilled and well-known translator, he called himself Hakob K'ṙnets'i t'argman [translator] vadapet. He is the author of most of the important translations produced at K'ṙna, where he probably taught foreign languages as well as the art of translating. In one of his unpublished works Hakob makes a number of valuable observations about methods of teaching. This experienced educator and translator wrote that for purposes of learning it was important to teach a subject not only "in word" but also "in writing." He wrote: "If a teacher teaches his pupils only orally, they will be unable to understand everything completely, since human perception is weak, but if he writes, it shall remain in their minds."[31]

One of the best-known personalities of the school of K'ṙna was Hovhannēs of K'ṙna, a leader of the Unitores who translated several books and wrote commentaries, a grammer, and more. *Hamaṙōt hawak'umn yaghags k'era-kanin* [A Compendium of Grammar] of Hovhannes is an important and exceptional work that has recently been published and made available for scholars. According to specialists, this work marks an important stage in the development of Armenian grammatical thought and is the first scholarly Armenian grammer book.

NAKHICHEVAN

The scriptoria adjacent to the religious centers of Nakhichevan played a special role in the cultural life of that city. On several occasions when Nakhichevan underwent the horrors of destruction, decay, and oblivion many of its libraries were destroyed. As a result only a few of the works produced in the scriptoria of the city have survived. In a colophon written in 1554 it is stated that Suleyman invaded Armenia and came to the city of Nakhichevan "ravishing and destroying the churches [on his way] and seizing books and gospels. . . . Paron Khach'atur went to Erzrum with the king's army and liberated from the infidels a large *mashtots'* [book of rituals], which he brought to . . . the city of Nakhichevan and handed over to St. Sargis Zōravar Church in 1554."[32]

There are several manuscripts copied in Nakhichevan that are known to scholars. Over ten of these are now in the Matenadaran of Erevan and bear testimony to the activities of a number of scriptoria between the twelfth and eighteenth centuries. Among the manuscripts copied and illuminated at these institutions were histories and commentaries. The scriptoria and the schools of St. Sargis and St. Errordut'iwn churches played a noticeable role as centers of calligraphy.[33] In the middle of the nineteenth century an elementary school was founded at St. Errordut'iwn Church and a girls' school at St. Gēorg Church, which was renovated at the same time and is still standing.

Codex no. 3722 of the Matenadaran of Erevan is a valuable example of calligraphy. The scribe Hakob copied it in 1304–1306 in one of the scriptoria of Nakhichevan. The numerous miniatures in it belong to the illuminator Simēon of Astapat. In the colophon of this manuscript Hakob states: "Being aware of the incomparable wealth of this book, I undertook the task of copying this God-made gospel with great hope and desire, since it is light and gives light to the eyes. . . . When you look at this, ask for forgiveness for the sins of Hokob, who copied it."

Of interest is also the gospel of 1324 copied by the scribe Hovsēp in the scriptorium of St. Sargis Church. Hovsēp states: "I accomplished this with great love and desire, seeking light for my soul and relief for my body."[34] Another gospel copied in the same scriptorium in 1351 used to be preserved in St. Karapet Church of Polu.[35] Among the scribes who copied manuscripts in the scriptoria of Nakhichevan were the "servant" Aṙak'el (fourteenth century), the priest Mesrob (sixteenth century), Hovhan Vardapet (seventeenth century), and Petros Aghamalian-Bert'umiants' (eighteenth century).

ASTAPAT

As a center of calligraphy Astapat played an important role from the fourteenth to the seventeenth century.[36] Its famed scriptorium was located at the school of St. Vardan Church, where Gēorg Tseruni and Vardan, the prior of that congregation, were active in the fourteenth century.

In 1379 Maghak'ia of Crimea and Hovhannēs of Orotn founded a higher institution of learning in St.

Step'anos or Karmir Monastery. The new school was in the tradition of the medieval seminaries of Armenia. Subsequent to the founding of the latter, the famed rabunapet Sargis Vardapet moved from the school of Aprakunis to Astapat, and during his tenure the schools of St. Vardan and Karmir Vank greatly flourished. Among the topics taught in these schools were painting, calligraphy, and the natural sciences.

Through the efforts of Maghak'ia of Crimea, Hovhannēs of Orotn, Sargis Vardapet, Grigor of Tat'ew, and their pupils, the schools of Astapat, Aprakunis, and other institutions in their vicinity became important centers of learning. Several students who studied in these went on to teach in various parts of Armenia, where they spread literacy and kept the literary and historical traditions alive among the Armenian people.

Several manuscripts were copied and painted in the cultural centers and the scriptoria of Astapat. Khach'atur of Erznkay, the scribe who copied a lectionary in the scriptorium of St. Vardan Church of Astapat, wrote in his colophon: "This was written . . . by the scribe Khach'atur of Erznkay in the year 767 [1318] . . . in the village of Astapat, under the protection of the holy soldier and martyr of Christ Vardan."[37]

The renowned illuminator Simēon, who painted and decorated a number of manuscripts during the fourteenth century, also lived in Astapat. One of the gospels he painted is now preserved in the Matenadaran of Erevan (no. 3722). This manuscript was copied by the scribe Hakob in 1304–1306, "in the metropolis called Nakhichevan; . . . this book was decorated in the great appenage of Astapat, which is situated on the bank of the swift and rainbow-like Arax River."[38] The miniatures and the decorations in this gospel express a festive mood, and its calligraphy and miniature art are closely related to the formative period of the art school of Van.[39] Among the scribes who worked in the scriptoria of Astapat were the clerk Aṙak'el (fourteenth century), the scribe Sahak (sixteenth century), Sargis Gtsogh [artist] of Shoṙot', and Abraham Vardapet of Astapat (eighteenth century).

KUK'I

In this well-known medieval village there were a number of scriptoria, among which St. Nshan or Hazarabiwrats' Monastery, where scribes gathered, was famous. Because of its active cultural life this monastery was one of the important religious and cultural centers of the district of Shahapunik'.[40] Only a small number of manuscripts have been preserved from this scriptorium and they are executed in an artistic tradition of high caliber. The oldest extant manuscript from there is Nersēs Lambronats'i's *Commentary on the Divine Liturgy,* which is dated 1276. Another copy of the same work was made in Kuk'i in 1322 by the scribe Markos Kronawor [cleric]. In the middle of the fourteenth century Daniēl of Kuk'i copied for Margarē Vardapet of Ōts'op' Hovhannēs of K'ṙna's *Girk' Dzhokhots'* [Book of Hell]. In 1409 the *Categories* of Aristotle were copied, and the scribe Manuēl copied and illuminated over ten manuscripts in the same scriptorium. Among his valuable works are a synaxarion (Matenadaran, no. 1511); a *gandzaran* [book of odes], copied in 1478; a *mashtots'* [book of rituals], copied in 1493; a gospel copied in 1495 and another one copied in 1496 at the request of the couple Gozal and Khontsin. In the colophon of the above *gandzaran* (Matenadaran no. 4433) Manuēl wrote: "This holy *gandzaran* was copied by the sinful, wretched *matnagēt* scribe Manuēl, a false priest." According to the Armenian lexicon *Baṙgirk' haykazean lezui* (2 vols., Venice, 1837), *matnagēt* means "one who knows about books and literature." The scribe Manuēl, who lived and worked in fifteenth-century Kuk'i, probably taught calligraphy and art in the local scriptorium. The artistic merits of the miniatures in the manuscripts copied by him bear testimony to his skill.

Among the noted scribes of the Monastery of Kuk'i were Bishop Hovsēp', the scribe Hakob, and the cleric Hovsēp' (fifteenth century). The school and the scriptorium of St. Nshan Monastery of Kuk'i were probably organized in the middle of the thirteenth century and survived until the middle of the eighteenth.

ŌTSOP'

This famous village in Shahapunik' was especially well known for its scriptorium, where a number of manuscripts were copied.[41] Unfortunately very few manuscripts copied there have survived. We know of a gospel that was copied there in 1292. Its skilled scribe, Bishop Shmawon of St. Astuatsatsin Monastery, notes in his colophon that "the divine word was copied in the district of Shahapunik', in the monastery near the all-blessed and God-protected village of Otsop' . . . by the sinful and impure scribe Shmawon." According to him, at the end of the thirteenth century the Monastery of St. Astuatsatsin was a well-known center with a large congregation. In his colophon he begs the reader to remember "also the brotherhood of this hermitage, its prior, the grandsacristan, the old and young members of this purgatory."

Besides the manuscripts copied by Shmawon at Ōtsop', there are others by the scribes At'anēs (fifteenth century) and the elderly Sargis Monozonik (sixteenth century). From the evidence in the works of these men one can tell that exegesis, grammar, and calligraphy were among the subjects taught at St. Astuatsatsin Monastery of Ōtsop', where special attention was given to binding and painting books. It is interesting to note that the scribe Shmawon decorated the manuscript that he had copied "with gold and silver, and with gold lines and flowery color; and I decorated both the inside and the outside with valuable stones and pearls that shone light."

The historical material and the epigraphical evidence from the Monastery of Ōtsop' suggest that the monastic school and the scriptorium were organized at the end of the thirteenth century and survived until the end of the eighteenth century.

BIST

The medieval centers of calligraphy here were located at St. Nshan or Kopatap' Hermitage and St. Astuatsatsin Monastery. Very few of the works produced at these places have been preserved, and these are from the fourteenth to the seventeenth century; three of the works are now preserved in the Matenadaran of Erevan (Mss. nos. 6257, 6531, 7481). From these manuscripts one can tell that the study of calligraphy and miniature art in the schools of Ōtsop' was quite advanced.

Like the several scriptoria in the district of Goght'n, those of Bist also were ravaged and destroyed by invaders. For example, in the colophon of a manuscript he copied, the scribe T'uma of Archēsh remorsefully wrote: "The time was bad because of the infidels so that one could not write for even one hour. We had all run away and under cover."[42] In such difficult circumstances "this holy gospel, which heals the soul and body, was copied by the sinful and impure scribe T'uma of Archēsh in the land of Goght'an, in the hermitage called Kopatap opposite the village of Rist . . . in the 785th year of the Armenian era [1336]."[43] In this manuscript, which has 540 leaves, there are 193 beautiful marginal decorations, 64 majuscules with flower decorations, 71 with bird decorations, 22 with animal decorations, and 26 with human images. Many of these decorations have been executed with exquisite art. The colophon of the manuscript states that the wooden cover "was prepared by Akob the carpenter," and "the worthless monk Sahak K'ajberuni bound the holy gospel." The same source also reveals that at that time there were among the monks and scribes of St. Nshan or Kopatap Hermitage "Shmawon, Yohanēs, who were all servants of Jesus Christ."[44]

Another extant manuscript from the scriptorium of St. Nshan was copied "by the sinful and unskilled scribe Grigor the Monk from the Hermitage of Bust in Goght'n, under the protection of the all-powerful St. Nshan, St. Astuatsatsin, and St. Sargis . . . in the year 1489."[45] From the same colophon we also learn that toward the end of the fifteenth century there were a number of renowned priors and monks in Bist: "the wonderful clerics Mesrob, Movsēs, Dawit', Nahapet, Yakob, Sargis the Monk . . ."[46] The manuscript has 528 leaves with 192 beautiful marginal decorations and an equal number of majuscules decorated with floral motifs. The images of the four evangelists and the tables give a special dignity to the book. The scribe Grigor begs the reader to remember the women who received the gospel and donated it to the churches of Bist: "The good lady Gharip Khat'un and Azat Khat'un with the crimson and gold-laced hair who received this. They gave this holy gospel to St. Nshan and St. Astuatsatsin Monastery of Bist as a sacred foundation and a gift."[47] The last extant manuscript from the scriptorium of the Hermitage of St. Nshan is a lectionary[48] copied by the monk Step'anos in 1689. In it there are 708 leaves, beautiful tables, marginal decorations, ornamental motifs, floral decorations, and miniatures.

One of the manuscripts from the scriptorium of the Monastery of St. Astuatsatsin is a gospel copied in 1439 by the scribe Khach'atur, which is now preserved in the Chester Beatty Library in Dublin and is catalogued under no. 565. This manuscript is described as having miniatures, images, and marginal decorations of a high artistic quality, which were executed by the painter Mkritch'.[49] The colophon of a *mashtots'* copied at St. Astuatsatsin Monastery states that "the prior of this holy order was Tēr Mesrop, a gentle and kind monk, and with him there were his companions, Movsēs, a noble monk, and the solitary Sargis, who was the abbot of this monastery. . . . The priests and the headmen of the all-blessed village of Bist, which deserves blessings, commissioned us to write this book in memory of themselves. . . . [This book was copied] by the feeble and unskilled scribe—the sinful and false monk—Karapet . . . in the year 1495."[50] It is clear from the evidence in the above manuscripts that at the end of the fifteenth century the monks Mesrop, Movsēs, and the solitary Sargis were the leading figures in the monasteries of St. Nshan and St. Astuatsatsin and were the directors of the schools and scriptoria in those institutions.

In the colophon of an undated manuscript it is stated that the person who received the present book was "the celibate priest Tēr Azaria from the village of Bist who lives at the renowned monastery called St. Nshan."[51] In the colophon of a *mashtots'* of 1634 copied at Ts'ghna by the priest Marut'a, the reader is asked to remember also "Tēr Simon of Bist, who worked with me copying [this] and smoothing [the surface of] the paper."[52]

There is no written testimony about the scriptoria of Bist in the sources of the ensuing period. In 1670, when Zak'aria of Agulis visited St. Nshan Monastery, its prior was the vardapet Alek'san of Bist,[53] and at the beginning of the eighteenth century, when Catholicos Abraham of Crete was passing through there, the prior was "Petros Vardapet, a wise and kind man, under whose supervision the monastery had been renovated in 1668."[54] In 1715 the latter visited Jerusalem and wrote about his visit in the colophon of a manuscript copied in Khlat' in 1575:

> I Tēr Petros, a humble man,
> . . . .
> A native of the district of Goght'n,
> From the village called Bist.
> This is the year 1715.[55]

During the fourteenth and fifteenth centuries, Yakob Vardapet of Bist, a learned scribe and commentator on the art of calligraphy and also a pupil of Grigor of Tat'ew, and Ghukas of Bist probably taught calligraphy in the scriptoria of Bist. In his famous *Book of Sermons,* written in 1407 at Tat'ew, Grigor of Tat'ew states that he composed that work at the request of the scribe Hakob and begs the reader to remember him, since he deserves it: "Moreover, Hakob Rabuni, the man who requested this book, my foster brother from the land of Goght'n, a native of Bist. May his memory be blessed."[56]

The artistic quality of the manuscripts copied and painted at the scriptoria of Bist indicates that in the late Middle Ages the calligraphy and miniature art taught there were very advanced.

P'AṘAKA

Unfortunately there are very few extant manuscripts from the scriptoria of P'aṙaka, and these are from the fifteenth, sixteenth, and seventeenth centuries. One of the oldest manuscripts "was copied in Goght'n, at the lesser hermitage of P'aṙakay called Dzoravank', which is under the protection of Saint George and the holy relic of the Wonderworker and all the saints who are assembled here . . . in the 924th year of the Armenian era [1495]."[57] The colophon of a synaxarion, which the scribe began to copy in Van in 1525 and subsequently the scribe Ghazar completed in P'aṙaka, gives the following information: "This holy synaxarion was completed in the Monastery of Jermuk, in the land of Goght'n, in the village of P'aṙakay, in the year 1654, on the tenth day of December when the sign of the zodiac was Virgo . . . during the priesthood of Tēr Martiros, who is the prior of the Monastery of St. Hakob. . . . Again remember with kindness the great orator and the ingenious poet and the learned rabuni Tēr Movsēs Vardapet from whom I learned the art of calligraphy."[58]

There are now only a few seventeenth-century manuscripts from P'aṙaka in the Matenadaran of Erevan. These are not only important for their contents but also for their marginal decorations and ornamented majuscules. One of these manuscripts (Matenadaran no. 8205), *Girk' Harts'mants'* [Book of Questions] by Grigor of Tat'ew, was copied by the scribe Martiros, the priest in 1638 at the scriptorium of St. Hakob Church: "This was completed in the land of Goght'n, in the village of P'aṙaka, under the protection of the order of Saint Hakob . . . in the 1,087th year of the Armenian era [1638]."[59] The scribe Martiros also began to copy a manuscript (Matenadaran no. 7758) when he was sixty years old and finished the task in 1653. In the colophon of the manuscript he noted: "Woe to you, stupid scribe, who became sixty years old, but you do not have any good qualities. Woe to you. . . . This book was copied by the unworthy scribe Martiros in the 1,102nd year of the Armenian era [1653] . . . in the village called P'aṙakay, under the protection of Saint George, which is called Dzoroyvank'."[60] At St. Shmawon Church of P'aṙaka the scribe Ghazar copied a gospel in 1665, and in its colophon he stated: "This holy gospel was copied in the village of P'aṙakay in the district of Goght'n under the protection of St. Shmawon Church."[61] Tirats'u Barsegh bound this manuscript in 1712.

The chronological and topographical data in the Matenadaran codex no. 604 indicate that the manuscript was copied at P'aṙaka in 1713 by the deacon Petros, the son of Ghatam, a native of P'aṙaka. In 1751 Bishop Barsegh, who is probably Tirats'u Barsegh, copied the work *Tsaṙ meṙoni, patmut'iwn kazmut'ean ew niwt'ots' meṙoni* [The Tree of Chrism, the History of the Making, and the Contents of the Chrism]."[62]

According to the evidence in the manuscripts, the scriptoria of P'aṙaka were located at the hermitage of St. George or Dzoravank', St. Shmawon Church, and St. Hakob Monastery.

The art of painting has a special place in Armenian culture. Since ancient times Armenian artists felt at ease painting and narrating their experiences in the language of colors and knew the art of expressing beauty. The ancient, medieval, and early modern historical sources contain much information on the art of painting in Armenia. The various branches of this art, especially medieval (tenth to fourteenth century) miniature art and wall painting, can be compared with those of other nations in their iconographical characteristics, colors, shades, and artistic features.

Armenian painting was not unaffected by the bitter destiny of the Armenian people. It suffered great losses because of the absence of an Armenian state for long periods of time and because of the barbarity of foreign oppressors, natural disasters, and unfavorable conditions. Nevertheless, thousands of valuable works and monuments, paintings, wall paintings, and miniatures produced in historic Armenia at different periods of time have survived the destruction wrought by the foreign oppressors and have reached us unscathed. These give us a good idea about the art of the Armenian people.

It is impossible to present a full picture of medieval and seventeenth- and eighteenth-century painting in Armenia proper without discussing the role and the contribution of the towns of Nakhichevan—namely Agulis, Shoṙot', Astapat, and old Julfa. The miniature art executed at these places, as well as at Bist, Abrakunis, Ts'ghna, Kuk'i, and Norashēn, is the expression of a single school that was the source of the art of the renowned Hovant'anian family. According to the testimony of the sources, from as early as the twelfth century there were many people in the districts of Nakhichevan who practiced calligraphy and miniature art. Besides the miniature artists, there were also muralists who skillfully painted the walls of monuments in a manner harmonious with their architecture.

Unfortunately, none of the murals of Nakhichevan from the twelfth to the fourteenth century has survived. At best only fragments of old murals or insignificant details have reached us, and on the basis of these it is impossible to write a complete history of the art of wall painting of Nakhichevan. The extant murals are from the seventeenth to the nineteenth century. The iconography of these reveals that the wall paintings of Nakhichevan were in the tradition of ancient Armenian art and that the themes for the most part came from the Old Testament; the decorations and the subjects were of a religious nature. This hindered the artists from displaying their worldly interests. Nevertheless, as in the miniatures and wall paintings from other regions of Armenia, so also in those from Nakhichevan we find more liberal and unrestricted compositions and new subjects, original interpretations of New Testament themes and especially lay motifs. Besides these characteristics, which reflect the changes in the socioeconomic conditions of the period, there is also plant ornamentation in these works of art, with examples of the fauna of Armenia: plants, bushes, numerous types of flowers, trees, and more. The beautiful ornaments and motifs derived from these are, in their composition and color, genuine representations of the originals as envisaged by the artists.

Most significant of the extant wall paintings on the architectural monuments of Nakhichevan are the ones either fully or partially preserved in St. K'ristap'or Church, St. T'ovma Monastery of Agulis, St. Karapet of Abrakunis, St. Lusaworich', St. Astuatsatsin, St. Hakob Hayrapet of Shoṙot', St. Step'anos or Karmir Monastery of Astapat, St. Astuatsatsin of Ṙamis, St. Grigor of Azna-berd, St. Hovhannēs Mkrtich' of Chahuk, and St. Astuats-atsin of Bist. Our own surveys and the literary sources reveal that St. Gēorg of Abrakunis (1603),[1] St. Hov-hannēs Mkrtich',[2] St. Shmawon, St. Errordut'iwn, St. Hakob Hayrapet of Agulis, St. Shmawon of P'aṙaka, St. Astuatsatsin of Norashēn, St. Lusaworich' of Gagh, St. Astuatsatsin of Tanakert, St. Vardan of Astapat, and other monuments also had wall paintings.

Surveys of these monuments reveal that from the middle of the seventeenth century their walls were painted by artists from the schools of Agulis and Shoṙot', where the art of the Hovnat'anian family reached its peak in the seventeenth and the eighteenth centuries. Modern studies and the extant wall paintings reveal that most of the seventeenth- and eighteenth-century archi-tectural monuments of Nakhichevan were painted by the Hovnat'anians, who have contributed a great deal to the development of Armenian art. Five generations of this family—Naghash Hovnat'an, Hakob and Harut'iwn Hovnat'an, Mkrtum, Hakob, Jr., and Aghat'on Hov-nat'an—succeeded each other for over a period of more than two hundred years and advanced Armenian art to a higher stage of development, enriching it with master-pieces of the brush.

The renowned Hovnat'anian family came from the town of Shoṙot' in the district of Ernjak. The early mini-ature art and wall paintings of certain members of this family—which also produced poets such as Naghash Hovnat'an and the brothers Hakob and Harut'iwn—and some of the creations of their mature period are closely connected with the wall paintings in the architectural monuments in their ancestral districts of Ernjak, Goght'n, and Nakhchawan, with the local scriptoria and especially with the art of the schools of Agulis and Shoṙot'. This period (seventeenth and eighteenth cen-tury) of the history of the family has been neglected by modern scholars.

Besides their many wall paintings in the monasteries of Armenia (in Erevan and Ējmiatsin) and Tiflis, Naghash Hovnat'an and Hakob and Harut'iwn diligently worked on the monuments of Shoṙot', Agulis, Abrakunis, As-tapat, Aznaberd, and other towns and villages. Only damaged remnants and fragments of these works remain, and they have never been studied.

The forefather of the Hovnat'anian family was Hov-nat'an (1661–1721), who is usually surnamed Naghash [painter]. He was born in Shoṙot' to the family of a teacher, the "philologist, scribe, and painter" Hov-hannēs of Shoṙot'. From the poems and meager biogra-phy of Naghash Hovnat'an we learn that he spent many years in Shoṙot', Agulis, Erevan, and Tiflis. He accom-panied the merchants of Agulis to Persia and visited a number of European cities, such as Venice, Marseilles, Amsterdam, Rome, and Trieste. Naghash Hovnat'an is well known in the history of Armenian civilization as a talented poet, musician, teacher, scribe, miniature artist, and painter of murals and portraits, whose art is closely tied with the land of Armenia and the Armenian ethnos. The title Naghash, given to him by the people and used by him in a number of his poems, and also used in reference to him by his son Hakob in his famous poem "I Lament with Tears, with Mournful Grief," bears witness to the fact that he was indeed a painter. Hakob wrote the above poem in 1721, on the occasion of the death of his father. It is a testament to the creative life of Naghash Hovnat'an. In the poem the artist is described as "the talented and wise master who was forever decorating the shrines of Armenian saints that stood like golden pil-lars"; "from his pen colorful flowers bloomed"; "he was a scribe who designed ancient and modern characters."

Summing up the accomplishments of the artist and his place in the history of art, Hakob writes:

He departed but his fame remained,
A renowned man, Naghash Hovnat'an.[3]

The surname of Hovnat'an remained in his family and his name became well known in the history of Armenian art and literature.

According to his biographers,[4] Naghash Hovnat'an was a graduate of the noted school of the St. T'ovma Monastery of Agulis, where he also worked as a teacher and a scribe. In manuscripts that he copied there he calls himself "the scribe Hovnat'an," or "Hovnat'an the clerk." In manuscripts painted by him in Agulis there are a number of miniatures with lay motifs, marginal ornaments, scenes, and flower motifs that reveal the worldly characteristics of the early art of the artist. The manuscript of 1682, which he copied in St. K'ristap'or Church[5] of Agulis, is of importance for its calligraphy. The miniatures on its cloth flyleaf are also assigned to Naghash Hovnat'an.

It was noted above that there were traces of the early wall paintings of Naghash Hovnat'an on the walls of the churches of Agulis and Shoṙot'. These were probably executed in the 1680s. Traces of Naghash's wall paintings have also been preserved in the church of St. T'ovma Monastery of Agulis and St. K'ristap'or Church. Unfortunately most of the paintings are now in a damaged state. The wall paintings inside the dome of St. T'ovma, as well as those on the areas below the dome and on the arches above the pillars and under the arch of the western portal of the church, have survived. These, together with the testimony of M. P'ap'azian in his short description,[6] indicate that all of the interior walls of St. T'ovma below the arches were covered with paintings in yellowish-gold color. The areas to the level of the arches were covered with paintings in white and blue. The arches and the entire ceiling of the church were painted in various colors with bright flower motives and vases full of flowers. The floral motifs on the walls of St. T'ovma (Figs. 95–98) are similar to Naghash's miniature floral decorations, in which the delicate images of birds give a peculiar animation to the colorful flowers.

The magnificent interior of the dome of St. T'ovma is unique. Here Naghash Hovnat'an has envisaged the ceiling as the sky (Fig. 97) and painted it in a light blue color. The stars painted on that background seem to twinkle and make the beholder believe he is looking into the depths of the universe. The style and the decorations of the paintings on the drum of the dome and the arches above the pillars of St. T'ovma, as well as those on the walls of St. K'ristap'or Church, are similar to Hovnat'an's paintings in the Cathedral of Ējmiatsin. According to M. P'ap'azian, the ceiling of the apse of St. T'ovma was also painted so that it represented the sky. In the four corners above the pillars of the apse there were four angels with their wings spread wide. On the upper parts of the stones of the bema there were reliefs and colorful paintings, and on the marbles at the two extremities of the bema, below the steps, was the relief of Saint Stephen the Protomartyr clad in deacon's garment.

Above the western portal of St. T'ovma there is a tall arch with striking reliefs. On the tympanum there is a relief (Fig. 95) depicting the doubt of the Apostle Thomas. Christ appears in the relief in standing position, embracing a large wooden cross. His right arm is raised and he is showing to Thomas his side, which was pierced by the lance. Thomas, who is depicted in a seated position, is carefully feeling the wound with his right hand in order to be certain. In addition to this biblical motif Naghash Hovnat'an has painted the image of God above Christ, and under and to the left of the curving arch he has portrayed an episode from the life of the Mother of God. To the right of the arch he has delineated the full image of Mary Magdalene. The radiant image of the sun with a female face above the head of the Mother of God and the representation of the half-moon sailing in the sky above the head of Mary Magdalene convey in this work the characteristics of easel painting. In order to create a connection between the relief and the paintings, Naghash Hovnat'an skillfully painted the relief so that at first glance it looks like a painting. The profiles above the western portal of St. T'ovma are unfortunately the only extant fragments of Naghash's iconography. These are in harmony with the architecture and ornamentation of the portal and enhance its beauty and magnificence. The art, coloring, and the floral motifs in the paintings of St. T'ovma and St. K'ristap'or churches of Agulis, the Cathedral of Ējmiatsin, Pōghos-Petros Church of Erevan, and other monuments indicate that Naghash Hovnat'an had

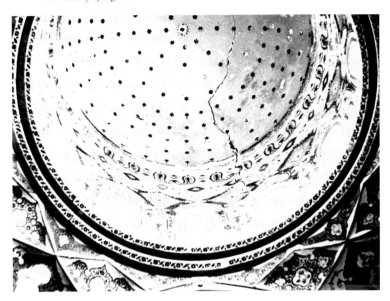

Fig. 97. Paintings inside the dome of the church of St. T'ovma Monastery of Agulis.

made an in-depth study of similar motifs used in miniature painting and especially in rug weaving. Naghash Hovnat'an based his art on the traditions of Armenian miniature painting and then moved in the direction of easel painting, which was already developed by the seventeenth century. There is also a connection between the art and poetry of Naghash. It is important to note that the floral ornaments in Naghash's wall paintings are full of worldly joy, the source of which is nature. Like the worldly sources of his poetic inspiration, the natural colors are the basic elements of Naghash's art. Natural scenes and expressions of vernal colors in his poetry also appear in the wall paintings. For example, some of his poetic images—"they shine with a starlike color," "red petal of rose," "pomegranate, red flower of pomegranate," "red rose," "floral lapis lazuli with golden petals," "bright red rose," "spring decorated with grace," "a vase painted in gold," "decorated with blooming

Fig. 98. Paintings inside the drum of the dome of the church of St. T'ovma Monastery of Agulis.

trees"—are themes that are also present in his wall paintings.

The miniatures and wall paintings of Naghash Hovnat'an bear witness to the fact that his art, like his poetry, burgeoned in Agulis and Shoṙot', his home, where he acquired the basic skills that gave him an opportunity to become known as "the talented and wise master."

Naghash Hovnat'an spent the last years of his life in his native Shoṙot'; he died and was buried there. At home he spent his time teaching and painting.[7] It is possible that he also worked with his sons on the wall paintings in the churches of his ancestral district, in the towns of Shoṙot', Abrakunis, and Astapat. For example, the extant wall paintings in the apse of the church of St. Karapet Monastery of Abrakunis, which consist of floral motifs, are in many ways similar to the flyleaf of the manuscript of 1682 copied by Naghash, according to M. Mkrtch'ian.[8] Our research on these and the paintings in the niches of St. Karapet leads us to guess that they are of three layers, the first of which probably belongs to Naghash Hovnat'an, whose two sons painted the walls in 1740.

One can also see the remains of seventeenth- and eighteenth-century wall paintings on the St. Hakob, St. Lusaworich', and St. Astuatsatsin churches of Shoṙot', which are traditionally ascribed to Naghash Hovnat'an. These paintings are at present in a badly damaged state. A small extant fragment, which is a section of a floral motif, in St. Lusaworich' Church is still visible on the arch of the southern pillar of the porch, which is attached to the western elevation of the church. The damaged remains of wall paintings in the beautiful interior of St. Hakob Church can be seen on the ceiling of the apse and on the drum of the dome. In the smaller, single-naved St. Astuatsatsin Church only the decorations in the apse and on the arches have been preserved. Besides floral motives on the arch of the apse, there are above the niches in the nine sides of the apse the portraits of nine apostles whose faces and other parts are now effaced (Fig. 99a–b). These portraits are enclosed by fine floral

Fig. 99a–b. Wall paintings in St. Astuatsatsin Church of Shorot'.

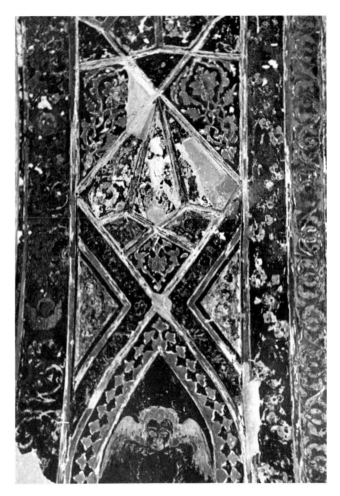

motifs. The garments of the apostles stretch down in folds, emphasizing their monumental stature. The compositional structure of the portraits in the apse of St. Astuatsatsin Church and the floral motifs are stylistically similar to the wall paintings of St. T'ovma of Agulis, St. Karapet of Abrakunis, and Karmir Vank' of Astapat.

At the end of the seventeenth century, Naghash Hovnat'an and his sons Hakob and Harut'iwn introduced a new momentum in the development of Armenian painting. The brothers Hakob and Harut'iwn, who were also talented, were since early youth taught by their father the art of painting and writing poetry, to which they devoted their entire lives. They transmitted to their heirs the secrets of their profession. Besides being a skilled painter, Hakob Hovnat'anian was also known as a poet. About thirty of his poems have survived. From the biographical ir.formation on Hakob and Harut'iwn we learn that they were born in Shoṙot' and received their elementary education there. Shoṙot' and its active cultural

life played a great role in the development of the two brothers. Like Naghash Hovnat'an, his sons also began their artistic careers by copying manuscripts and painting miniatures. There are at present a number of manuscripts copied and decorated by the two brothers preserved in the Matenadaran of Erevan (nos. 11533,

Fig. 101. The paintings of Hakob and Harut'iwn Hovnat'anian in the apse of St. Karapet Church of Abrakunis.

Fig. 100. The paintings of Hakob and Harut'iwn Hovnat'anian inside the dome of St. Karapet Church of Abrakunis.

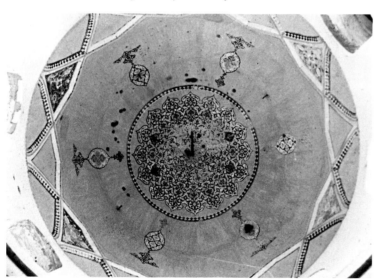

Fig. 102a–b. Paintings in the apsidal niche of St. Karapet Church of Abrakunis.

ligraphy and miniature art. It contains more than 240 images, 220 compositions, and many floral and marginal decorations.

In the history of eighteenth-century Armenian art Hakob and Harut'iwn Hovnat'anian are also known as skilled wall painters who first worked with their father and then by themselves. They painted the walls of a number of churches and palaces in various districts of Armenia. The brothers helped their father decorate the walls of the Cathedral of Ējmiatsin, painting a group of portraits—those of "the patriarch Hayk," King Trdat, Queen Ashkhēn, Princess Khosrovidukht, the Virgin Hr̄ip'simē, and others. According to the literary sources, Hakob and Harut'iwn also participated in the project of decorating the palace of King Vakhtang VI in Tiflis, a task that was undertaken by their father. In 1750 they decorated with fine artistic taste the monastic guest house of Ghazarapat (in Ējmiatsin), the newly constructed buildings in the monastery, and more.

21624, 8645). These are richly decorated with numerous kinds of lay and religious motifs, miniatures, portraits, and marginal ornaments. The synaxarion (509 pages)[9] that the two brothers copied in 1729–30 at Ējmiatsin is a unique example of eighteenth-century Armenian cal-

Fig. 103a–e. The paintings of Hakob and Harut'iwn Hovnat'anian in St. Grigor Church of Aznaberd.

(continued)

Fig. 103a-e (continued)

The brothers Hakob and Harut'iwn also did some work on the monuments of Ernjak and its vicinity. There are fragments of wall paintings executed by them in the churches of Abrakunis, Astapat, and Aznaberd that have survived. The wall paintings and decorations of the church of Karmir Vank' of Astapat, which were renovated and restored in 1860, made the interior of the church more picturesque and expressive through a synthesis of colors. At present the dome and a great part of the roof are destroyed and most of the wall paintings are effaced. One can still see remains of paintings in the apse, on the pillars, and on the upper parts of the walls. E. Lalayian states that in the dome, on the drum, and on the squinches there were the portraits of apostles and saints.[10] The ceiling of the apse and the arches of the church of Karmir Vank' were covered with magnificent paintings and the portraits in the niches were in a frame of colorful floral decorations.

One of the important stages in the art of Hakob and Harut'iwn were the paintings on the walls of St. Karapet Monastery of Abrakunis. The inscription that they left on the western wall of the second story of the southern vestry of the church stated that the task was accomplished in 1740. This inscription was still visible in a damaged state until the end of 1978. Fragments of floral motifs in the dome, the apse, and the two niches of the hall have also survived (Figs. 100–102a–b). On the upper parts of the apse and above the niches there used to be portraits of the Mother of God, Saint Paul, and Saint Peter in fully erect position. The painting style of the murals of St. Karapet of Abrakunis is related to that of the works of Naghash Hovnat'an in the Cathedral of Ējmiatsin insofar as principles of composition, iconography, and coloring are concerned. The Hovnat'anian brothers even utilized the floral motifs of Naghash in the Cathedral of Ējmiatsin and strove to decorate the interior of the church of St. Karapet as a single unit.

The ornamentation inside the dome of St. Karapet of Abrakunis is composed of multi-colored flowers enclosed in a regular frame (Fig. 101). On the entire inte-rior area of the dome, which is painted in gold, there are twenty-four geometric designs and decorations resembling trees that begin at the perimeter of the dome and are evenly distributed. These draw the onlooker's eye to the center of the dome. The fragment of wall painting preserved in the apse of the church (Fig. 102) is distinguished by its fine composition and coloring. The composition of the painting inside the dome of St. Karapet Church reminds one of that in the dome of the famed cathedral of St. Step'anos Monastery (now on the Iranian side of the Arax River) of Magharda or Shamb, which is the district adjacent to Ernjak. There are also similarities between the paintings on the arches of St. Step'anos, St. T'ovma, and St. K'ristap'or churches of Agulis.[11] Unfortunately the paintings on the walls of St. Step'anos Monastery of Magharda have not been studied by specialists. Similarities in compositional and coloring details lead us to surmise that the Hovnat'anians also painted the walls of St. Step'anos Monastery during the seventeenth and the eighteenth centuries.

The remnants of the paintings of Hakob and Harut'iwn Hovnat'anian have also been preserved in St. Grigor Church of Aznaberd.[12] Here the portraits and the compositions on the arches of the apse, the southern wall of the hall, the areas above the entrances to the vestries, and the twelve Apostles on the facade of the bema, as well as those on the four pillars of the church, are surrounded with floral decorations and enclosed in black lines. In 1867, new paintings were executed in the tradition of the art of Hakob and Harut'iwn Hovnat'anian, and the older ones were restored. The restorer, according to the inscriptions inside the church, accomplished this task during July and August of 1867. He tried to preserve the details, color tones, and characteristics of the earlier portraits. One can especially notice this in the portraits of Saint Mashtots', Saint Sahak Part'ew, Saint John Chrysostom, the Mother of God, the twelve apostles, and Saint George that are on the facade of the bema, the apse, and the wall of the southern vestry. In the wall paintings of the church of Aznaberd (Fig.

103a−e), one can feel the artistic conception characteristic of the mid-eighteenth-century painters of the Hovnat'anian family, especially that of Hakob and Harut'iwn. In comparing the different sections of the wall paintings in the church of Aznaberd with those preserved in St. Karapet of Abrakunis and Karmir Vank' of Astapat, which were executed by Hakob and Harut'iwn Hovnat'anian, we notice many common features shared by them in the interpretation of forms, the style of details, and the artistic unity of the paintings throughout the interior of the monument.

Besides working on miniatures, wall paintings, and portraits, Harut'iwn Hovnat'anian was also involved in the applied arts. He is known to have carved different kinds of floral decorations, images of birds, and other ornaments on wood. Master craftsmen used these to stamp decorations on cloth, carpets, rugs, drapery, and tablecloths.

Fragments of nineteenth-century wall paintings have also been preserved inside St. Astuatsatsin basilican church of Bist, which has a nave and two aisles. One can still see the damaged wall paintings above the niches and on the ceiling of the apse. The inscriptions under the icons of saints and heads of angels testify that these were painted in 1877.

We must also mention that there are fragments of wall paintings preserved in St. Astuatsatsin Church of Ŕamis in which new paintings, made after the middle of the nineteenth century, covered the eighteenth-century work. At that same time various icons of saints, enclosed in rectangular black frames, were painted in the apse and on the facade of the bema, and the arches of the nave as well as the ceiling of the apse were decorated with floral motifs and images of angels. Today one can see only fragments of these. Fragments of floral motifs have also survived in the niches of the apse and on its ceiling. Certain fragments on the western wall appear to be floral decorations comprising bunches of flowers placed in vases that have handles in the form of chirping birds.

In concluding this brief sketch on the extant wall paintings in the architectural monuments of Nakhichevan, we would like to note that the art of the renowned Hovnat'anian family and that of the school that flourished in New Julfa (Isfaan) were offshoots of the magnificent ancient artistic traditions of the scriptoria and schools of Agulis, Shoŕot', Nakhichevan, Astapat, old Julfa, Abrakunis, Norashēn, Ts'ghna, Bist, and Kuk'i. Generations of painters from this tradition traveled beyond the borders of historic Armenia and reached Saint Petersburg and Moscow, decorating the palaces and galleries of those cities with their masterpieces.

As in the different districts of Armenia, so also in Nakhichevan there are extant and ruined bridges on the ancient highways. These monuments were built at times of prosperity when commerce flourished. The study of bridges is important to any reconstruction of the patterns of the ancient commercial routes and the socioeconomic history of Armenia. From our survey we know that since ancient times the highways built in Nakhichevan had a local and international significance for transit trade and played an essential role in the development of local cultural ties with the outside world and in the expansion of the channels of communication inside the country. The roads along the Arax River pass through plains and fields (the plains of Sharur, Nakhichevan, and Julfa), and in the mountains they cross a number of mountain passes and defiles (the passes of Sisian and Arp'a), and the Gilan, Ernjak, Nakhichevan, and Arp'a rivers. The ancient paths connecting the dwelling sites in these plains or near the mountain passes and the mouths of rivers served as the groundwork for the major as well as secondary medieval and early modern highways of Armenia.

Our survey of the sites mentioned in this book shows that there were several large and small stone bridges in various parts of Nakhichevan that were built over swift rivers, brooks, and deep defiles in the valleys. Unfortunately most of these bridges have reached us in ruins and insignificant remains. In present-day Nakhichevan there are fifteen to seventeen bridges, some still standing, others in a semidilapidated state. Despite the lack of information in the historical sources, most of these bridges were built or rebuilt in the seventeenth and the eighteenth centuries. Geographically most of the bridges are located on the Gilan and Ernjak rivers and their tributaries, and their structures range from those that have a single arch to those with five arches.

We should first note a number of bridges on the Arax River that unfortunately were destroyed. The most famous of these was the magnificent bridge with four arches that had been built near Julfa. The ruins of its piers can still be seen today on the Persian side of the border. According to sixteenth-century Kurdish historian Sharif ad-Din, this bridge, which was on a major highway passing through Julfa and was internationally important ever since the early Middle Ages, "is founded on polished rock. . . . Its top is amazingly smooth and the stones are firmly joined to each other so that the most skillful architect will be amazed. The arches are so high and wide that the pier of one of them is sixty Persian cubits and that of the other is fifty cubits. Below the arch there is a caravanserai on the two sides of which there are amazingly beautiful doors."[1] According to a number of historical sources, this famous bridge "was [still] standing until 1400 or 1500, but at the time of the deportation of the [Armenian] inhabitants of Julfa [in 1604] it was in ruins. Passing through Julfa, the travelers Tavernier in 1655, Chardin in 1673, and Tourneford in 1700 crossed the river by boat and noted that the bridge was in ruins."[2] Ghewond Alishan notes that "later sources say [the bridge] was [still] standing until Shah Abbas destroyed it."[3]

Among the famous bridges of Nakhichevan we must also mention that of Aza, or Der, in the village of Aza, which is in the region of Ordubad. This bridge is still standing and open to traffic. It can support up to eight or ten tons easily. The bridge of Aza is built over the Gilan, the largest river in Goght'n, and is 2.3 kilometers from the Arax River. The bridge has five arches and is built of polished blocks of stone. The width and height of the arches differ because of the terrain. The width of the road passing over the bridge is 4.5 meters. The road is lined with side walls that are 0.60 meters high. In the lower parts of the three central piers that face the current of the river there are projections that produce a secure hydraulic system near the bridge. In order to relieve the heavy, dense mass of the structure an arcaded corridor was built inside the bridge. The sources say nothing about the earlier form of the bridge of Aza. Geographically the bridge served as a connecting point on one of the major highways of early medieval Armenia. Consequently the earlier structure was probably built in the early Middle Ages. It was rebuilt a number of times, with the present bridge rebuilt in the seventeenth century. Its structure, with its five arches, is similar to that of the bridge of Oshakan on the K'asakh River. According to Ghewond Alishan, the bridge of Aza was renovated in the nineteenth century "with the support of Awetik' Tēr Mkrtdch'ian of Agulis."[4]

The next important bridge on the Gilan River is located a little below the historic village of Bohrut, or Bekhrut and is now in ruins. The structure had three arches and connected a number of important villages and towns of Goght'n and Ernjak. The bridge's piers rest on the rocky banks of the river. The structure was built of polished blocks of basalt and semipolished blocks of sandstone and is 4 meters wide. From its architectural characteristics one may assume that it was built in the fourteenth or the fifteenth century and was renovated in the seventeenth or the eighteenth century. The two arches of the bridge were destroyed by floods in the second half of the nineteenth century.

About 3 to 4 kilometers beyond the bridge of Bohrut and to the east of the village of P'ařaka there is another bridge, which stands on the P'ařaka Brook, a tributary of the Gilan River. This structure has one arch and its piers rest on the rocky banks of the river. It is built of polished and semipolished blocks of stone. Through this bridge Shořot', Mesropawan, Tewi, and other towns and villages maintained a constant tie with Agulis, Ts'ghna, Orduar, and other places. The arch of the bridge was destroyed by floods. There is no information on the date of its construction. Our guess is that it was built in the seventeenth century.

There are two seventeenth-century bridges in the village of Bist, which is located to the northeast of P'ařaka. The first one is on the Norakert Brook, which flows along the northern border of Bist and is a tributary of the Gilan River, and the second one is on the Mesropawan River, which flows along the southern border of the village. The piers of the bridge on the Norakert Brook rest on high, rocky hills along the banks of the brook. This bridge, which has one arch (Fig. 104), is built of polished and semipolished blocks of stones and is still in operation. Since ancient times it connected the village with the renowned Hermitage of St. Nshan, with several towns and villages in the district of Ernjak, and especially with the town of Shořot'. There is no information on the date of its construction or renovation. From its structural

Fig. 104. Bist bridge over the Norakert Brook.

characteristics one may assume that it was built or re-built in the seventeenth century.

The second bridge of Bist on the Mesropawan River also has a single arch. Its piers, which are built of polished blocks of stone, rest on the rocky banks of the river. Being operative and wide, it is to this day the only means of approach for traffic to and from Bist. Trucks weighing as much as eight to ten tons travel over it easily. There is no information on the date of construction of this bridge. Our guess is that it was built in the middle the seventeenth century. The date 1869 appears on a stone set in the upper part of the eastern facade of the southern pier and facing the arch; this is probably when the bridge was renovated.

To the west of the historic village of Oghohi-Aghahets'ik, which is 2.5 kilometers to the northeast of Bist, there is another beautiful bridge with two arches on the Norakert Brook. The width of the arches are not identical because of the terrain. The bridge is built of

Fig. 105. Lak'at'agh Bridge over the Ernjak River.

semipolished and polished blocks of stone and flagstone. The vaulted arches and the facades were built so sturdily that the bridge is still in a good condition and continues to function. There is no information on the date of its construction. Our guess is that it was built before 1663, since it is mentioned in the inscription of 1663 at the Monastery of St. Khach' in Aghahets'ik.

For centuries the bridge of Aghahets'ik, which stands on one of the mountain highways of Goght'n, has connected the towns and villages of Goght'n and Ernjak. Since one of the roads going to Karabakh passed over it, it is called ''the bridge on the road to Karabakh'' in the inscription of St. Khach' Monastery.

The survey of the region and the historical sources indicate that there were also a number of bridges on the Ernjak River. The bridges in Shahkert, Norashēn, Khanagha (Parontēr), K'r̄na, and Lak'at'agh (Fig. 105) were considered important monuments between the seventeenth and nineteenth centuries. Unfortunately only the bridge in Shahkert had survived the wear and tear of time.

The Shahkert bridge spans the Ernjak River near the village. It has one arch and is built of polished blocks of stone and lime mortar. It is still in operation today. According to its building inscription, it was constructed in 1551 by Pōghos Ghazanch'ets'i of Shahkert.

The bridge near the village of Norashēn is in ruins. But according to A. Sedrakian, ''It was built with magnificently polished stones. . . . An extraordinarily devastating flood in the August of 1871 destroyed half of it.''[5] According to M. Smbatian, two brothers from Norashēn, Khoja Mkrtich' and Khoja Hanēs, built this monument in 1663. They also donated to St. Karapet Monastery of Abrakunis a gospel that they had received.[6]

One can see the insignificant traces of a number of destroyed medieval bridges on the Arp'a, Nakhichevan, Truneats', and Vanand rivers and their tributaries. All of these had single arches. On the highway connecting Nakhichevan with Sisian, over the Saghuasonk' rivulet, the modern Salasuz, which is a tributary of the Nakhichevan River, there is a bridge with a single arch erected at the beginning of the nineteenth century and built of polished blocks of tuff and lime mortar. Until 1970 the traffic from Nakhichevan to Sisian crossed over this bridge. The ruins of the bridges on the Truneats' or Van-and River—those at K'aghak'ik, Trunis, Khanagha, Disar, and other villages—are well known monuments with single arches.

A number of large and small bridges have also survived in the major towns of Nakhichevan—Agulis, Orduar, Ts'ghna, Shoṙot', and others. These bridges span brooks that flow through the above cities and connect the different quarters on both sides. The remains of the piers of such a bridge are found in the central quarter of Ts'ghna, which is called Karmunji hraparak [bridge square]. One can also see the ruins of bridges in the northeastern and western parts of the town of Shoṙot'. These connected the ancient town with the monasteries and the nearby villages.

In Verin [Upper] Agulis there are two bridges that are still standing and a number of others in ruins. The first of the extant bridges is in Vank'i T'agh [monastic quarter] and is located in a small glen on the side of the mountain to the south of that quarter. The second bridge is well known in history and stands over the Agulis River, which bisects the city of Agulis. The bridge is near the marketplace. The structure that preceded it was rebuilt in the seventeenth century. On July 2, 1872, "the arch of the bridge, which was built of stone, was destroyed by a flood." It was rebuilt and destroyed again by the flood of 1884.[7] It was rebuilt once again and is still in operation.

The bridges described in this chapter are part of the architectural testament of Nakhichevan. Their structural characteristics and artistic features are closely connected to those of the bridges of medieval Armenia. No work on the bridge-building techniques of medieval Armenia would be complete without a detailed study of all the bridges in Nakhichevan.

Map 1. Historical Nakhichevan.

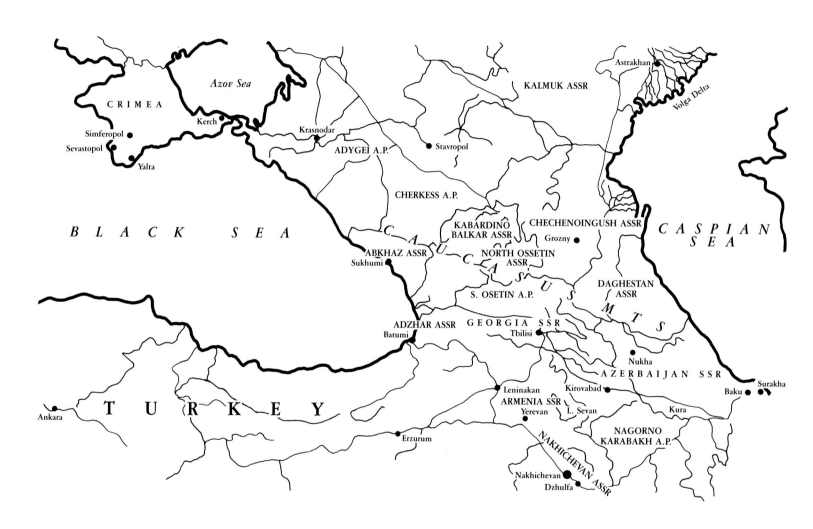

Map 2. Present-day Nakhichevan ASSR.

INTRODUCTION

1. Samvelian, *Hin Hayastani kulturan*, vol. 1 (Erevan, 1931), p. 118.

2. O. Abibulaev, *Arkheologicheskie raskopki Kiul'-tepe* (Baku, 1959); idem, "Nekotorye itogi izucheniia kholma Kiul'-tepe," *Sovetskaia arkheologiia* (Moscow), no. 3 (1963), pp. 157–68.

3. Samvelian, *Hin Hayastani kulturan*, p. 28.

4. *Komunist* (Armenian newspaper published in Baku), 24 December 1976.

5. A. Ayvazian, "Arba ew Chahuk berderě," *Lraber hasarakakan gitut'yunneri*, no. 9 (1976), pp. 88–91.

6. *Hay zhoghovrdi patmut'yun*, vol. 3 (Erevan, 1976), pp. 115–25.

7. *Hay zhoghovrdi patmut'yun* (hnaguyn zhamanaknerits' minch'ew mer ōrerě) (Erevan, 1972), p. 341. *Obozrenie rossiiskikh vladenii za Kavkazom*, part 3 (Saint Petersburg, 1836), pp. 328–29.

8. *Atlas Azerbaidzhanskoi SSR* (Baku, Moscow, 1963), p. 12.

9. H. Manandian, *K'nnakan tesut'yun hay zhoghovrdi patmut'yan*, vol. 2 (Erevan, 1960), pp. 146, 152–55, 333–37.

10. A. Salamzade, *Adzhemi Abubekr oglu i arkhitekturnye pamiatniki Nakhichevanskoi ASSR* (in Azerbaijani) (Baku, 1976).

11. T'urkakan aghbyurnerě Hayastani, hayeri ew Andrkovkasi myus zhoghovurdneri masin, vol. 1 (Erevan, 1961), p. 34.

12. V. Step'anyan, *Yerkrasharzherě haykakan leřnashkharhum ew nra merdzakayk'um* (Erevan, 1964), pp. 218–41.

13. The plans of the monuments are ours. The plans of the churches of Astapat and Aznaberd were prepared by the architect Murad Hasrat'yan.

THE DISTRICT OF GOGHT'N

1. *Movsēs Khorenats'i, Patmut'iwn Hayots'* [Moses Khorenats'i, *History of the Armenians*, trans. and comm. on the literary sources by Robert W. Thomson (Cambridge, Mass.: Harvard University Press, 1978)], pp. 120–21.

2. E. Aghayian, "Goght'n-Goght'an teghanuně," *Lraber hasarakakan gitut'yunneri*, no. 12 (1957), pp. 51–52.

3. Koriwn, *Vark' Mashtots'i* [Koriun, *The Life of Mashtots*, trans. Bedros Norehad, Armenian General Benevolent Union of America, 1964)], p. 28.

4. *Movsēs Khorenats'i*, p. 143.

5. *Step'anosi Siwneats' episkoposi Patmut'iwn tann Sisakan*, ed. Mkrtich' Ēmin (Moscow, 1861), p. 15. (Hereafter Step'anos Orbelean.)

6. Nicholas Adontz, *Armenia in the Period of Justinian*, trans. Nina G. Garsoian (Lisbon, 1970), pp. 67*, 69*. According to Adontz, both lists are fictional.

7. A. G. Abrahamian, *Anania Shirakats'u matenagrut'yuně* (Erevan, 1944), p. 350.

8. *T'ovma Artsruni, Patmut'iwn tann Artsruneats'* (Tiflis, 1917), p. 404.

9. Ghewond Alishan, *Sisakan* (Venice, 1893), pp. 324–25.

10. S. Eremian, *Hayastaně ěst "Ashkharats'oyts'i"* (Erevan, 1967), p. 74. According to Movsēs Khorenats'i, Tigranes the Great settled the offsprings of Astyages in Oskiogha and the other appanages in Goght'n and Nakhchawan. Movsēs Khorenats'i, *History*, trans. R. W. Thomson, p. 120.

11. *Zak'aria Agulets'u oragrut'yuně* (Erevan, 1938), pp. 5, 7, 110 passim.

12. E. Lalayian, *Goght'n kam Ordubadi kam Verin Agulisi ostikanakan shrjan* (Tiflis, 1904), pp. 61–62. This is an offprint from *Azgagrakan Handēs*. (Hereafter *Goght'n.*)

13. M. T'aghiadian, *Chanaparhordut'iwn i Hays*, vol. 1 (Calcutta, 1847), p. 66.

14. Lalayian, *Goght'n*, pp. 66–67.

15. *Pazmaveb*, vol. 52 (Venice, 1894), pp. 534–35.

16. M. Sarian, *Graṙumner im kyank'its'*, vol. 1 (Erevan, 1966), p. 141.

17. *Mshak* (newspaper published in Tiflis), no. 36 (1872), p. 2.

18. P. Pṙoshian, *Erkeri zhoghovatsu*, vol. 7 (Erevan), p. 276.

19. Alishan, *Sisakan*, pp. 331–33.

20. Leo, *Hayots' patmut'yun*, vol. 3 (Erevan, 1946), p. 763.

21. *Ardzagank'* (weekly published in Tiflis), no. 25 (1884).

22. See A. Ayvazian, "Agulisi chartarapetakan hushardzannerě," *Lraber hasarakakan gitut'yunneri*, no. 2 (1978), pp. 72–86.

23. *Abraham kat'oghikos Kretats'woy Patmagrut'iwn ants'its'n iwrots' ew Natr-Shahin parsits'* (Vagharshapat, 1870), p. 77.

24. V. M. Sysoev, "Nakhichevanskii krai—Nakh. ASSR (otchet o poezdke letom 1972 g.)," *Izvestiia Azkomstarisa,* issue 4, part 2 (Baku, 1929), p. 162.

25. *Hayeren dzeṙagreri ZHĒ dari hishatakaranner (1621–1640 t't'.),* vol. 2, comp. Vazgen Hakobian, Ashot Hovhannisian (Erevan, 1978), p. 826.

26. Lalayian, *Goght'n,* p. 66.

27. *Banber Matenadarani,* no. 12 (Erevan, 1977), p. 263.

28. Ibid., p. 265.

29. A. Araskhanian, "Pekhi-aghbiwr ew Snasents'-Khov," *Aghbiwr,* no. 11 (Tiflis, 1886), p. 399.

30. *Zak'aria Agulets'u oragrut'yunĕ,* pp. 140–41.

31. Ibid., p. 141.

32. Ibid., p. 14.

33. Ibid., pp. 128, 147.

34. A. Ghanalanian, *Avandapatum* (Erevan, 1969), p. 12.

35. Ibid., p. 37.

36. S. Ēp'rikian, *Patkerazard bnashkharhik baṙaran,* vol. 1 (Venice, 1903), p. 514.

37. *Kalvatsagrer ew tntesakan ayl gortsark'neri veraberyal arkhivayin vaveragrer,* comp. Harut'yun Abrahamian, fasc. 1 (Erevan, 1941), p. 6.

38. Khamdullakh-Kazvini, *Nuzaat-al-Kulub,* Rukopisnyi Fond AN AzSSR, rukopis' S-110/37–46.

39. S. Ter-Avetisian, *K arkheologicheskomu obsledovanniu Khoraba-Giliana* (Tiflis, 1927). The area was surveyed in 1975 by an expedition sponsored by the Academy of Sciences of Azerbaijan S.S.R.

40. A. Ayvazian, "Goght'n gavaṙi ch'inarnerĕ ew nrants' nahapetĕ," *Hayastani bnut'yun,* fasc. 2 (1975), pp. 53–55.

41. I. Ozarovskii, *Opyt voennogo obozreniia Zakavkaz'ia* (Saint Petersburg, 1883), p. 90.

42. I. Shopen, *Istoricheskie pamiatniki Armianskoi oblasti* (Saint Petersburg, 1852), p. 335.

43. *Pazmaveb,* 52 (1894), p. 495.

44. Lalayian, *Goght'n,* p. 60.

45. V. M. Sysoev, "Nakhichevanskii krai (Nakh. ASSR)," *Izvestiia Azkomstarisa,* issue 4, part 2 (Baku, 1929), p. 150.

46. Alishan, *Sisakan,* p. 321.

47. Shopen, *Istoricheskie pamiatniki Armianskoi oblasti,* p. 335.

48. Alishan, *Sisakan,* pp. 319–20. Alishan also published the photograph of the ruins of St. Step'anos Church of Anapat. See Plate 87 in *Sisakan.*

49. Lalayian, *Goght'n,* p. 60.

50. *The Catalogue of Mesrop Magistros,* Matenadaran of Erevan, Gospels, folder 2, p. 253.

51. M. Smbatian, *Nkaragir surb Karapeti vanits' Ernjakay ew shrjakayits' nora* (Tiflis, 1904), p. 150.

52. M. Barkhudariants', *Arts'akh* (Baku, 1895), p. 147.

53. Sanjain, Avedis, *A Catalogue of Medieval Armenian Manuscripts in the United States* (Berkeley: University of California Press, 1976), pp. 778–79.

54. Lalayian, *Goght'n,* p. 59.

55. Sysoev, "Nakhichevanskii krai," pp. 153–54.

56. For details on Ṙamis and its monuments, see A. Ayvazian, "Ṙamisi eṙanav bazilikan ew nra vimagrutyunnerĕ," *Patma-banasirakan handes,* no. 3 (1979), pp. 182–88.

57. Sysoev, "Nakhichevanskii krai," pp. 171–72.

58. Matenadaran, no. 604, p. 199ᵛ.

59. A. Abrahamian, *Mi ēj Andrkovkasi zhoghovurdneri ew hay-ṙusakan haraberut'yunneri patmut'yunits'* (Erevan, 1953), p. 232.

60. A. Ayvasian, "Ts'ghnayi chartarapetakan hushardzannerĕ," *Ējmiatsin* (March 1978), pp. 49–56; (July 1979), pp. 47–51.

61. Alishan, *Sisakan,* p. 342.

62. Alishan, *Sisakan,* p. 343.

63. *Abraham kat'oghikos Kretats'woy Patmagrut'iwn,* 77.

64. A. Ayvazian, "P'aṙakayi chartarapetakan hushardzannerĕ," *Banber Erevani Hamalsarani,* no. 1 (1979), pp. 207–16.

65. Alishan, *Sisakan,* p. 345.

66. Matenadaran, no. 604, p. 199ᵛ.

67. Matenadaran, no. 604, p. 200ᵛ.

68. Abrahamian, *Mi ēj Andrkovkasi zhoghovurdneri ew hay-ṙusakan haraberut'yunneri patmut'yunits',* p. 234.

69. *Sbornik svedenii o Kavkaze,* vol. 5, part 1 (Tiflis, 1880).

70. Alishan, *Sisakan,* p. 345.

71. Ibid., p. 345.

72. Aṙak'el of Tabriz, *Patmut'iwn Aṙak'el vardapeti Dawrizhets'woy* (Vagharshapat, 1896), p. 280.

73. Smbatian, *Nkaragir Surb Karapeti vanits' Ernjakay ew shrjakayits' nora,* p. 490; Lalayian, *Goght'n,* p. 92.

74. *Abraham kat'oghikos Kretats'woy Patmagrut'iwn,* p. 78.

75. Matenadaran, no. 6531, p. 264ʳ.

76. H. Acharian, *Ts'uts'ak hayerēn dzeṙagrats' T'awrizi* (Vienna, 1910), p. 125.

77. N. Pogharian, *Mayr ts'uts'ak dzeṙagrats' Srbots' Yakobeants',* vol. 1 (Jerusalem, 1966), p. 123.

78. *Abraham kat'oghikos Kretats'woy Patmagrut'iwn,* p. 78.

79. Aṙak'el of Tabriz, p. 630.

80. Lalayian, *Goght'n,* p. 90.

81. Matenadaran, the Catalog of Mesrop Magistros, Gospels, folder 2, p. 573.

82. *Abraham kat'oghikos Kretats'woy Patmagrut'iwn,* p. 78. On the monuments of Bist, see A. Ayvazian, "Goght'n gavaṙi Bist avani chartarapetakan hushardzannerĕ," *Patma-banasirakan handes,* no. 1 (1978), pp. 283–89.

83. *Abraham kat'oghikos Kretats'woy Patmagrut'iwn,* p. 78.

84. L. Khach'ikian, *ZHE dari hayeren dzeṙagreri hishatakaranner* (Masn aṙajin, Erevan, 1955), p. 73.

85. Step'anos Orbelean, p. 378; Alishan, *Sisakan*, p. 344.

86. Aṙak'el of Tabriz, p. 280.

87. H. Oskian, *Vaspurakan-Vani vankeṙ*, vol. 2 (Vienna, 1942), p. 715.

88. *Zak'aria Agulets'u oragrut'yunĕ*, p. 125.

89. Alishan, *Sisakan*, pp. 338–41; Lalayian, *Goght'n*, pp. 76–79.

90. Sysoev, "Nakhichevanskii krai (Nakh. ASSR)," pp. 174–83.

91. Lalayian, *Goght'n*, p. 76.

92. Alishan, *Sisakan*, p. 341.

93. Ibid., p. 338.

94. Smbatian, *Nkaragir S. Karapeti vanits' Ernjakay*, p. 489.

95. *Zak'aria Agulets'u oragrut'yunĕ*, p. 109.

96. L. Khach'ikian, *ZHE dari hayeren dzeṙagreri hishatakaranner*, part 3, 1481–1500 (Erevan, 1967), pp. 115–16.

97. Lalayian, *Goght'n*, p. 77.

98. Movsēs Khorenats'i, *History*, trans. R. W. Thomson, p. 188.

99. B. Piotrovskii, "Hay zhoghovrdi tsagman harts'i shurjĕ," *Teghekagir HSSH GA, hasarakakan gitut'yunner*, no. 6 (1945), p. 13.

100. K. Basmajian, "Hay nakhararutiwnnerĕ beweṙayin ardzanagrut'eants' mej," *Banaser*, nos. 8–9 (Paris, 1902).

101. N. Adontz, *Armenia in the Period of Justinian*, trans. N. Garsoian, pp. 68*, 69*. According to Adontz, the *Throne List* and the *Military List* are from the seventh century. Cf. chap. 10 in the above work.

102. Alishan, *Sisakan*, p. 338.

103. H. P'ap'azian, *Matenadarani parskeren kalvatsagrerĕ*, fasc. 1 (Erevan, 1968), pp. 290–91.

104. Alishan, *Sisakan*, p. 341.

105. Smbatian, *Nkaragir S. Karapeti vanits' Ernjakay*, p. 149.

106. H. P'ap'azian, *Matenadarani parskeren kalvatsagrerĕ*, fasc. 1 (Erevan, 1968), p. 93.

107. Ibid., p. 120.

108. Step'anos Orbelean, p. 13.

109. Ibid., p. 14.

110. Ghewond Alishan, *Hayapatum* (Venice, 1901), pp. 250–53.

111. Alishan, *Sisakan*, p. 311.

112. Ibid., p. 339.

113. Alishan, *Hayapatum*, p. 253; translation of "More Astonishing" by Diana Der Hovanessian from Diana Der Hovanessian and Marzbed Margossian, eds., *Anthology of Armenian Poetry* (New York: Columbia University Press, 1978), pp. 43–44.

114. On the publications of the printers from Vanand, see Alisan, *Sisakan*, pp. 339–40; Leo, *Erkeri zhoghovatsu*, vol. 2 (Erevan, 1969), pp. 459–72.

115. Smbatian, *Nkaragir S. Karapeti vanits' Ernjakay*, p. 491.

116. Lalayian, *Goght'n*, p. 79.

117. Sysoev, "Nakhichevanskii krai," p. 178.

118. Smbatian, *Nkaragir S. Karapeti vanits' Ernjakay*, p. 491.

119. Alishan, *Sisakan*, pp. 340–41.

120. Step'anos Orbelean, p. 242.

121. Alishan, *Sisakan*, p. 341.

122. *Zak'aria Agulets'u oragrut'yunĕ*, p. 7.

123. Lalayian, *Goght'n*, p. 79.

124. Alishan, *Sisakan*, p. 338.

125. Smbatian, *Nkaragir S. Karapeti vanits' Ernjakay*, pp. 310–11.

126. Sysoev, "Nakhichevanskii krai," p. 183.

THE DISTRICT OF ERNJAK

1. Alishan, *Sisakan*, p. 348.

2. Ibid., p. 349.

3. A. G. Abrahamian, *Anania Shirakats'u matenagrutyunĕ* (Erevan, 1944), p. 350.

4. H. Achaṙian, *Hayeren armatakan baṙaran*, vol. 2 (Erevan, 1930), pp. 859–60.

5. Alishan, *Sisakan*, pp. 363–66; I. Shcheblykin, *Pamiatniki Azerbaidzhanskogo sodchestva epokhi Nizami (Materialy)* (Baku, 1943), pp. 68–70.

6. Step'anos Orbelean, p. 7.

7. A. Ayvazian, "Ernjak berdĕ, *Lraber hasarakakan gitutyunneri*, no. 2 (Erevan, 1979), pp. 61–73.

8. H. Hakobian, *Ughegrut'yunner*, vol. 1, 1253–1582 (Erevan, 1932), p. 116.

9. Step'anos Orbelean, p. 139.

10. *Hishatakaran aghētits' Grigor Khlat'ets'woy* (Vagharshapat, 1897), pp. 9–11.

11. Smbatian, *Nkaragir S. Karapeti vanits' Ernjakay*, p. 359.

12. Step'anos Orbelean, p. 378.

13. A. Sedrakian, "Hnut'iwnk' i gawaṙin Ernjaku (Vagharshapat, 1872), p. 102.

14. Alishan, *Sisakan*, pp. 409–28; S. Ter-Avetisian, *Gorod Dzhugha* (Tiflis, 1937). A. Vruyr, "Jugha," *Patma-banasirakan handes*, no. 4 (1967), pp. 169–80; A. Ayvazian, "Jughan ew nra patmakan hushardzannerĕ," *Hayastani bnut'yun*, fasc. 2 (Erevan, 1976), pp. 34–37.

15. Alishan, *Sisakan*, p. 413.

16. H. Aṙak'elian, *Parskastani hayerĕ, nrants' ants'ealĕ, nerkan ew apagan*, part 1 (Vienna, 1911), p. 30.

17. Ṙ. P'ashaian, "Aram Vruyri antip namaknerĕ Nikolay Maṙin," *Garun*, no. 12 (Erevan, 1975), p. 75; Ṙ. P'ashaian, *Aram Vruyr* (Erevan, 1976), p. 87.

18. Alishan, *Sisakan*, p. 413.

19. Aṙak'elian, *Parskastani hayerĕ*, p. 413.

20. M. Smbatian, *Nkaragir S. Karapeti vanits' Ernjakay*, p. 484.

21. *Kalvatsagrer ew tntesakan ayl gortsark'neri veraberyal arkhivayin vaveragrer*, fasc. 1, comp. Har. Abrahamian (Erevan, 1941), p. 6.

22. M. Sarian, *Graṙumner im kyank'its'*, book 1 (Erevan, 1966), p. 140.

23. Alishan, *Sisakan*, p. 424.

24. A. L. Iakobson, "Ob armianskikh khachkarakh," *Istoriko-philologicheskii zhurnal*, no. 1 (1978), p. 222.

25. Sedrakian, *Hnut'iwnk*, p. 40.

26. Smbatian, *Nkaragir S. Karapeti vanits' Ernjakay*; A. Ayvazian, "Abrakunisi S. Karapet vank'ĕ," *Ējmiatsin* (July 1976), pp. 45–52.

27. Alishan, *Sisakan*, p. 369.

28. Step'anos Orbelean, p. 378.

29. Alishan, *Sisakan*, p. 370.

30. On this complex and its abbots, see Alishan's *Sisakan*, pp. 370–74.

31. Sedrakian, *Hnut'iwnk'*, p. 71.

32. Sedrakian, *Hnut'iwnk'*, p. 72; Alishan, *Sisakan*, pp. 369–70.

33. Matenadaran of Erevan, codex no. 68, p. 103ʳ.

34. *Sbornik svedenii o Kavkaze*, vol. 5, part 1 (Tiflis, 1880).

35. Sedrakian, *Hnut'iwnk'*, p. 81.

36. A. Ayvazian, "Norasheni chartarapetakan hushardzannerĕ," *Lraber hasarakakan gitut'iwnneri*, no. 8 (1980), pp. 110–15.

37. Step'anos Orbelean, p. 378.

38. Sedrakian, *Hnut'iwnk'*, p. 117.

39. H. Aṙak'elian, *Hanragitak baṙaran*, vol. 1 (Tiflis, 1915), pp. 1058–59.

40. Alishan, *Sisakan*, p. 366.

41. Ibid.

42. Ibid.

43. Smbatian, *Nkaragir S. Karapeti vanits' Ernjakay*, p. 177.

44. Ibid., p. 225.

45. Alishan, *Sisakan*, p. 366.

46. *Handes Amsorya*, vol. 71 (Vienna, 1957), pp. 170–71.

47. Alishan, *Sisakan*, p. 366.

48. Ibid., p. 367.

49. Ibid.

50. Smbatian, *Nkaragir S. Karapeti vanits' Ernjakay*, p. 261.

51. Alishan, *Sisakan*, p. 367.

52. Sedrakian, *Hnut'iwnk'*, p. 139.

53. Smbatian, *Nkaragir S. Karapeti vanits' Ernjakay*, p. 488.

54. Sedrakian, *Hnut'iwnk'*, p. 139.

55. A. Ayvazian, "Shoṙot'i ew Gaghi ekeghets'akan chartarapetakan hushardzannerĕ," *Ējmiatsin* (May 1977), pp. 46–51.

56. Shopen, *Istoricheskie pamiatniki armianskoi oblasti*, p. 325.

57. M. Hasrat'ian, *Syunik'i 17–18 dareri chartarapetakan hamalirnerĕ* (Erevan, 1973), p. 90.

58. Sedrakian, *Hnut'iwnk'*, pp. 124–25.

59. Ibid., pp. 125–26.

60. Ayvazian, "Shoṙot'i ew Gaghi ekeghets'akan chartarapetakan hushardzannerĕ," pp. 51–56.

61. *Staticheskoe opisanie Nakhichevanskoi provintsii* (Saint Petersburg, 1833), p. 75.

62. *Materialy dlia opisaniia mestnostei i plemen Kavkaza*, issue 2, section 2 (Tiflis, 1882), p. 46.

63. Step'anos Orbelean, p. 378.

64. Shopen, *Istoricheskie pamiatniki armianskoi oblasti*, p. 325.

65. Leo, *Patmut'yun Hayots'*, vol. 3 (Erevan, 1946), pp. 762–65.

66. M. Ch'amch'iants', *Patmut'iwn Hayots'*, vol. 3 (Venice, 1736), pp. 842–48; H. Aṙak'elian, *Hay zhoghovrdi mtavor mshakuyt'i zargats'man patmut'yun, 14–19rd dd. aṙajin kesĕ*, vol. 2 (Erevan, 1964), pp. 124–26.

67. Sedrakian, *Hnut'iwnk'*, pp. 108–9.

68. Ibid., p. 110.

69. H. Oskian, *Ts'uts'ak dzeṙagrats' Mkhit'arean Matenadaranin i Vienna*, vol. 2 (Vienna, 1963), p. 476.

70. Step'anos Orbelean, p. 378.

71. Matenadaran of Erevan, codex no. 4154, p. 220ᵛ.

72. Ibid., p. 221ʳ.

73. Smbatian, *Nkaragir S. Karapeti vanits' Ernjakay*, p. 152.

74. Step'anos Orbelean, p. 378.

75. Sedrakian, *Hnut'iwnk'*, pp. 115–16.

76. *Sbornik svedenii o Kavkaze*, vol. 5, part 1 (Tiflis, 1880).

77. Smbatian, *Nkaragir S. Karapeti vanits' Ernjakay*, p. 147.

78. *Staticheskoi opisanie Nakhichevanskoi provintsii*, 145.

79. See n. 76.

80. Smbatian, *Nkaragir S. Karapeti vanits' Ernjakay*, p. 357.

The District of Nakhichevan (Nakhchawan)

1. E. Lalayian, *Nakhijewani ostikanakan shrjan* (Tiflis, 1906), pp. 14–15. (Hereafter *Nakhijewan*.) *T'urk'akan aghbyurner*, trans. A. K. Safrastian, vol. 3 (Erevan, 1967), p. 71.

2. Movsēs Khorenats'i, *History of the Armenians,* trans. R. W. Thomson, p. 139.

3. Adontz, *Armenia in the Period of Justinian,* pp. 462–63.

4. A. G. Abrahamian, *Anania Shirakats'u matenagrut'yunĕ* (Erevan, 1944), p. 350.

5. T'ovma Artsruni, *Patmut'iwn tann Artsruneats'* (Tiflis, 1917), p. 404.

6. Movsēs Khorenats'i, *History,* p. 120.

7. P'awstosi Buzandats'woy patmut'iwn hayots' (Venice, 1914), p. 222.

8. H. Hakobian, *Ughegrutyunner,* vol. 1 (Erevan, 1932), p. 16.

9. *HSSH Patmut'yan Petakan Kentronakan Arkhiv,* fund 429, file 97, paper 4.

10. U. K. Nikitina, "Gorod Nakhichevan' i Nakhichevanskii uezd," *Materialy dlia opisaniia mestnosti i plemen Kavkaza,* issue 2 (Tiflis, 1881), pp. 112–13.

11. *Pazmaveb,* vol. 53 (1895), p. 160.

12. Lalayian, *Nakhijewan,* p. 41.

13. Step'anos Orbelean, p. 8.

14. T'ovma Artsruni, p. 105.

15. K. Samvelian, *Hin Hayastani kulturan,* vol. 1 (Erevan, 1931), p. 28.

16. See the details in M. Hasrat'ian, "Astapati vank'i chartarapetakan hamalirĕ," *Patma-banasirakan handes,* no. 1 (1975), pp. 126–48.

17. Alishan, *Sisakan,* pp. 507–8.

18. Lalayian, *Nakhijewan,* pp. 48–50.

19. Alishan, *Sisakan,* p. 508.

20. *Hayrenik'i dzayn* (Erevan weekly), no. 52 (74) (December 1966).

21. Lalayian, *Nakhijewan,* pp. 11–12.

22. O. Abibulaev, *Arkheologicheskie raskopki Kiul'-tapa* (Baku, 1959).

23. Lalayian, *Nakhijewan,* p. 61.

24. Aŕak'el of Tabriz, p. 190.

25. *Sbornik svedenii o Kavkaze,* vol. 5, part 1 (Tiflis, 1880).

26. Lalayian, *Nakhijewan,* p. 43.

27. P. Bedirian, "Baŕeri 'kensagrut'yunits'," *Hayots' lezu,* no. 1 (1977), p. 43.

28. Ibid., p. 44.

29. Movsēs Khorenats'i, *History,* p. 120.

30. Sebēos, *Patmut'iwn i Herakl* (Erevan, 1939), p. 120.

31. *Movsēs Kaghankatuats'i, Patmut'iwn Aghuanits'* (Paris, 1860), p. 44. [English trans. C. J. F. Dowsett, *The History of the Caucasian Albanians by Movsēs Dasxurançi* (London, 1961), p. 208.]

32. Ghewond, *Patmut'iwn Ghewondeay metsi vaŕdapeti hayots'* (Saint Petersburg, 1887), p. 33.

33. T'ovma Artsruni, p. 105. Cf. Vardan Patmich', *Hawak'umn patmut'ean* (Venice, 1862), p. 72.

34. *Ashkharhats'oyts' Vardanay Vardapeti* (Paris, 1960), p. 16.

35. Aŕak'el of Tabriz, pp. 523–24.

36. Mik'ayēl Ch'amch'ian, *Patmut'iwn Hayots',* vol. 2 (Venice, 1785), pp. 841–42.

37. Lalayian, *Nakhijewan,* p. 13.

38. On the monuments of Aznaberd, cf. A. Ayvazian, "Aznaberd," *Erevani hamalsaran,* no. 3 (1978), pp. 23–27.

39. For details, see A. Ayvazian, "Arba ew Chahuk berderĕ," *Lraber hasarakakan gitut'yunneri,* no. 9 (1976), pp. 87–92.

THE DISTRICT OF CHAHUK

1. Step'anos Orbelean, pp. 378–79.

2. A. Abrahamian, *Anania Shirakats'u matenagrut'yunĕ* (Erevan, 1944), p. 350.

3. On the other historic villages not covered in this work, see A. Ayvazian, "Nyut'er Nakhijewani patmakan gyugheri teghagrut'yan ew patmakan hushardzanneri veraberyal," *Patma-banasirakan handes,* no. 2 (1972), pp. 258–66.

4. See A. Ayvazian, "Arba ew Chahuk berderĕ," *Lraber hasarakakan gitut'yunneri,* no. 9 (1976), pp. 92–95.

5. A. Ayvazian, "Nyut'er Makhichevani haykakan patmakan hushardzanneri veraberyal," *Patma-banasirakan handes,* no. 2 (1971), p. 272.

6. Ghazar Chahkets'i, *Girk' Astuatsabanakan, or koch'i drakht ts'ankali* (Constantinople, 1735), p. 330.

7. Hakobian, *Ughegrut'yunner,* vol. 1, 206.

8. G. Kapantsian, *Khaiasa-Kolybel' armian* (Erevan, 1947), p. 183.

9. A. Gharibian, *Hayots' lezvi patmutyan usumnasirut'yan neratsut'yun* (Erevan, 1937), p. 62.

10. *ZhD dari hayeren dzeŕagreri hishatakaranner,* comp. L. Khach'ikian (Erevan, 1950), p. 567.

11. G. Hovsēp'ian, *Khaghbakeank' kam Pŕosheank' Hayots' patmut'ean mēj* (Vagharshapat, 1928), p. 54. STI, which G. Hovsēp'ian considered a ligature, is from Arabic and means "lady."

12. See A. Ayvazian, "Ōtsop'i ew Kuk'ii hushardzannerĕ," *Patma-banasirakan handes,* no. 2 (1976), pp. 262–65.

13. Step'anos Orbelean, p. 379.

14. *Staticheskoe opisanie Nakhichevanskoi provintsii* (Saint Petersburg, 1833), p. 145.

15. Step'anos Orbelean, p. 379.

16. Ayvazian, "Ōtsop'i ew Kuk'ii hushardzannerĕ," pp. 257–62.

17. Smbatian, *Nkaragir S. Karapeti vanits' Ernjakay,* p. 485.

18. Ibid., p. 150.

19. Matenadaran of Erevan, *The Catalogue of Magistros,* "Gospels," folder 2, p. 854.

20. Step'anos Orbelean, p. 378.

21. S. Barkhudarian, *Divan hay vimagrut'yan,* vol. 2 (Erevan, 1960), p. 129.

22. Step'anos Orbelean, p. 378.

23. Smbatian, *Nkaragir S. Karapeti vanits' Ernjakay,* p. 150.

24. A. Ayvazian, "Nakhnadaryan kayan Nakhichevani ISSH hyusisum," *Bander Erevani hamalsarani,* no. 3 (1974), pp. 238–41.

SCRIPTORIA

1. Alishan, *Sisakan,* p. 364.

2. *Ts'uts'ak dzeṙagrats' Mashtots'i anvan matenadarani,* vols. 1–2 (Erevan, 1965–70).

3. Matenadaran, codex no. 1571.

4. *ZhE dari hayeren dzeṙagreri hishatakaranner,* part 1, 1401–50, comp. L. Khach'ikian (Erevan, 1955), p. 423. (Hereafter *ZhE dar.*)

5. Smbatian, *Nkaragir S. Karapeti vanits' Ernjakay,* p. 205.

6. A. Ch'opanian, *Naghash Hovnat'an ashughĕ ew Hovnat'an Hovnat'anean nkarich'ĕ* (Paris, 1910); G. Lewonian, "Hovnat'anyan naghashnerĕ hay nkarch'ut'yan patmut'yan mej," *Khorhrdayin arvest,* no. 2 (1938); Garegin Hovsep'ian, *Niwt'er ew usumnasirut'iwnner hay arvesti ew mshakoyt'i patmut'ean,* fasc. 5 (Antelias, 1951); M. Mkrtch'yan, *Naghash Hovnat'an* (Erevan, 1957).

7. A. Aṙak'elian, *Hay zhoghovrdi mtavor mshakoyt'i zargats'-man patmut'yun,* vol. 2 (Erevan, 1964), p. 294.

8. Leo, *Patmut'yun Hayots',* vol. 3 (Erevan, 1946), p. 278.

9. P. Pṙoshian, *Verin Aguleats' erku seṙi usumnaranneri bats'vilĕ ew kanonadrut'iwnk'ĕ* (Moscow, 1868); *Taraz,* no. 47 (Tiflis, 1892), pp. 606–7.

10. Matenadaran, codex no. 1571, p. 285ʳ.

11. Alishan, *Sisakan,* p. 326; *ZhE dar,* p. 337.

12. Matenadaran of Erevan, "*Mesrop Tēr-Movsisian,* Mayr ts'uts'ak hayeren dzeṙagrats' (dzeṙagir); Avetaranner," folder 2, p. 546; Alishan, *Sisakan,* p. 326.

13. Matenadaran, codex no. 4517, p. 101ʳ.

14. See A. Ayvazian, "Aprakunisi surb Karapet vank'ĕ," *Ējmiatsin* (July 1976), pp. 45–52.

15. *ZhD dari hayeren dzeṙagreri hishatakaranner,* comp. L. Khach'ikian (Erevan, 1950), p. 592. (Hereafter *ZhD dar.*)

16. *ZhD Dar,* p. 559.

17. *Handēs Amsoreay* (Vienna, December 1899), p. 269; Smbatian, *Nkaragir S. Karapeti Vanits' Ernjakay,* p. 117. On Ghazar Vardapet and Esayi Varzhapet, see Matenadaran, "*Magistrosi ts'uts'ak, Magistrosi ts'uts'ak,* Awetaranner," folder 2, p. 752; "*Magistros,*

Gandzaranner,*" p. 178; Smbatian, *Nkaragir S. Karapeti vantis' Ern-jakay,* pp. 148–49.

18. Matenadaran, "*Magistrosi ts'uts'ak,* Awetaranner," p. 859.

19. A. Ayvazian, "Shoṙot'," *Grk'eri ashkharh,* no. 11 (1974).

20. Smbatian, *Nkaragir S. Karapeti vanits' Ernjakay,* pp. 282–83.

21. Alishan, *Sisakan,* p. 353.

22. A. Ayvazian, "Norashen-Norakert," *Grk'eri ashkharh,* no. 9 (1976).

23. *ZhD dar,* p. 424.

24. Smbatian, *Nkaragir S. Karapeti vanits' Ernjakay,* pp. 138–39.

25. Matenadaran, "*Magistrosi ts'uts'ak,* Awetaranner," folder 2, p. 209.

26. Smbatian, *Nkaragir S. Karapeti vanits' Ernjakay,* p. 127.

27. Matenadaran, no. 6235, p. 165ᵛ.

28. Smbatian, *Nkaragir S. Karapeti vanits' Ernjakay,* p. 140.

29. A. Eremian, "Tasnhingerord dari mi anhayt nkarch'uhi," *Ējmiatsin* (July 1952), pp. 48–50; *ZhE dar,* part 2 (Erevan, 1958), p. 64.

30. For details, see Hovhannēs K'ṙnets'i, *Haghags k'erakanin,* ed. L. S. Khach'ikian (Erevan, 1977), "Introduction," pp. 5–51.

31. A. Movsisian, *Urvagtser hay dprots'i ew mankavarzhutyan patmut'yan (10–14-rd darer)* (Erevan, 1958), p. 345.

32. *Mayr ts'uts'ak hayerēn dzeṙagrats' Matenadaranin Mkhit'ar-eants' i Venetik,* vol. 3, comp. B. Sargsian and G. Sargsian (Venice, 1966), p. 312.

33. A. Ayvazian, "Nakhchavan," *Grk'eri ashkharh,* no. 1 (1977).

34. *ZhD dar,* p. 189.

35. *Ts'uts'ak hayerēn dzeṙagrats' Nikomidioy ew shrjakayits',* comp. S. Hovakimian (Venice, 1969), p. 11.

36. A. Ayvazian, "Astapat," *Grk'eri ashkharh,* no. 11 (1976).

37. Matenadaran, "*Magistrosi ts'uts'ak,* Chashots'," 1, p. 36.

38. *ZhD dar,* p. 25.

39. *Haykakan manrankarch'ut'yun* (Erevan, 1967), pp. 208–9.

40. A. Ayvazian, "Ōdzop'i ew Kuk'ii hushardzannerĕ," *Patma-banasirakan handes,* no. 2 (1976), pp. 264–65.

41. Ibid., pp. 259–260.

42. Matenadaran, codex no. 6257, p. 269ᵛ.

43. Ibid., p. 267ᵛ.

44. Ibid., p. 269ʳ.

45. Matenadaran, codex no. 6531, p. 262ʳ.

46. Ibid., pp. 125ʳ, 269ᵛ.

47. Ibid., p. 262ᵛ.

48. Matenadaran, codex no. 7481.

49. *ZhE dar,* part 3 (Erevan, 1967), pp. 391–92.

50. Ibid., p. 215.

51. *Ts'uts'ak hayerēn dzeřagrats' T'avrizi,* comp. H. Achařian (Vienna, 1910), p. 125.

52. Matenadaran, codex no. 4475, p. 376ᵛ.

53. *Zak'aria Agulets'u oragrut'yunĕ,* p. 95.

54. *Abraham Kat'oghikos Kretats'woy patmagrut'iwn,* p. 78.

55. *Mayr ts'uts'ak dzeřagrats' srbots' Hakobeants',* comp. N. Pogharian, vol. 1 (Jerusalem, 1966), p. 403.

56. *ZhE dar,* part 1 (Erevan, 1955), p. 73.

57. *ZhE dar,* part 3 (Erevan, 1967), p. 215.

58. Matenadaran, "*Magistrosi ts'uts'ak,* Haysmawurk'ner," p. 98.

59. *Hayeren dzeřagreri ZhĒ dari hishatakaranner, 1621–1640 t't'.,* comp. V. Hakobian and A. Hovhanisian, vol. 2 (Erevan, 1978), p. 738.

60. *Ts'uts'ak hayerēn dzeřagrats' Nor-Bayazeti,* comp. H. Achařian (Vienna, 1924), p. 30.

61. Matenadaran, "*Magistrosi ts'uts'ak,* Awetaranner," folder 2, p. 840.

62. Smbatian, *Nkaragir S. Karapeti vanits' Ernjakay,* p. 122.

Wall Painting

1. Alishan, *Sisakan,* pp. 355, 367.

2. *Zak'aria Agulets'u oragrut'yunĕ,* p. 65.

3. Naghash Hovnat'an, *Banasteghtsut'yunner* (Erevan, 1951), p. 215.

4. See A. Ch'opanian, *Naghash Hovnat'an ashughĕ ew Hovnat'an Hovnat'an Hovnat'anian nkarich'ĕ* (Paris, 1910); N. Akinian, *Hovnat'an Naghash ew Naghash Hovnat'aniank'* (Vienna, 1911); G.

Lewonian, "Hovnat'anian Naghashnerĕ hay nkarch'ut'yan patmut'yan mej," *Khorhrdayin arvest,* no. 2 (Erevan, 1938); M. Mkrtch'ian, *Naghash Hovnat'an* (Erevan, 1957); E. Martikian, *Haykakan kerparvesti patmut'yun,* book 1 (Erevan, 1971); M. Ghazarian, *Hay kerparvestĕ 17–18-rd darerum* (Erevan, 1974).

5. Matenadaran, codex no. 3628.

6. M. P'ap'azian, *Hnut'iwnk' vanōrēits' Goght'an gawař, lusankarch'a-kan albom* (Vagharshapat, 1891).

7. Naghash Hovnat'an, *Banasteghtsut'yunner,* p. v.

8. Mkrtch'ian, *Naghash Hovnat'an,* p. 57.

9. Matenadaran, codex no. 1533.

10. Lalayian, *Nakhchavan,* pp. 54–55.

11. See the two photographs of the wall paintings of St. Step'anos Monastery in L. Minasian's *Irani haykakan vank'erĕ* (Tehran, 1971), pp. 123–24.

12. For details, see A. Ayvazian, "Aznaberdi S. Grigor ekeghets'u ormnankarnerĕ," *Banber Erevani hamalsarani,* no. 1 (1977), pp. 246–52.

Bridges

1. *Handēs Amsoreay* (Vienna, 1899), p. 66.

2. Ařak'elian, *Parskastani hayerĕ, nrants' ants'ealĕ, nerkan ew apagan,* pp. 35–36.

3. Alishan, *Sisakan,* p. 413.

4. Ibid., p. 346.

5. Sedrakian, *Hnut'iwnk',* p. 87.

6. Smbatian, *Nkaragir S. Karapeti Vanits' Ernjakay,* p. 116.

7. *Ardzagank'* (Tiflis weekly), no. 25 (1884), p. 383.